The Woman Book of Love and Sex

DEIDRE SANDERS

SPHERE BOOKS LIMITED
London and Sydney

First published simultaneously in Great Britain by
Michael Joseph Ltd and Sphere Books Ltd 1985
30–32 Gray's Inn Road, London WC1X 8JL
Text Copyright © 1985 by Deidre Sanders
Surveys Copyright © IPC Magazines Ltd

**TRADE
MARK**

Set in Times

Printed and bound in Great Britain by
Cox & Wyman Ltd, Reading

This book is dedicated to the 15,000 women who took part in the surveys. Thank you for your help and trust.

Contents

	Acknowledgements	ix
1	The Woman's-Eye View of Sex	1
2	Nice Girls Still Don't	17
3	Learning to Love	31
4	As You Like It	49
5	Who Needs Orgasm?	65
6	Real and Fantasy Lovers	83
7	The Fertility Trap	98
8	Is Motherhood Bad For Sex?	116
9	Why Do Women Have Affairs?	127
10	Women Who Love Women	144
11	Women Alone	160
12	Women – and Children – Abused	172
13	Unlucky?	193
	Help Directory	210
	Further Reading	230
	The *Woman* questionnaires: 1) The Love Life of the British Wife	233
	2) Love and the Unmarried Woman	243
	Note on Methodology and Sample	254
	Index	257

Acknowledgements

This has been a very demanding project. Not only did we have to analyse 1,044 detailed tables of statistics but read and collate thousands of personal accounts sent in by readers. I could not have managed it without a great deal of help.

Above all, my thanks to Anne Rigg, research consultant, who was responsible throughout these surveys for the methodology, questionnaire design and statistical analysis, and who helped beyond her brief with so much creative energy. Thank you to psychologist Susan Martin, who so carefully coded all the questionnaires, and to Dataflow, who worked overtime completing the computer analysis to our tight schedule.

I am grateful to Jo Foley and Dee Nolan, then editor and assistant editor of *Woman*, whose commitment and enthusiasm made the whole project possible, and to Anne-Marie Sapstead, assistant features editor, for all her constructive suggestions and hard work in the early stages.

Thank you to Patt Purdy, Yvonne Hammond, Jacqueline Runeckles, Sheila Bass and Mary Wilson, also Cathy Aird (in Australia), Janet Gunns (in Canada) and Margaret Smith (for the South African details), who all helped with research, and to Pat Henderson and Simone Waldock, who helped type – and retype – the manuscript.

I am grateful to Robert Shreeve of Sphere Books and Henrietta Heald of Michael Joseph for their valuable suggestions and help with editing, and to the following people, who all took the trouble – at a time when most of them were meant to be on holiday – to read through the manuscript or specific chapters and made helpful comments: psychologist and sex therapist Anne Dickson; Dr John Bancroft of the Medical Research Council Reproductive Biology Unit and Dr Judy Greenwood of the Royal Hospital, Edinburgh; Dr J. M. Kellett of St George's Hospital, London, and Professor Michael Adler, professor of genito-urinary medicine at the Middlesex Hospital Medical School; Toni Belfield of the Family Planning Association, and Deborah Bowmer and Stephen Saunders of the National Marriage Guidance Council; to the Rape Crisis Centre and the Incest Crisis Line.

A special thank you to my husband Rick, who not only lived with the survey as well as me for months but also gave me invaluable help in keeping the manuscript to a reasonable length; to my daughter Susie, who put up with a mum who kept saying, 'Yes, when I've finished the book . . .' and cheered loudest when I could say I had typed the final page, and to Jeannie Sperry, without whose cheerful support in the home all this would have taken a lot longer and been far more of a strain.

1 The Woman's-Eye View of Sex

Despite all that has been written about sex in recent years, until *Woman* magazine commissioned the two surveys on which this book is based we had very little reliable information about women's sex lives today.

At what age do girls start having intercourse? How promiscuous are they? How much do they enjoy sex? How many women always or usually reach orgasm? Do any still fake it? Do wives find that sex after marriage becomes dull? How many wives have affairs? How do women rate their men as lovers? How many prefer to make love with other women?

All of us involved in the initial planning of the project brought far more to it than just a professional interest in what could obviously be a fascinating and challenging piece of research. As women, we were all conscious of pressures, doubts and uncertainties that affect us in our personal lives.

With all the emphasis there has been in the past couple of decades on the importance of a fulfilling sex life, many of us now set ourselves a very high standard. Of course, we often have to accept that our sex life will be less than perfect – just as we usually have to accept that our relationships generally both at home and at work are less than perfect. We can count ourselves lucky if we are reasonably content.

However, we knew that many women feel under pressure to be sexual superwomen. They often feel failures – because they can't live up to current popular images of what a sexy woman should be like, and/or because when their sex lives were less than wonderful their partners often seemed to blame them for having faulty sexual responses, for being under-sexed, for not being like other women.

We saw the surveys as a valuable service to women generally. For all the general talk about sex, few of us feel safe enough to talk in detail about our sex lives. Even if we do, we still only confide in a handful of our closest friends.

I can't speak for the others involved in the project, but I have

1

found many of the results of our surveys very reassuring and helpful in my personal life. It's not only that knowing many other women share your feelings stops you feeling like a freak. The size of these surveys and the detailed analysis we carried out on the findings meant that we were able to spot many trends and patterns of behaviour among men and women that lead to our love relationships being less happy and fulfilled than they might be. Once you understand some of the blocks and problems, it opens the path to making changes.

I want to emphasize that this book does not intend to blame men. The surveys were carried out on women: the book is written from the women's point of view, and any suggestions are primarily directed at women who feel they want to bring about changes in their relationships. Of course it contains criticisms of men voiced by women who took part in the surveys, and they may make some men feel uncomfortable or indignant.

However, the women weren't slow to criticize themselves, and I have certainly tried to avoid any tendency to put all the responsibility for good sex on to men's shoulders. I hope that men will find this book a valuable insight into women's sexuality and bear in mind that the women's views on love and sex were expressed when they felt free to speak their minds without fear of criticism or blame.

Our first questionnaire was aimed at wives. Its ninety questions covered everything from how easily they are sexually aroused to how satisfied they are, from whether they like making love with the lights on to whether they are having an affair. We were careful that the questions were as open as possible, encouraging replies from wives who are enjoying their sex lives and those who aren't, from those to whom sex is important and those who don't care for it much.

We would have been content with a thousand returned questionnaires, which would have provided a reasonably reliable statistical sample. In fact, the response was astonishing. More than seven thousand married women replied, thousands of them attaching letters explaining more about their feelings, their pleasures, their anxieties.

The quotations reproduced in this book are from the letters which accompanied the questionnaires. They are all insights into private lives. To protect the anonymity of the writers, I have allotted them fictitious names and ages only approximat-

2

ing to their own. Where I have quoted one person more than once, I have sometimes changed the name again, and I have changed the names of partners, where mentioned.

Some women filled in the questionnaire with their husband: 'We both found your questionnaire fascinating. We work hard at our marriage and have answered your questions very truthfully. Thank you for an interesting evening!'

Some found it had improved their sex life: 'Since letting him see my answers to your questionnaire our sex life has improved. It gave us an opening to discuss some of the differences in each other's ideas about sex.'

Some made it clear that they had never before revealed their feelings to anyone, not even to their husband:

'It's been nice to tell someone the truth for a change!' 'I have never sought advice from a magazine or filled in a questionnaire, but I really wanted to after looking at this one. I often think I am the only young married woman today who thinks like I do about sex.' 'My husband would be livid if he knew I was filling in this questionnaire.' 'Thank you for giving me the chance to get it all off my chest. I'm dying to see the results and find out if I'm the norm. I hope your report will help me to get closer to my husband.'

The size of the response showed that we had struck a chord among wives: sex obviously does matter to a great many of them.

More than nine out of ten wives said that sex is important in their marriage.

Pauline, 29: 'I don't ask for new clothes or to be taken out, money is very tight and I'm tied down with three children under four. Sex is my anchorage. The one thing that's free, satisfying and totally mine.'

Jenny, 32: 'We are two individuals in everyday life and one person in love. We both feel when we make love we are joined as one body. It really is the greatest feeling there is, and to find someone who fills your life as my husband does is something precious to hold on to for ever.'

Nine out of ten believe that understanding each other's sexual needs is important in marriage and eight out of ten that sexual fulfilment matters as much to women as it does to men.

However that doesn't mean they all consider themselves fulfilled.

May, 44: 'Imagine the scene. Husband reads paper all evening. 10.30 p.m. Table to lay for breakfast, have hot drink.

3

Bed. He reads technical magazines or library book. 11.00 p.m. lights out. What kind of a sexy mood would *you* get? I've had a vision of myself as a hole in the mattress! Lovemaking for him is no more important than the chores before bed. The act has never taken more than ten minutes in all.'

Some hoped that the results of the survey would improve their sex life: 'If my husband knew more about women, he would understand my needs are not unusual.' Some asked for guidance: 'I shall look forward to reading the results of your survey and perhaps you can offer some further help.'

Having received such a massive and varied response from wives, we thought we should widen our research to include all those women without a husband: young unmarried women, those who have chosen never to marry or perhaps simply never met the right man, those who are separated, divorced or widowed.

Again we included a lengthy questionnaire in *Woman*, this time consisting of more than one hundred questions. We expected fewer replies. It might be difficult for young women living at home with their parents to fill in the questionnaire confidentially and return it to us. Would older women realize that it was aimed at them, too?

In the event, the second survey received just as large a response as the first: from women of all ages, those living with their parents and those not, the single, and the formerly married. Again thousands of letters detailing feelings and experiences flooded in with the completed questionnaires.

'Your survey is a fabulous idea – allowing women to express their views without fear of criticism from friends, colleagues, family or anyone else.'

'We're glad you're bringing the subject of unmarried lovers into the open. Just because we don't have marriage licences doesn't mean we're cold and unloving. I hope my answers don't make me out to be a raving nymphomaniac – I certainly am not – but I answered them as frankly as possible.'

'Those of us who are divorced or widowed are not often catered for in many aspects of life. We are still human and most of us do have an active sex life.'

Among unmarried women having sexual relationships, nine out of ten also say that sex is important to them. Eight out of ten agree that sex is as important to women as it is to men. These were the same proportions revealed by the survey of wives.

Mary-Anne, 23, had intended to wait for marriage but eventually decided to have intercourse with her present boyfriend. 'He's so caring and gentle, and now it's absolute bliss. I think making love is the best thing since sliced bread. When my boy-friend's away I'm always thinking about sex with him.'

Some, like Debbie, 23, feel their needs are ignored. 'Sex to him was like a prescription. I was to be taken four times a day whether I felt like it or not. As long as he was achieving satisfaction, it was fine. He was too busy concentrating on his own pleasure to worry about mine. I felt like a piece of meat. The saying "Lie back and think of England" was never so true.'

Some, like Lindsay, 25, feel that sex is important to them but they enjoy their most fulfilling relationships with other women. 'It is a total sensory experience. There is always wonder at the sameness and softness of the other's body. You know what feels good and it can vary from quiet and gentle to passionate as much as any sexual relationship. There's as much joy in giving as receiving.'

Even though the overwhelming majority of the unmarried women replying to our survey had relationships with men, *one in ten had made love with another woman*. We also heard from many wives whose lovers are women.

Few people, men or women, can talk easily and openly about sex. When such stress is laid on sexual success it's very hard to admit to worries. With 15,000 completed questionnaires returned by women of all ages, we had a unique opportunity to learn more in depth about the sexual joys and disappointments of women today.

In order to ensure that our findings were as statistically reliable as possible, we selected at random for detailed analysis 2,000 questionnaires from wives and 2,000 from unmarried women in correct proportions for ages and regions. Eventually we had 1,044 detailed tables of statistics. For more explanation of our research method and sample, see page 254, but it's worth mentioning here that we found almost no regional variation. What we did discover was that, where the questions in the two surveys overlapped, there was often remarkable consistency in the results – as already illustrated in the examples given above – though on the whole there is more sexual satisfaction reported among unmarried women than among wives.

Most women say that they are at least reasonably content. Sixty-nine per cent of unmarried women with a special man-friend say they enjoy their lovemaking a great deal; 27 per cent

5

say they enjoy it reasonably well; only a tiny 4 per cent say 'not very much' or 'not at all'. However, *only 39 per cent of wives say they are very happy with their sexual relationship; 37 per cent are reasonably satisfied; leaving 23 per cent – more than one in five – definitely dissatisfied.*

The latter figures do not just reflect couples caught in unhappy marriages. In general, wives feel their sex lives are worse than their marriages. Of course, sex is just one part of a whole relationship, and a wife who says she is very happily married is more likely to be very satisfied with her sexual relationship. But more than half of wives say their marriage is very happy, far more than are very satisfied with their sexual relationship. And, as the figures below show, only one in ten say they are *un*happily married, half as many as are unhappy with their sex lives:

	Marriage	Sexual relationship
Very happy	51%	39%
Reasonably happy	37%	37%
Not very happy	8%	15%
Not at all happy	3%	8%

The main reason why wives express more dissatisfaction than unmarried women seems to be that they set higher standards. They are in relationships they expect to last, they are usually more knowledgeable, they are more discriminating lovers. Being more aware of what is possible, they are more aware if their own love life is falling short, and they are more prepared to put their discontent into words. It also seems that marriage itself has a dampening effect on some couples.

Linda, 21, said, 'If you really care about each other, you can live together happily with an irregular sex life. But it isn't as frequent or exciting as it used to be. I believe my husband feels the same. It isn't ruining our marriage, but we aren't satisfied with our sex life.'

What bothers women is not so much a raging discontent but a persistent, niggling feeling that this important part of our lives isn't as pleasurable and exciting as we'd like it to be. This list gives some idea of the most common problems reported to us.

- *More than half of unmarried women and nearly three quarters of wives want to make changes in the way they and their partner make love.*

- *Half of unmarried women, and a slightly larger proportion of wives, worry that they don't enjoy sex enough and sometimes make love wishing they weren't.*

- *Four out of five wives experience difficulties becoming sexually aroused. (For more than one in three this is a problem on at least half the occasions they make love.)*

- *One third of unmarried women with partners wish they were less inhibited or more enthusiastic when making love.*

- *More than half of unmarried women find it hard to talk freely to their partner about sex.*

It's quite a list! Obviously there are all sorts of particular relationship problems which can get in the way of sexual pleasure, but when this many women report similar anxieties, clearly something more general is at work.

It's interesting how women rate themselves and their partners as lovers. I felt rather uneasy about this question because treating sex as a performance test can cause problems in itself. However, we did need to get some measure of whether women felt they were sexually short-changed by their partners. Quite the opposite is the case – see Figure 1.

Women are very appreciative of their men, and rate them more highly as lovers than they rate themselves. *Only one in ten women overall believes she is an excellent lover, but four out of ten unmarried women and three out of ten wives give their partners top marks.* Women are much more likely to rate themselves as average than they are their partners.

What makes someone a good lover is usually thought to be their willingness and ability to ensure that their partner enjoys sex as well as themselves. Yet, according to our survey, the tendency is for men to enjoy sex more than women, for men to be more likely to want sex more often.

Even among the wives who would like to make love more, what blocks them is often their own lack of desire – *they* don't feel like it, *they* find it hard to be responsive, *they* are too tired. The most common change wives would like to make in their own lovemaking is to be keener to make love more often.

7

Figure 1

How good a lover?

Unmarried women

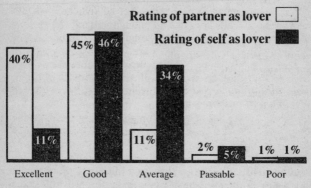

Rating of partner as lover ☐
Rating of self as lover ■

	Excellent	Good	Average	Passable	Poor
Partner	40%	45%	11%	2%	1%
Self	11%	46%	34%	5%	1%

Wives

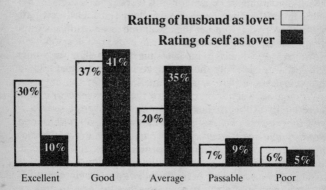

Rating of husband as lover ☐
Rating of self as lover ■

	Excellent	Good	Average	Passable	Poor
Husband	30%	37%	20%	7%	6%
Self	10%	41%	35%	9%	5%

When women rate themselves down as lovers, it is usually because they think that there is something wrong with them. As Fay admitted, 'I often feel I am an inadequate wife although my husband does not agree. I always seem to be the one who is "too tired" for lovemaking, whereas my husband is always ready. If I tell my husband I feel too tired and he talks me round, I usually enjoy sex, but it's the initial arousal I find difficult.'

If men are thought to be 'better' at sex, more likely to enjoy it, and more likely to want more of it, then our ideas of sex may be too slanted towards our image of masculine sexuality. If so, it's hardly surprising that many women have trouble fitting in with it. As we've seen, half of unmarried women worry they don't enjoy sex enough; and three out of five believe that women's sexual needs are not well enough understood.

Blaming men is not the answer. Some men are indifferent or selfish lovers, just as some women are. But most men want to bring their partners as much sexual pleasure as they themselves enjoy, and if possible to increase enjoyment for both of them. Men are as much trapped by the current image of what goes to make successful sex as are women.

For example, according to the women who responded to the surveys, *it's twice as important to men that women should usually reach orgasm* – ironic, isn't it?

'My husband believes that, as he has an orgasm every time we make love, then I should also,' said Marian, 28. 'Although on most occasions I do, he feels he has somehow failed, or thinks I have not enjoyed lovemaking, if I do not get there. I have explained that I do not feel it is terribly important for me to reach orgasm, as I find lovemaking enjoyable with or without it, and that, for me, the emotional satisfaction is always equally intense.'

Another pressure felt by both partners is that, not only should the woman usually climax, but that she should do so during intercourse, like a man. But this is not the common pattern among women. Three quarters of wives and two thirds of unmarried women reach orgasm on at least half the occasions they make love, but more commonly this is not during intercourse. *Fewer than half of wives and only a quarter of unmarried women usually reach orgasm through intercourse.* Yet we are so swayed by the masculine model of sexuality that we think that intercourse is the 'right' way to reach orgasm. If we don't 'succeed' in this way, we feel we've failed; and men too unnecessarily feel they are failing as lovers.

I hope this survey will reassure many such as Claire: 'I always have an orgasm either before or after intercourse, but sometimes I feel pressured by the press and films and books because I have never had an orgasm during intercourse. I need manual stimulation. It is my husband I feel sorry for because I think he blames himself. I am satisfied – I would be even more so if I knew that other women were the same.'

9

Pretending to reach orgasm when you don't makes it harder to discover which sort of stimulation would be more effective. *Only one in five wives never has difficulty reaching orgasm when she wants to.*

One point that came across loud and clear from our questionnaires is that good sex for most women is not something that starts with the first caress and ends with orgasm. 'A lot of men think that making love is simply intercourse,' said Aileen, 25. 'They should learn that it is a combination of many things.'

The surveys confirmed that for most women good sex is part of a good relationship and inextricably interwoven with it. It is a physical expression of the feelings, not a mere appetite to be satisfied or a sport for recreation, though fun and satisfaction certainly play their part.

Eighty-four per cent of unmarried women believe that sex is best with one man you love; only 5 per cent believe that it is more exciting if you have many different partners. 'I really enjoy sex when I am in love.' 'I have to be emotionally involved with a man to enjoy sex with him.' 'Pleasures of the body are a bonus to a good relationship.' 'When I do have sex it is always with someone who is important to me and who I care a great deal about.'

It's not just our general happiness or discontent with our relationships which affect our sexual desires, either. Our level of sexual response is governed by our immediate feelings about our partner.

Caroline, 23: 'If he is bad-tempered or unlikable during the day, then expects me to make love passionately at night, I cannot respond – to me it would seem hypocritical. Sex is certainly an important part of marriage but liking (not just loving) your partner is even more important.'

'When our sex life is good it is always because our relationship is going well,' wrote Maureen, 38. 'If we are at odds with each other, the sex deteriorates.'

Because for most women sexuality is a reflection of our entire relationship with our partner, arousing our sexual desires is not just a question of skilful foreplay. We need to feel loved, desired, appreciated, respected throughout the day, through words, deeds and physical contact.

Lilian, 45: 'I yearn for a good sex life with someone who treats me properly all the time. My husband only kisses me during sex, never for a hello or goodbye mornings and evenings. The only time he touches me is for sex. Even though I am middle-aged, I would still like a cuddle on the settee, even with the children in the room, but that would embarrass him. The moment he starts to paw me I'm expected to feel like making love, and I don't.'

Both wives and unmarried women lay more stress on kissing and cuddling as compared to intercourse than they believe their men do.

More than one third of wives would like more kissing and cuddling. They want to feel appreciated as people, not just wooed for sex. Joy, 47, resented her husband 'only making up to me when he wants sex, patting me on the bottom when we're getting ready for bed and saying, "Am I all right for tonight?!" or something similar.'

Likewise, *nearly one third of unmarried women would like more kissing and cuddling from their lovers.* Fiona, 22: 'I often say to my boyfriend, "I love you." I like to hold hands and kiss and fondle him but he sometimes shrugs me off, especially if we are in company. I always like him to show me affection and never shrug him off. We make love less often now than we used to.'

While only 11 per cent of unmarried women say they don't kiss and cuddle much with their partner apart from before intercourse, for wives the figure is 31 per cent.

Even as a prelude to intercourse, men seem to find it hard to give their partners all the kissing and cuddling they need; some had told their partners they thought it 'soft'. The most common change wanted by married and unmarried women alike in the way their partner makes love is that he should kiss and cuddle them more. It left the next most popular change wanted – that he should be more skilful – way behind.

Janice, 35, complained, 'The one thing that shuts me up completely is being approached suddenly and without verbal contact (hand straight to groin, or straight to removing knickers), often whilst washing up or cooking, or other difficult-to- leave tasks. My needs include tenderness and mental contact but my husband is unable to communicate his feelings and I am shutting off mine.'

Many women find that sexual arousal depends on all of their body being loved, not just the 'sexual' parts.

Sandra, 32: 'My husband tended to dive straight in and I started to jump/jerk away whenever he touched my personal parts.

'We talked and over a couple of months realized that it was

because he wasn't cuddling and loving other parts of me first. He had to make me believe that *all* of my body was important, by paying it as much attention as possible.'

But if men are inhibited about showing tenderness, women are often equally inhibited about showing sexual desire – or even allowing that it's a possibility. Men need to feel that kissing and cuddling will be welcome if they are not to retreat behind a bluff exterior, but women are still brought up in a tradition that it's not 'nice' for a girl to be openly sexual.

Jean, 28: 'I have always been rather tense when my husband approaches me. I do not seem to need to have intercourse often but I am sure my husband and I would be a lot happier and more contented if I did. My parents did not mention sex in front of me; in fact, they never mentioned love. They were happy but were very inhibited about anything physical. I never saw them kiss and cuddle.'

Fewer than 50 per cent of wives make the first move sexually, even half the time.

Wives may be dissatisfied sexually but they find it hard to share their feelings with their husband (which might enable him to do something about it). They suffer in silence. While three quarters of wives would like changes in the way their husband makes love, only a third talk openly about sex or sexual feelings. More than half the wives who are dissatisfied with their sexual relationship have held back from making a request that would have brought them greater pleasure.

Davina, 32: 'I would like to be able to ask for oral sex and get carried away, but I feel too shy, like a tart, if I ask. Even if he does it I cannot let myself go, or show any pleasure, in case he thinks I'm sex-mad or something. It's hard to explain. I just can't enjoy myself in front of him. I would like to be a different person – more sexy, more forward, less inhibited – but I feel guilty afterwards.'

This is a problem among unmarried women, too. *The most common change they would like to make in their lovemaking is to become less inhibited.*

The question of how often you make love is commonly a touchy point between couples. *More than half of husbands and two out of five of wives would like to make love more often; so would nearly half the unmarried women in sexual relationships and more than half of their partners – though in the case of the 'unmarrieds' what prevents them appears to be lack of opportunity and privacy rather than problems linked with their*

How often do you usually make love?

Wives, aged:	Under 25	Under 35	Under 45	Under 55	55+
Every day	10%	4%	4%	3%	3%
4 or 5 times a week	21%	16%	10%	6%	5%
2 or 3 times a week	37%	36%	35%	25%	16%
Once a week	18%	21%	21%	29%	27%
Less than once a week	13%	17%	24%	18%	22%
Less than once a month	1%	5%	4%	12%	10%
Never make love these days	—	1%	2%	7%	17%

Unmarried women in a sexual relationship aged:	16 – 18	19 – 21	22 – 25	26 – 40	41 – 60
Every day	6%	7%	8%	6%	5%
4 or 5 times a week	19%	21%	18%	16%	10%
2 or 3 times a week	33%	32%	35%	36%	38%
Once a week	23%	19%	18%	19%	15%
Less than once a week	13%	12%	11%	13%	13%
Less than once a month	4%	7%	6%	9%	13%
Never make love these days	3%	2%	4%	1%	5%

Unmarried women in a sexual relationship:	Living with parents	Living with partner	Overall	Wives (overall)
Every day	3%	14%	7%	5%
4 or 5 times a week	16%	26%	19%	10%
2 or 3 times a week	35%	33%	34%	29%
Once a week	23%	14%	19%	25%
Less than once a week	14%	9%	12%	18%
Less than once a month	8%	4%	7%	8%
Never make love these days	2%	—	3%	5%

Figure 2

relationship or differing sex drives. Figure 2 shows how frequently couples of different ages say they have intercourse.

Successful sex is often equated with frequent intercourse – and that leaves many of us worrying whether we are woefully inadequate. Yet the tables show that *the average married couple makes love somewhere between once and twice a week*. While frequency of making love is linked to age – there being a slight falling off as couples grow older – what is more striking is how consistently couples seem to find their pattern and keep to it. Clearly, many couples make love once, twice or three times a week virtually all their married life, though one in seven wives under 25 makes love once a fortnight or less, one in five of the under-35s.

We used rather different age-bands for our survey on unmarried women because there are many questions relating to single women where it is relevant to know whether they are 16 or 21. However, again we can see a tendency for the younger woman to make love slightly more often.

Unmarried women with sexual partners make love more often than married women. Those living with their partners are more likely to make love every day or nearly every day; 19 per cent of those living with their parents do so with the same frequency, and another 39 per cent of these make love two or three times a week.

An unmarried woman now living with her parents, expecting as nearly all of them do to marry one day, may think that it is only because she still lives at home that she isn't making love more often, but in fact she is only a little more likely to make love more often as a bride under 25, and by the time she is 30 will probably be making love with the same frequency she is at present.

Of course, it doesn't matter if you only make love on Saturdays while the couple next door makes love every night (unless they're so noisy they disturb your sleep!), as long as you and your partner feel content with the frequency. As we've seen, however, this is a common cause for concern. There may be many reasons why couples do not make love more often – *more than half of the wives who wanted to make love more frequently said their husband is too tired*.

Rosemary, 28: 'My husband is a self-employed workaholic. I fell for a chap I work with part-time. Although my husband loves me and works all the hours God made so we can "live well", this chap who has no money, no car, never bought me anything, gave me more love and happiness than my husband ever has.'

Probably by now you will have recognized many of your own feelings about sex in the comments and statistics provided by the women who answered the questionnaires. And that is what this book is about: revealing the common experiences of women in order to give us the confidence of knowing that, if we are not entirely happy, it's rarely because there is something wrong with us.

However, not blaming ourselves or our partners doesn't mean that we should feel complacent if we know that we or they are unhappy. We cannot expect someone else to take on the responsibility for our sexual happiness. People often think they can't talk about sex, but sadly, if one of us is unhappy and we don't try to make changes, it can put our relationship under a great strain. As we see in Chapter 8, *three out of ten wives have at least one affair – half of these have had two or more.*

Perhaps some husbands need to look again at their priorities, but some wives might think again before having an affair (rather than trying to improve their sex life with their husband), if they realized how tough life can be when you're a woman alone over the age of 25 or 30.

While only half of those who have been married once want to try it again, nine out of ten want a special man in their life if they haven't got one already. But he's hard to find. *More than 80 per cent say it's hard to meet the right kind of man.*

Socializing is difficult for women on their own and many complain that men have sex on their minds rather than love. Margot, 39: 'Typical male – he knew I was divorced so thought I must be absolutely gasping for it. It took an hour of fighting for my honour to convince him I was not an easy lay.'

We were startled to discover how common sexual harassment and assault are among all age groups.

Hilary, 34, was twice assaulted: 'I felt filthy. On neither occasion did I entice anybody! This is my body and I hate it being grabbed. I certainly was not trying to be provocative. It wasn't a see-through blouse and I had a cardigan on. One time I was even wearing a cape. What am I supposed to wear not to attract this type of attention? Both times I was just minding my own business.'

One in ten women had been sexually assaulted, many of them far more seriously than this. *In one fifth of cases they were*

15

raped. Equally chilling was the discovery that *one in twelve had been sexually abused by a member of her own family*.

Bridget, 26: 'My dad went to work away from home for eighteen months. The visit to my GP was not talked about. Every time I spoke to my mum about "the hand that grows big of a night-time when I'm in bed," I was told, in effect, to shut up. I have never had a boyfriend. I'm scared of men and relationships. I'm still a virgin. I would quite like a man friend but I can't stand being touched in any way. I definitely don't want sex.'

Such experiences, though far more common that is generally acknowledged, still only happen to comparatively few. However, for those of us who want to enjoy happy, fulfilled relationships with men, and want our daughters to do the same, it's uncomfortable to realize how few girls can grow up without having come across – if not at first hand, then through a friend's or sister's account – some rather frightening aspect of male sexuality: cat-calls, flashers, warnings of men loitering near the playground. Of course, men who use threats in this way are only a tiny minority, but they indirectly affect the majority of women and colour our early impressions.

How deeply we will be affected usually depends on our parents, on whether they manage to help us link sex with loving and caring and pleasure rather than with fear and guilt. How far most of them succeed is the subject of the next chapter.

2 Nice Girls Still Don't

Parents and daughters: the legacy of guilt

Your sexuality doesn't begin with your first kiss but on the day you're born. The way you are taught to regard yourself through infancy and childhood establishes a lasting pattern.

Andrea, 24: 'I wish I could be more adventurous, but my mother brought me up to be shy and acted as though sex didn't exist. I wish I could break away from her narrow-mindedness and have more self-confidence and self-respect, and I wish my sex life was better.'

Inside many a modest, inhibited woman is imprisoned a strong, sexy one. Knowing she's there makes it all the more infuriating if we can't find the key to set her free. She's expected to live up to the 'nice girl' image: a woman who is unselfish, doesn't make criticisms and tries to please others.

The nice girl does not talk about sex. She will not say what she really wants; she tries to keep the sexual woman bound and gagged – with bad results.

Over half the wives who say they are not at all satisfied with sex also say they never talk about it with their husbands. *Nearly half of those who never talk about it have sexual difficulties, four times the proportion of those who can put their thoughts into words.*

Putting it into words means owning up. It's like making love with the lights on: we can't pretend that we don't know what's happening, that we just got carried away, that sex is nothing to do with us. We have to accept responsibility.

Couples who can talk about sex still have problems, but they manage to resolve them more easily. Couples who can't talk are left in the dark.

'My husband seems to do it all wrong, but I can't bring myself to tell him.' 'I feel like a tidy and convenient receptacle for sperm. I'm self-righteous in not demanding satisfaction and angry with myself too. I resort to masturbation, which is enjoyable and satisfying.'

Some feel that putting it into words takes the magic out of sex: 'I would like my husband to fondle my breasts more, but I'm too romantic to discuss the mechanics of sex.'

But partners may not be mind-readers. Not only do men and women have different tastes and responses; we all vary as individuals.

Who says that it spoils sex to talk about it? Is it the full-grown woman or the nice girl? It is easy to put the responsibility for sex with our partner, easy to blame him if we are unsatisfied. But what use to play Sleeping Beauty, waiting for our prince to wake us with a kiss, if he hasn't got a clue which castle we're in?

Talking with parents

Babies enjoy sexual sensations. Exploration and curiosity continue through childhood. If your parents found you playing with your genitals or playing doctors, you will have learned what they thought of sex. Did they accept it as natural, something you could talk about, or did it worry or anger them? Did you learn to keep it dark and secret?

At puberty sexuality emerges as an unavoidable issue for you and your parents; teenage years are stressful. You start to wonder about your body – not how healthy it is or how it feels to you, but how it looks to others.

'We are bombarded with beautiful sexy women on TV who makes us feel we should be slimmer/prettier/bigger breasted/ blonde/brunette etc. Most of my friends feel inadequate about their looks and bodies.'

Hormonal changes at puberty cause sudden mood-shifts and more conscious sexual feelings. Relationships with boys change. So do relationships with parents.

Every mother, by definition, knows something of what her daughter is going through. But few can talk comfortably and frankly about it. More than half the unmarried women living with their parents say talking about sex with their mothers is impossible or very hard. Only 11 per cent are able to talk openly and 27 per cent fairly openly (and fairly openly probably means it's the most personal aspects that are hardest to discuss). In other words, *only one young woman in eight living with her parents can rely on her mother for sexual guidance.*

18

Even fewer are able to talk about sex with their fathers. Two per cent find it easy, 8 per cent fairly easy, 19 per cent difficult, and more than half can't raise the subject at all. (Twenty-one per cent say they don't know or the question doesn't apply, presumably because their fathers no longer live with them.) But who better than a girl's father to give insight into how a boyfriend is feeling, how sincere he may be, what his anxieties are? It is little wonder that so many women can't talk about sex to their husbands when throughout childhood and adolescence they never spoke frankly to the most important man in their life.

It may be hard for fathers to deal with a daughter's emerging sexuality. Some ignore the issue, some are strict and try to keep her away from boys. A few themselves put sexual pressure on their daughters. (See Chapter 12.)

Most fathers, however, are proud to see their daughter becoming a woman. If they could talk openly it would be a valuable contribution to her future well-being.

Julie, 19: 'My parents backed me up when I told them I was sleeping with my boyfriend. My father took him out for a drink and came back saying he knew I was in genuinely affectionate hands. They let us sleep together at home, and both my brothers, who are 14 and 16, were consulted when this was decided. I owe my parents my ease and pleasure in my body and making love.'

The effects of silence

Even if few are able to go as far as Julie's family, parents owe their children some sexual education. Girls whose parents say nothing usually take their silence as an expression of disapproval and distaste; and such silence can be dangerous.

Laura, now 21: 'When I was 10 my sisters and I went every Sunday for tea with a man in his sixties called Uncle Mike. Eventually I started going on my own. He gave me dolls and clothes and had intercourse with me. I used to protest – I didn't know what was happening, but it hurt. Now I feel sick whenever I think of it. I wish I could kill him. If my parents had told me the basic facts of life, it would probably never have happened.'

Parents who, as their daughter reaches puberty, talk only of the basic facts, with no mention of feelings of desire or pleasure, often hamper her ability to weigh up situations and make decisions she won't regret. They do not stop the feelings.

Dawn, now 39: 'I was 14. I'd never been properly kissed and it made me feel weak and giddy. My mother had told me how babies were made but I didn't connect it with this. I was never told about being aroused and was amazed at this flood of good feelings.

'Afterwards he asked why I hadn't told him I was a virgin and how old I was. I loved him, so I told him. I couldn't understand his panic and I never saw him again. At home I managed to work out that what we'd done could have made me pregnant. When I realized the enormity of it, I wouldn't date anyone for about eighteen months.'

If a girl finds herself pregnant through ignorance, her parents not having told her about the reality of sex, it is extremely difficult for her to seek their support and advice.

Felicity, now 23: 'My mother never told me the facts of life, I suppose because she didn't think I was mature enough. I was 17 and totally confused. I didn't think you could get pregnant the first time. When I missed a period I was too scared to tell her. I was sick every morning and she kept asking if I'd had a period. I said yes but I was two months' pregnant and my stomach was big. She took me to the doctor, who said birth control pills would help if my periods were irregular. I was too petrified to say anything.

'When I was four months gone, I gave in and told her I was going to have a baby. She suggested abortion, but it was too late. She said they'd see me all right anyway. It was a great relief. My dad said I'd been a silly girl but he'd stand by me.'

In a real crisis, most parents act out of love and concern; but girls like Felicity interpret silence about sex as condemnation and are frightened of rejection.

Parents who won't discuss sex openly make it hard for a girl to find her sexual identity. They undermine what her body and emotions are telling her. Most teenagers are under pressure from boys and from their own desires to experiment; young girls mostly want and expect to end their teens as sexually active women. If parents admit this, they can offer realistic guidance in handling relationships. If their attitude is 'thou shalt not', implied or direct, they will be disregarded; their daughter will enter sexual relationships with only whatever knowledge she has learned elsewhere.

One strong message young girls receive is that sex equals intercourse. Most schools explain sex as the means of reproduction rather than as a pleasurable experience. (But our survey shows that most women do not find their greatest satisfaction in simple intercourse; they say that kissing and cuddling is at least as important.) Meanwhile, the media tell women that their primary task is to appeal to and arouse men.

Lynette, 18: 'Men are led to believe that any woman is available. Too much emphasis is put on beauty, dizzy blondes and fantastic figures, not enough on brains, personality and the overall person. Women's feelings are not understood. Many women get themselves into stupid situations because they lack confidence in a man's world.'

It is hard to say no, hard to say what you want; it is easy to feel there's something wrong with you if you don't want or enjoy intercourse.

Rosalie, 18: 'My first sexual experience was a disaster. My friend came round with her boy and my boyfriend. I had no intention of going all the way, but my friend dragged her boyfriend upstairs and I was left trailing along, not daring to be accused of being frigid. So I went with him.'

Tracey, now 20, had intercourse at 15: 'Nobody told me about the wider aspects of sex, that it's nicer to wait until you're sure and you love your partner. The boy was persuasive and I was fond of him; I put up some resistance then agreed. It was painful, boring, and I later felt sorry I'd done it.'

Roma, now 24: 'It was awful. I was 15, the boy was older, and I wanted to impress him. I thought everybody did it. I had dreadful guilt afterwards and fear of pregnancy. I thought females shouldn't enjoy it, that it was fun for the man only. I don't know whose fault it was – my parents', my own, or school sex education. I was very curious.'

Female sexuality and guilt

It is natural to want to explore your sexual responses, by, for example, masturbation; but this is another subject that parents find it hard to talk about. *Nearly two thirds of the unmarried women in our survey said they masturbate, as do 56 per cent of wives.* Many feel guilty (39 per cent of the unmarried).

Sonia, 19: 'I have masturbated since I was eight. As a child I was convinced it was very wrong. Now I don't think that, but not through talking to anyone about it. It's a real taboo.'

Terri, 20: 'I feel uneasy if it's mentioned. Everyone must do it, but the only person I ever told is my lover, and only because he asked.'

If parents can let their daughter know that masturbation is

21

normal, they can avoid making her feel guilty – and guilt about sexual matters often plagues women later in life.

Similarly, parents who can speak about the penis and vagina may never have mentioned the clitoris – which is, after all, an organ purely for female sexual pleasure.

There are good reasons for girls not to rush into making love too young, but few for condemning masturbation or petting. If a girl learns ways of enjoying sex without intercourse, it lessens the pressure to 'go all the way' and smooths the path to mature sexual enjoyment. But many parents make daughters feel ashamed.

Linda, 17: 'I had my first relationship with a boy when I was 14. I was overjoyed. We petted, but never had intercourse. I wrote about it in my diary, which my mother read. She was very upset. She and my father told me to stop seeing the boy. I hadn't done anything wrong but I lost their trust, which hurt me deeply. I've never been forgiven. My mother brings it up discreetly about twice a year and it still hurts.'

The idea that nice girls don't is hard to dislodge and can mar an otherwise happy relationship.

Carol, 23: 'Parents and society condition people against enjoying sex. When I started sleeping with my (much loved) boyfriend, I didn't reach orgasm through intercourse and, though he often asked me, I couldn't pluck up courage to say what I really enjoyed. I was afraid he might find it boring or, in the case of oral sex, distasteful. I didn't say anything because I wanted him to take all the decisions, so I wouldn't feel demanding and unfeminine.'

It is unrealistic to expect a girl to deny sex until she finds a long-term partner and then, at the flick of a switch, become an uninhibited, imaginative and communicative creature of passion.

Eleanor, 28, is married with children: 'Sex was *never* mentioned in our house. When I started menstruating at 11, I nearly called an ambulance, as I was on my own and thought I was dying. If it hadn't been for my friend's mother I wouldn't have known what was happening. It took four days before I dared tell my mother. She gave me a book that explained periods, nothing else.

'Sex was a dirty word, so I learned from books, girls' comics and friends. At 13, I started to rebel against my parents. When I was 15, I met my husband and we had sex after three weeks, and from then regularly until we married. Then it got worse. I liked it less and less. The excitement had gone and I no longer had to rebel against my parents.

'I can't forget what I learned from my upbringing – that sex is dirty – and find it very hard to relax and let go. If we do anything different or unusual, I feel guilty and upset. I hate my body and don't like myself as a person, although I have lots of friends and my husband loves me dearly.'

Today's unmarried women believe that the old double standards still apply, no matter what is written about the modern sexually liberated woman. Often a boyfriend's parents allow a couple to sleep together when the girl's parents do not. Seventy-three per cent think that girls who have sex with several boys get a bad reputation; only 17 per cent feel the same applies to boys. Men who sleep around are virile studs. Women who sleep around are tarts and slags.

Jill, 17: 'My boyfriend has had several affairs, for which his friends admire him. I haven't. He says that if I had he would never have been interested in me!'

It is not that young women crave promiscuity. They want to feel free to express their sexuality in a happy, stable relationship; they want to feel confident about making the first move, and they are fed up with feeling guilty. They think men should treat sex with the same respect that most women do, not as notches on the bedhead. But most parents' attitudes unintentionally reinforce the double standard.

Parents and contraception

Obviously parents worry about the risk of pregnancy for their daughters, but these days this should be minimal. I am not advocating that all young girls should be put on the pill, nor ignoring the health risks. But young pregnancy is hardly advisable.

In the opinion of the women who responded to our survey, withholding information about contraception will not prevent early sex; rather, reticence is likely to increase the risk of girls not using it or not using it properly. More than four out of five unmarried women believe that if contraception is hard to obtain it leads to more pregnancies, not less sex.

The parents of almost half our married women, regardless of age, have never spoken to their daughters about contraception. Of the rest, only 16 per cent discussed it fully. What's alarming is that parents are hardly more likely to have discussed contraception with a young woman who is having intercourse than with one who is not.

For their part, daughters are afraid of raising the subject. For example, Kristel, 17, a virgin: 'I can talk fairly openly with my mother but I'm afraid that if I tell her I want to go on the pill she'll try and talk me out of it. She might stop me going to stay with my boyfriend or him with me.'

Claudia, 20: 'I got pregnant at 16. My parents were reasonably understanding and paid for an abortion. Afterwards the FPA gave me the pill. After about eight months my mother asked me to come off it as she thought it would encourage me to sleep around. Subsequently I got pregnant and had a second abortion.'

Rosemary, 20: 'My mother's favourite line is that it's always the nicest girls who get caught; the bad ones know exactly what to do. How on earth can making love with somebody you love and are planning to marry, being responsible enough to prevent an unwanted pregnancy, be classed as bad? I wish I could speak like this to my parents.'

If parents can make it easy for their children to discuss and use contraception, their early sexual experiences are more likely to be pleasurable.

Emma, 18: 'With the summer holiday ahead and plans to go camping together, Mum advised me to get some form of contraception. I wasn't particularly bothered, but for my parents' peace of mind I went to the local GP. When we did make love there was no worry – but not using contraception would have taken any enjoyment away.'

Sometimes there are health reasons why parents should discuss contraception.

Nicky, 18: 'My GP gave me the pill – luckily my mother found them before I started taking them. She was very upset that he'd not checked our family medical history. Two of my cousins died on it, and though my mother came off before any damage was done, she now has thrombosis. Also, I have high blood pressure.'

Some girls are so scared of their parents finding out that they risk pregnancy instead: 'I first made love at 20. I went to the family planning clinic and was given the pill. I flushed the packets down the toilet, scared my mother would find them.'

Thirty per cent of those living at home would be too frightened to see their doctor about contraception if they thought he might tell their parents, and some take a chance instead, though under present guidelines a doctor will *not* tell parents about a consultation without a girl's permission, even if she's under 16.

If parents do find out, it's often by prying. Jody was angry when her mother found her pills. 'It wasn't accidental. She was snooping while I was at work. I'm 19, and she had no right. I hadn't told her because I knew she would be upset – she's jealous of boyfriends; she thinks I'm going to run away and leave her.

'Now she's convinced I've cheapened myself – that I've blackened my soul and won't ever be forgiven. There's always an atmosphere between us. I don't think she'll ever accept that I'm an adult. But taking the pill was mature and responsible.'

Secret sex

Parents' attitudes often make early sexual experiences anxious, guilty and unenjoyable. Not a good augury for satisfying sex later on. Their prohibitions rarely prevent sex – just ensure that it happens in secret. Four out of ten parents whose daughters are living at home and having sex don't know. Two out of ten know but are unhappy about it, and more than three out of ten know and accept it – though sometimes this is a more or less resigned acceptance rather than an openly discussed issue.

Making love secretly often means that the act itself is rushed, concluding before the woman is fully aroused, assuming she can relax enough to feel aroused at all.

Denise, 20: 'My fiancé and I have little privacy – we both live with our parents. I couldn't make love in our house, but we do in his living room. I must be honest and say I don't enjoy it much. I feel guilty and tense in case the door opens.'

One way to get privacy is to do it elsewhere. Jackie, 21: 'It's difficult for us with no home or car of our own. We have made love in a boat, in a railway station, outside some shops at night, by a church, in a garage, in a friend's bathroom and in the back of the British Legion loos.'

Some variety of venue is exciting – many couples later deliberately rediscover the thrill of courting by making love in unusual places – but the back of the British Legion loos in winter sounds less than idyllic.

Of daughters living at home, 12 per cent don't know how their parents would react to their boyfriend sleeping with them at the family home, 10 per cent say their parents accept it, and 8 per cent will only accept a regular boyfriend.

Some parents strongly disapprove even when girls have left home, making it impossible to talk about the subject honestly and probably putting strains on their own relationship with their daughter which they'll later regret.

Marilyn: 'My mother wrote to me at college asking where my fiancé stays when he visits. I told her he stays with me. She wrote back saying she assumed he shared my bed and she was saddened and disgusted. I'm 22 years old! I was disappointed in her cheap view of me and my fiancé.'

The role of religion

Some wives blamed religious upbringing for sexual difficulties.

Nicola, 31: 'I am very shy. My strict Catholic upbringing was the main factor when my first marriage broke up and now it seems my second is going the same way. Neither of my husbands has seen me naked. I think I'm pretty and have a good figure, but I can't take off my clothes even for a doctor. If it was left to me, we would never make love. It's not that I don't want to. I just can't take the first step.'

Anna, 27: 'My husband is a theology student and wants to be celibate. He only makes love to please me or after I've had a go at him, and gets very upset that he still enjoys it. He thinks it is sinful. He can't see that this is a reason to end a marriage. We've only been married a year but I'm leaving him.'

Hannah, 55: 'I was a nun for fifteen years but left because I did not want to die *wondering*. I was 32 when I came out and met Peter at the hospital drama club. Later I learned he had studied for five years for the priesthood. He was very shy; I made the advances and asked for a goodnight kiss, which he gave when he was sure no one was about. We grew fond of each other. I enjoyed it when we excited each other and liked feeling his erection. But after we married he would refer to this and say I made him commit sin.

'I am a loving person but he didn't want sex once we were married. Even the night of our wedding, sailing on a ship to Ireland, he locked himself into his cabin (we couldn't get a double) and wouldn't let me in. I was heartbroken.'

Religious teaching often makes people ashamed of sexual feelings. But parents can choose which parts to stress. Judging by accounts of women to whom religion is important, the belief that intercourse should be confined to marriage need not deny a happy exploration of sexuality.

June, 22: 'We are both practising Catholics, and believe that, while "making love" is more important than sex, sex and marriage go together. I am thrilled that he can get so excited. It feels delightful for us to be moving together with him very hard so close to me. We can talk frankly about it and he's learning not to be inhibited. We're teaching each other how we tick, how we cope when things go wrong, how to say sorry and forgive; also about what sex can and can't do.'

Samantha, 23: 'We don't believe in sex before marriage, but we enjoy all forms of it apart from penis–vagina intercourse. We are satisfied and happy.'

Simply prohibiting sex as sinful can make it seem desirable for all the wrong reasons. Anne Marie, 20: 'Coming from a strict Catholic family, having sex was rebellion. I wanted to see what all the fuss was about. Love was an afterthought. It saddens me now.'

Bridging the gap

Few of us were blessed with parents who talked easily about sex, but the first step to improving our sex lives – a goal sought by so many women – is verbal communication: we must learn for ourselves how to overcome embarrassment and *talk*. Not just women; men too.

There is a simple exercise used by sex therapists to break down initial shyness. Make two identical lists of these medical terms relating to sex on the left-hand sides of two pieces of paper: intercourse, copulation, coitus, masturbation, onanism, oral sex, fellatio, cunnilingus, orgasm, climax, genitals, vagina, clitoris, labia, penis, testicles, breasts, menstruation, period, ejaculate, semen.

Without comparing notes with your partner, write down on the right-hand side all the other related words you know – making love, fucking, fanny, etc. – marking with a tick the words you don't like. See who comes up with the most words. Then swap your lists and read them aloud. Talk about the words you like, where you first heard them, why you like them; talk about the ticked words you don't like. Possibly, for example, you may not like your partner to refer to your cunt – like prick, it's a word often applied to stupid or unpleasant men.

It is an important first step in sexual communication to find a vocabulary you are comfortable with. Kathy, 25: 'Why be embarrassed to speak to someone you sleep with? Talking about my life with my partner improved it 100 per cent. It's great to be open. Step over the first hurdle and it's easy.

'You love him, don't you? He's probably as shy as you are. Make it easy for both of you. Men are shyer than women. Give them a break from their masculine image!'

Why are parents silent?

No mother wants her daughter to be troubled and confused about sex. The trouble is that poor sex education is passed from one generation to the next. If our parents were ashamed to talk, we are often hampered by the embarrassment they taught us when it comes to talking to our children.

There is often a natural reticence between the generations in talking about sex, but if our upbringing has left us with guilt and inhibitions, we may ourselves try to deny that our children have sexual feelings and pass on our own anxieties.

Jane found that talking with her parents meant she didn't start having sex until she felt ready: 'I was under enormous pressure to have sex, and didn't know how not to without damaging some good friendships. Talking with my mother and father helped me to extricate myself from such situations.'

Some parents fear that talking about sex will lead to earlier experiment. According to the popular media, young people are wildly promiscuous from an early age, risking increasingly horrible diseases, pregnancy, abortion and ruin. Actually the rate of teenage pregnancies hasn't risen for years, but parents fear for their daughters.

Maureen, 39: 'With all this talk of sexual athletics and contraceptives, youngsters today are under great pressure to have as much sexual experience as possible.'

But we found that whether or not parents speak openly about sex makes no difference to whether their daughter has sex under the age of 16, and has surprizing little effect generally. As we have seen, what it does influence is the quality of the sex she is likely to experience.

Parents fear promiscuity, like Wendy, 42: 'With contraception, the younger generation can only find excitement with a constant change of partners. I deplore this. Women are basically romantic and emotional, not sexual. I believe young girls are forced into sex.'

Actually, today's young women aren't as different from

earlier generations as their mothers fear. They may not wait for marriage to have sex, but they overwhelmingly believe in fidelity. *Of those with a steady partner, only 9 per cent think fidelity unimportant, 9 per cent aren't sure, and 81 per cent say it does matter.* Only a few could be said to be promiscuous: 7 per cent had one other lover, 4 per cent had two or more.

No woman said contraception caused her to have sex too early or to be promiscuous. Many said their reasons for first having sex, and sometimes regretting it, were for the love, warmth and security lacking at home.

Kim, 25: 'My parents had been arguing. I felt desperately in need of affection and fell to a man who supplied it. I didn't think of it as a sexual experience but received much warmth and comfort. I suppose I wasn't ready and maybe I was used, but it didn't feel like that.

'It wouldn't have happened if I hadn't felt so deprived of love and comfort. How many parents are aware of their child's feelings? If they gave them more time their children wouldn't be so grateful to find comfort elsewhere.'

Paula, 17: 'I was 15 and very naive. My parents were divorced. My boyfriend eventually talked me into it around the time my father stopped seeing me. I felt lost and vulnerable and thought I would lose him too so I gave in. I hated it. It was over quickly and I felt dirty and used.'

Periods of promiscuity were repeatedly linked to feelings of rejection. Mandy, 18: 'I realized I was doing it to feel wanted. I had to know that someone liked me.'

Undemanding love

It seems that the best way to prepare our daughters for a happy love life is to love them – to give an undemanding love that respects their individuality and ability to make their own decisions, giving them the necessary information to make those decisions.

Talking openly about sex doesn't rush girls into it, but it does make it more likely that the experience will be a happy one. This is not because parents have thrust manuals of sexual technique into their daughters' hands but because they've been encouraged to see sexuality as part of a bigger whole – part of themselves, part of a relationship, and something worthwhile. Not as some dirty, hole-in-the-corner secret.

Parents often underestimate how much influence they carry.

Some, acting with the best intentions, seem to block all chances for their daughter to develop her sexuality in a caring relationship.

Lucy, 18: 'My boyfriend and I had talked about having sex for a long time. I was never pressurized. We planned it. I went on the pill. It was important to both of us as we were both virgins. By this time we knew each other's bodies well and what we liked. It was really lovemaking. We were both so happy we cried. It lasted five hours before I went home. I couldn't stop touching his body even when we were dressed. It made us feel even closer.

'But my mother found a packet of pills. We had a long row. I cried all night and most of the next day. In the morning I could hardly see as my eyes were so swollen. I had to go and tell my boyfriend I couldn't see him again. I nearly killed myself that night. For six months I was very depressed and put on two and a half stone. I failed all my lower VIth exams. I saw him occasionally but we never spoke.

'I see him now for half an hour a week. It's very hard but now I have hope in life. We aren't going out, we don't make love. I ache to be with him. Writing this is making me cry. I know to most people we must seem very young but the intensity of feeling is just the same. I just long for a time when I can run my own life.

'Please don't think my mother is horrible. She was doing what she thought best and I still love her.'

Being the parent of a teenage girl is not an easy role. You can be caring, open, honest, willing to discuss anything, and your daughter may still be awkward and rebellious and in trouble.

The very essence of being a teenager is learning to be an adult and making mistakes. It's often a matter of luck whether these mistakes are minimal or drastically unhappy. But blaming yourself or your daughter is as wise as blaming a baby for crying or an old person for going grey.

3 Learning to Love
The first time – and lessons learned with hindsight

The first time you have intercourse is an important event. In retrospect, what happened on that occasion may not seem in any way typical of your later sex life – but, surprisingly often, the reasons that led to our first time being delightful or feeling like a dreadful mistake can still be affecting our sexual happiness today.

One woman in ten says she enjoyed the first time a great deal, three liked it reasonably well, four didn't enjoy it much and two not at all. So overall, six out of ten didn't enjoy their first time, though among today's 16-to-18-year-olds, who are perhaps more sexually knowledgeable and confident than past generations, this figure falls to just under half.

These days, 68 per cent of women have intercourse before their 19th birthday. Perhaps more surprising is that 44 per cent of their mothers' generation did too. Figure 3 shows at what ages twenty women from the two generations are likely to have had their first experience.

Three quarters of women of all ages, including the over-forties, think it's reasonable for girls to start having intercourse by the age of 18. Where opinions have changed is that more 16-to-21-year-olds think that it is acceptable to start having sex at 16, whereas older women prefer 18. It looks as though they have reason on their side, too. The later you leave it, the better it is likely to be.

Seventy per cent of those who first had intercourse under the age of 16 did not enjoy it, compared with 60 per cent at 16 to 18 years old and 50 per cent at 19 to 25.

Intercourse when you aren't ready is not only unpleasant at the time but can damage an otherwise happy relationship and create unnecessary fears in the future.

Debra, 19: 'We were great friends and in love. I was 14. We thought we were grown up. One day we agreed to try it. We solemnly undressed and got into bed; then I said we couldn't

31

because we didn't have any sheaths. He said not to worry because he would withdraw. I didn't know what he meant but it sounded convincing.

'He tried to put his penis in several times before giving up. Because I felt it was my fault for being too tight I decided to suck it instead, which I'd read about. It was awful. He took ages to come and when he did I was almost sick. After that we never did have sex because I was always so tense.'

Lisa, 21: 'I was 16. The relationship was fine at first, but we did too much too soon. He was just as green as me but he would read about things like oral sex in girlie magazines and then come over and try it out on me. Consequently I'm still scared of getting too intimate with boyfriends. I'd like a full sexual relationship but I'm afraid I would regret it afterwards.'

Figure 3

At what age do young women now first have intercourse – and when did their mother's generation?

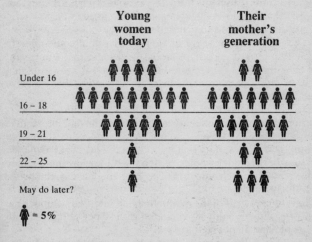

* (The older women – aged 41 to 60 – on whom I based these figures took part in our survey on unmarried women but more than four out of five of them had been married in the past. Figures for today's young women are based on those now aged 22 to 25, but those for today's teenagers will not prove very different.)

Why do women say yes?

Age is far from the only factor which affects enjoyment of first-time intercourse. As Louise, 18, pointed out: 'Age is of little importance. Maturity, stability and love are more important.' We found that the *reasons* women gave for having intercourse the first time were crucial to their enjoyment of it. (See Figure 4) Age is relevant mainly because the younger you are, the more likely you are to have intercourse for reasons you later regret.

We can't separate emotions from sex; the more you like or love your partner, the better your first experience is likely to be.

Megan, 18: 'I enjoyed the first time very much, both sexually and emotionally. It was the final missing bond in our relationship.'

Figure 4

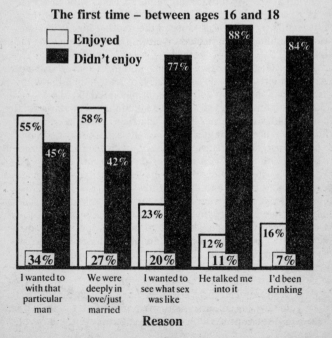

The first time – between ages 16 and 18

☐ Enjoyed
■ Didn't enjoy

Reason	Enjoyed	Didn't enjoy
I wanted to with that particular man	55%	45%
We were deeply in love/just married	58%	42%
I wanted to see what sex was like	23%	77%
He talked me into it	12%	88%
I'd been drinking	16%	84%

(additional figures at base of bars: 34%, 27%, 20%, 11%, 7%)

Reason

Trisha: 'I was 19 and my husband 17. It was our wedding night. As Christians, though we had talked about it, we didn't want to do it before. We had no hang-ups. We enjoyed it the first time and we still do.'

However, not many women these days believe in waiting for their wedding night. Only 3 per cent of 16-to-25-year-olds believe that a couple should wait even until they have *plans* to marry before having intercourse. The common reason they give is that sex is too important to be left to chance.

Robyn, 23: 'I now know my first partner didn't satisfy me. I think both partners should have had sex with others, so they're not ignorant, and sex with each other, to see if they're good together.'

'It's a good thing to have sex before marriage,' said Jan, 21. 'Different sexual appetites can break up a relationship.'

Again, older women back them up. Among those aged 41 to 60 only one in ten thinks sex before marriage wrong. Sometimes they speak with experience.

Cynthia, 42: 'My mother taught me that once you gave in to a boy he lost all respect, so I said no. But I wish we had. Frustration by both of us finished the relationship. It was sad, very unfulfilled, and affected my attitudes and feelings for the future.'

Isabel, 44: 'Lovemaking means nothing to my husband. Although girls today may start early, at least they'll know the kind of man they want and not be disappointed like me.'

In fact, in our survey of wives we found that whether or not a couple had sex together before marriage made remarkably little difference to whether the wife felt sexually satisfied now. *Three quarters of those who are sexually satisfied had sex before marriage, but so did two thirds of those who are dissatisfied.* Whether a wife had had other lovers before her husband made virtually no difference to these figures.

Our ideas about what makes for good sex change and develop. The couples who enjoy a mutually happy sex life now aren't necessarily those who started off enjoying it the most. Factors such as whether a couple are affectionate and kiss and cuddle a lot, and how easily they can talk together about changing sexual feelings, play a large part in determining whether they continue to enjoy sex together.

And those same factors affect whether you enjoy the first time you have intercourse, too – regardless of whether it's before or after your wedding night. If you care for the boy you are with, he's likely to care for you, be more gentle and loving, and you're more likely to be able to share feelings and anxieties.

Lee, now 20: 'It was great. Not like the movies, not an earthquake, but I've never loved anyone so much as that night. We'd been going out for three months before he started to kiss and cuddle and touch. Because someone once tried to force me to have sex, he said it was important for me to know that he loved me and didn't just want me for that. Over the next two months he taught me how to excite us both but still steered away from sex – until I was ready, he said.

'One night in a pub I made up my mind, but I was still frightened. We drove to a quiet place and he did his best to calm me. Then we made love. As I lay in his arms afterwards, he asked if he'd hurt me; I said it had at the very beginning but I soon got over that. We've been happy ever since.'

Even if the first time is not successful from a purely physical point of view, it can still be a happy experience for emotionally close partners.

Hilary, 20: 'We were both totally inexperienced, but it was OK to feel inadequate together – even if it was a bit bungled, it brought us closer. Neither of us put pressure on the other to perform so we were relaxed.'

Fay: 'Without love, the first time would have been ghastly. Since then, it's got better and better.'

Though 84 per cent of unmarried women think sex is best with one man you love, many have intercourse for the first time with men they hardly know. Under these circumstances, first-time sex is rarely pleasant and can cause long-term problems.

Netta, now 27: 'I was 16 and just left home; I can't even remember his name. Because he was older I thought he knew it all. It was a disaster – my first time, in someone else's house, scared stiff. I was too tight. One quick stab which hurt like hell. For years after I thought my vagina was too small to make love.'

Katie, 20: 'It was extremely painful and I wondered what all the fuss was about. He was only interested in himself. He even tried to convince me I had come. Fat chance – he had all the technique and refinement of a tumble drier.'

One in five have intercourse mainly out of curiosity.

Marie, now 17: 'I was 14. I can't remember much, but I was excited and curious, and it was totally different from what I had expected. I remember feeling very smug in school, sitting in

35

maths and thinking, Nobody knows what happened to *me* last night.'

If friends say they are having sex, you can feel left behind, like Sally, now 24. 'When my friend told me about sex with her long-standing boyfriend, I felt I was missing a good thing. I was 16 and started to go out with a boy the same age. He didn't excite me, but I decided to have sex with him. It was not pleasant – I was unaroused, scared and, looking back, not ready for such an important experience. I should have let it happen naturally instead of forcing it on myself.'

Some deliberately have sex with virtual strangers, afraid of making a fool of themselves with someone they care for.

Lesley, 26: 'I was afraid of making a right mess of it, so I decided to practise on someone I didn't care about.

'I got drunk at the disco and was picked up. It was revolting. All I could think was hurry up. I opened my eyes to have a peek at his thing. God, how ugly, I thought. I felt sick. Everything's hazy after that. I woke up next morning in my own bed, hardly able to walk, I was so sore and swollen. My white trousers were covered in blood and I washed them in the bath. I was disgusted with myself. I kept thinking it wasn't meant to be like that – what about the four-poster bed and the champagne? A disaster. I didn't even learn anything.'

A stranger is far less likely to be careful of us and our feelings and, in circumstances like this, who could hope to be relaxed and happy enough to be able to learn?

Of those who have sex for the first time out of curiosity, three quarters don't enjoy it.

Miranda, 28: 'It was loveless and mechanical, anxious and painful. I felt inadequate, unable to move in the right way, unsure what I should be feeling. It happened because I couldn't stand the ignorance of virginity any more. I never saw him again and was left with only the worry that I must be absolutely awful in bed.'

Sandra, 20: 'I just wanted to know what it was all about. He couldn't get it in. When he finally did, it hurt. I didn't think much more about it. I'd rather have had a bag of chips.'

Sex can't be more than an expression of what's already in a relationship, or latent in it. If you don't share affection, romance, trust and humour, sex is unlikely to conjure these qualities out of thin air. Usually it will highlight their lack.

Alison, 20: 'I was curious – I wanted to try this wonderful thing that everyone was so het up about. Afterwards I just thought: is that it? I'd been really excited, but what a let-down. Looking back, I regret my calculating coldness and that I didn't even fancy the guy much. I should have waited. I knew about sex, but I didn't know about relationships, respect and responsibility. Why don't they teach that in school?'

Some schools do, inviting visitors from the Family Planning Association, for example, so girls can feel safe 'and talk about their problems and mistakes. But in many schools, apart from lessons on reproduction, discussion about sex means bragging and the fear of losing face in the cloakroom, adding to the pressure to rush into sex.

Ellie, now 27: 'It was lousy. But the next day at school my friend wanted to know what it was like. "Great!" I said.'

Just over one in ten 16-to-18-year-olds have sex for the first time because they were talked into it, and 90 per cent of them don't enjoy it.

If you're talked into it by a man who doesn't care so much for you as for adding notches to his bedhead and bragging to his mates, it can be a crushing experience. Zoe, now 21: 'I was 18. He took me to his room and all the sweet-talk began. Next minute I was in bed and then it was all over. Scowling, he asked if I was a virgin. I said yes. He said I wasn't tight enough and didn't bleed. I was good, he said; not very good, but not bad. I was very hurt, especially when I found he'd bet with his mates he'd get me into bed. The bet was £150 for a new drum kit.'

Sometimes young women with little knowledge of sex don't know what's happening enough to protest effectively.

Marjorie, now 46: 'I was strongly against sex before marriage. Even heavy petting took me by surprise. Nobody had told me about it and I was worried and confused. I was also very shy and didn't stand up for myself. Eventually my scruples were overcome in a field and it's something I've always regretted, though the man later became my husband.'

If you feel unsure about what's what, talk to somebody. If not your parents, maybe an aunt or an older relative, maybe a teacher. Lots of us are puzzled when we're young. You could talk to your GP or family planning clinic doctor – even if you don't want contraception, they should be pleased to help – or you may be able to reach a young people's advice centre. For further details see the addresses at the back of this book.

Some men accuse girls of not loving them if they won't do it; others threaten to find their sex elsewhere.

Iris, 21: 'I was 17. He said if I didn't sleep with him he'd have to find someone else. He made me feel childish. We had sex and it took both of us about two minutes to come. One minute I felt pain as he entered and the next I was in bewilderment as it was my first orgasm. The orgasm was good but that's about all.'

Time and again young women wrote about putting the man's desire before their own, being worn down by his arguments.

Rosalind, 21: 'He kept on and on at me until I got so fed up I agreed. All I wanted was to get it over with. Afterwards I hated my lack of self-respect and I hated him.'

Unwillingly having intercourse, putting someone else's demands before your own, and resenting them for it, does eat away at self-respect. Yet girls are usually brought up to be helpful and obedient; they see their mothers putting husband and family first, and often find refusing – even refusing intercourse they don't want – particularly hard.

More and more women these days feel they need to learn how to be assertive – how to have more self-confidence and stand up for themselves. (If you want to learn more, see the Help Directory and Further Reading.) Being assertive doesn't mean aggressively disregarding your partner's feelings but taking responsibility for your own. In this case it would simply mean deciding for yourself and saying if you want to have intercourse or not.

If you're ever under pressure to have intercourse you don't want, remember you've *always* the right to change your mind. Just because you said you would last time doesn't mean you have to this time; just because he's got an erection doesn't mean compulsory intercourse. When you say no, the message is *not now*. Don't bring the future into it; let tomorrow look after itself.

Saying no will stir up many feelings in you. We all tend to be nervous in circumstances like this. You may fear his anger or rejection; fear that you are sexless and abnormal. Given that girls are supposed to say no when they mean yes, he may press you all the harder. But again, simply say what you feel – tell him you're frightened of making him angry. Getting whatever fears you have out of the closet will make you more confident.

Don't apologize. There's no crime in not wanting intercourse. You may regret hurting his feelings. If so, say so, but you have nothing to be ashamed of.

Once he has received the message, don't justify your decision with endless talk. Move on; if you care for your partner, tell him so.

It's not only teenage girls who agree to intercourse they don't want at the time. Many women continue to do this all their lives. *More than half of all wives sometimes have intercourse wishing they weren't.*

Isabel, 34: 'The woman has a part of somebody else's body put inside her – unless I actually want sex, I feel invaded. If I don't feel secure and loved enough to relax, I resent my partner.'

Sex that you don't want can make you feel used. Petra, 21: 'He expected us to make up in bed after a row. It was a disaster. Afterwards I told him I still wanted to talk – I had so much on my mind that I had behaved mechanically and it was no pleasure.'

Gina, 57: 'Gifts often seem connected with a sexual advance. It seems churlish to say no – but if I could wait until I really wanted sexual love, I would give myself more passionately. Faking pleasure is an easy way out.'

There are those who believe that a woman should *never* openly refuse her husband, but faking or just putting up with it leads to women experiencing a lot of sex they don't enjoy – hardly an incentive to want to make love more often. To make your body act out something you don't feel damages your self-esteem. You are, in effect, saying, 'My feelings don't matter,' when they do – very much. Feeling unable to say no also leads to excuses and roundabout ways of avoiding sex – for example, going to bed extra early so you can be asleep when your partner joins you or, like Christine, 'I keep him talking until he's too tired and can't be bothered.'

In the long run, dishonesty doesn't even help your partner. Your partner feels rejected but is uncertain of the cause; resentment makes him imagine all sorts of inaccurate explanations. He doesn't know how to improve things; he might be relieved by a straightforward refusal and an explanation of your true feelings.

Consider whether the reason you don't want to make love is that some other problem is getting in the way. Talk about your feelings – see if kissing and cuddling arouse you. If you still don't want intercourse, don't force yourself – this rarely helps – but if the problem continues you probably need some expert advice (See Help Directory).

Wives who *can* say no comfortably speak warmly of their sexual relationship and understanding husbands.

Libby, 29: 'Where we live, women are expected to want sex

whenever their husbands do. My husband used to be that way but we have talked a lot, and now he realizes that women are more than machines.'

Seven per cent of 16-to-18-year-olds say it was drink that led them to have intercourse the first time and 84 per cent of these didn't enjoy the experience.

If you're with a boy with whom you were ready for sex anyway, a drink may be part of the fun. 'It was on a beach one hot summer's evening, thanks to a mixture of curiosity, teenage infatuation and a pint of lager and lime,' said Margaret.

But if you're drunk, a man who doesn't know you well isn't likely to treat you with respect. You may find yourself out of your depth; he'll probably be less than sober himself.

Pattie, 17: 'I was at a disco with a friend. We were drinking heavily with different blokes. He kissed me hard and put his hands up my skirt and told me he wanted to take me to a quiet room. I thought it was going to be a bit of kissing and I went along.

'It turned out to be a toilet. Next thing I knew he was undoing my trousers. I remember the pain and I must have screamed because he put his hand over my mouth. Next day I noticed a bloodstain on my trousers. I worried about what diseases I might have caught or if I was pregnant.'

If you know it's going to be a long evening in a hot disco try to alternate alcohol with soft drinks. The danger with alcohol is that it takes twenty minutes to take effect. It's easy to be drunker than you realize.

Taking a chance

You can get pregnant the first time; we heard from women who did. *More than three out of five of those who first had intercourse under 16 used no contraception; two out of five of those between 16 and 25 also took a chance.*

If you're talked into sex, if you've had too much to drink, or are simply too young, you're less likely to use contraception.

Danielle: 'I was 15 and too young for a sexual relationship, but I was proud to have caught this particular boy. I was very nervous, because he'd already got one girl pregnant. We didn't use any contraception.'

Even in a stable relationship, you may be tempted to ignore the increasing likelihood of sex. It can be hard to admit that you want it. Couples talk of getting carried away when intercourse had clearly been on the cards for some time – as they may admit with wry hindsight.

Kirsten: 'There was no holding back. It was the natural thing to do. I thought I would explode with happiness. We never gave a thought to contraception; we couldn't think of anything, which shows how important it is to have contraception worked out as soon as you start going out seriously.'

This is easier, of course, if contraception can be discussed in a confidential, comfortable atmosphere with a sympathetic relative or advisor.

Stella's period was late after her first time: 'I have never been so scared in my life. I dared not speak to my parents or friends. I thought of suicide, abortion with a coat hanger, falling downstairs or walking under a car. When I started my period I was so relieved; the thought of other girls going through what I did is terrifying.'

Schools aren't managing to fill the need for education about birth control. It's not enough to say what methods of contraception exist; girls need to be told that their GP will respect their confidentiality, and where the family planning clinic is. It helps if they can discuss the advantages of different methods and the risks attached.

A girl who *can* take responsibility for contraception is more likely to enjoy her first time.

Caroline: 'We petted, but I wouldn't go any further until the pill was effective. When we did make love, it was one of the most wonderful experiences of my life. I also got a big thrill when he climaxed. I felt such power – it was me, my body and my actions which had caused it.'

Sex we regret

Two out of five sexually experienced unmarried women have had sex and regretted it; an overwhelming number said that this was because there was no good relationship with the man. One in five regretted it because it was a disaster sexually; rather less than one in five because they'd had too much to drink.

Willa, 20: 'At college the attitude was sex for physical pleasure, or so people said. I did it twice, to prove myself. It may have been physically good at the time, but the next morning it was bloody awful.'

Only 1 or 2 per cent of unmarried women believe in

intercourse on the first date. Over half of the more romantic 16-to-18-year-olds think you should at least be in love before you have intercourse, but a majority of the older age groups think sex is reasonable once a couple have simply got to know each other.

Gwen, 27: 'I've learned I have to be involved with a man to enjoy sex. I no longer feel I *have* to do it. I shall wait until I really want to in future. We put too much pressure on ourselves to have sex with men we don't really know.'

Women may have a desperate need for love when affection is lacking in life or at times of crisis. Coral, now 22: 'My parents had just been divorced and I would have been a pushover for any father figure. He seduced me. It was a disaster which upset me for ages – embarrassing, degrading and the biggest regret of my life. When I bump into the man now I feel like vomiting.'

It helps to know the difference between desire for sex and the need for affection. Be honest – if you're miserable and unsure, say no. A man who likes you will respect this. If a man can't be an understanding friend, he's unlikely to be an understanding lover.

If you're sad, give family and friends a chance to comfort you. You may think they don't care, but it could be that you haven't let them know how unhappy you are. If you feel utterly desperate and alone, all you have to do is pick up a phone, dial the operator, and ask for the Samaritans. You won't even have to say who you are; you'll be able to talk to a sympathetic listener.

The myth of promiscuity

Though two out of five unmarried women have had intercourse and regretted it, few could be called promiscuous. Nearly half the 16-to-18-year-olds now in a sexual relationship have had no previous lover, a quarter have had just one or two. One in ten has had five or more.

But starting intercourse young can mean that later relationships include intercourse too soon.

Sally, 18: 'I regret starting at 15. Once you've experienced sex it encourages you to sleep with other boys.'

Stacey, 23: 'If I have daughters I'll try to stop them having sex at 14, as I did. If they're like me and really enjoy it, it's hard to say no after the first time.'

Women who have been through periods of promiscuity – one

in ten 19-to-21-year-olds and one in eight 22-to-25-year-olds have had eleven or more lovers – often look back on such times with regret.

May, now 23: 'I was extremely loose between the ages of 15 and 19. I still don't know whether I was insecure or just immature, but I wish I'd waited until I was grown up before I started having sex.'

Popular images of sex often make it sound like a sport. You practise, improve your technique, and look for a skilled partner. Some women try to lead this kind of life, and then blame themselves when it doesn't bring happiness.

Serena, 18: 'When I finished with my boyfriend I had one-night stands with half a dozen men, and regretted it. I was drunk every time. All I wanted was a meaningful relationship.'

The right kind of man

Which qualities in a man are most likely to lead to a good relationship and how easy are they to find?

Fifty-seven per cent of unmarried women from 16 to 25 say it's hard to meet the 'right kind of man'. Two per cent say it's easy; 41 per cent say fairly easy.

We asked which they would say were the most likely ways of meeting them (see Figure 5). Dances and discos came top of the list, followed by through friends and then through school, college or work. But we also asked them how their own most successful relationship started and the reality contrasts revealingly with their expectations.

Unmarried Women aged 16 to 25 *Figure 5*

What do you think are the most likely ways of meeting the right kind of man?		Where did your most successful relationship start?	
Discos/dances	48%	Through friends	30%
Through friends	45%	School/college/work	28%
School/college/work	41%	Discos/dances	22%
Through hobbies/ interests	19%	Through hobbies/ interests	6%
Social clubs	9%	Other ways (pubs, holidays etc.)	14%

The superficial atmosphere of discos and parties doesn't necessarily reveal your deeper qualities.

Linda, 19: 'Discos are disheartening. I'm not pretty or slim and men aren't interested, while my friends are tremendously successful in the boyfriend stakes even though I've got as much to offer. I hate that way of being chatted up, even by someone attractive.'

Most happy sexual relationships are based on friendship and formed like other friendships – through mutual friends, by working or studying together.

Tricia, 19: 'I was attracted to him but we were just friends in a group. Eventually the relationship grew more serious and we've been going steady for two and a half years. I'm glad we were friends before we became lovers.'

Valerie, 24: 'You can get to know someone better at work than at a disco. Let's face it – we don't always look glamorous and drink affects the way we act in a club. At lunch we could discuss things and relax, which gave me an insight into him as a person. At a disco you just think "he looks nice" or "he'll do". It's more of a physical thing.'

Love at first sight does happen, but rarely because of macho good looks or bravado. 'I fancied his great big cheesy grin from the moment I saw him.' 'He was rather quiet.' 'We met going swimming with friends. Afterwards we walked along a riverbank and shyly touched each other. Then we held hands and fell in love.'

Women tended to speak ruefully of hunting he-men types. Michelle, 21: 'He treated me as a second-class citizen. Leaving him was the best thing I could have done. Now I'm going out with someone who is his opposite – gentle, caring and loving. That's what I want. It took two and a half years to realize I am worth loving.'

Often, women said their best relationships were based on mutual trust and respect. Rachel, 22: 'He treated me as an equal human being. There's no substitute for that. All the orgasms in the world don't help if you're treated like a dog.'

Learning through touch

If you first have intercourse with a boyfriend you have been developing a friendly relationship with for some time, it is likely you will first have shared a gradually deepening physical intimacy – good old-fashioned 'petting'.

44

Anne, 19: 'Besides being madly attracted to each other we found we could communicate exceptionally well. Our courtship has progressed from first shyly holding hands to the lovely warm, funny, sexually intimate relationship we now have. I didn't go to bed with him until I'd known him a year, and even then he didn't pressurize me – more like the other way round.

'Our first time happened when I'd left home and gone to university. Conditions weren't ideal. The bed was small and squeaky and I was in a very emotional state, so it wasn't sexual pleasure that it brought so much as a feeling of closeness and having shared first our minds and now our bodies. We'd progressed to the point where all our petting left out was intercourse.

'Now we sleep together regularly and our physical command of the situation has vastly improved. Learning through touch we now enjoy our sex life a great deal more.'

Jane, now 26: 'Over the course of a year we'd moved from kissing – all I'd ever done before – to just stopping short of intercourse. My parents went away for the weekend so we planned to make love. I suffered from the giggles but apart from that it was pretty successful. Slight lack of fireworks and 1812 overtures, but much, much more fun than I imagined and a lovely feeling. Why does nobody tell young girls that it's meant to be fun? It would save an awful lot of worries.'

If there hasn't been enough of this gradual exploration and development of understanding, even couples who are very fond of one another may not be sexually relaxed and have a nasty shock the first time they attempt intercourse.

Hazel: 'We'd made a conscious decision and I'd gone on the pill. We were completely naked for the first time. I was horrified by the size of his penis. I didn't realize how big they got. I thought I'd be split in two. It hurt. I wasn't keen on leaking semen afterwards either.'

Many women are unpleasantly surprised how messy sex is. Men, for their part, often confuse myth with reality.

Lena, 17: 'There was no pain, no blood, nothing. I thought nothing of it but it was really important to my boyfriend. We argued for days. He said I'd lied to him, there'd been someone else, I wasn't innocent. I felt so terrible, that there was something wrong with me. Eventually we sorted it out and now we have a perfect relationship. But losing my virginity was a nightmare.'

It is quite common not to feel pain or bleed. Using tampons, petting and leading an active life can stretch or tear the hymen so when intercourse takes place all it may need is a little further stretching. If you are aroused and confident, the muscles at the entrance to the vagina will probably be relaxed and make the entry of the penis comfortable.

The power of petting

Progressing from kissing and cuddling to caressing breasts, nipples and clitoris can bring women to orgasm, and is almost always crucial to women's sexual pleasure and satisfaction.

But the clitoris is so sensitive that a man has to learn what kind of touch is right. It is one thing to reach orgasm alone – and many women haven't discovered how to do that – and another to relax and respond to a partner, saying what feels good (see Chapter 5).

It's always important to be aroused and relaxed before attempting intercourse. Only when you feel ready and have had enough stimulation does the vagina unfold and lubricate. Men often underestimate how long this takes since their own erection usually occurs more quickly, and sometimes couples forget all their bodies have been telling them when they decide to have intercourse. Instead of adding intercourse to their petting, they substitute it.

Vicky, 19: 'Because everything was so planned it wasn't as enjoyable as it might have been. It would have been better as a logical step from mutual masturbation – instead, it was quite clinical. I was thinking more of what was going to happen rather than getting turned on.'

Petting is not just a second-rate substitute for the real thing, nor simply preparation for intercourse. It's valuable in itself. Many women all their lives find clitoral stimulation more exciting than intercourse. 'The only way I reach orgasm is through direct stimulation of my clitoris.' For women, intercourse is only one ingredient of sex, and often not the most important one. It's quite possible for a woman who never had intercourse to have a more exciting and satisfying sex life than one who has it every night and twice on Sundays. Moreover, seeing petting merely as foreplay to 'the real thing' leads many girls into intercourse too soon. Lucy, 18: 'I really lusted after him, and thought sex would be like masturbation only better. It wasn't; it hurt, and I got cystitis.'

Married couples, too, often forget the value of petting.

Heather, 33: 'I'd like him to touch me all over a lot more – more foreplay, more heavy petting, more kissing everywhere and more oral sex.'

Alice, 21: 'I love my breasts and nipples to be fondled and caressed, and I always wondered if I could have a climax just by being played with, but he's too impatient.'

Elaine, 22: 'We used to spend more time kissing and petting, and I used to have orgasms during intercourse fairly often. Now he doesn't take the time. I haven't had an orgasm with him for five years. I always fake it. I wish I wasn't such a failure.'

Anne, 29: 'If he wants sex he just turns over and starts to pull at my nightie or undies. I'm supposed to be turned on and take them off. Five minutes and it's all over. He goes back to sleep, or gets up and I'm left lying there. He thinks it's "soft" to kiss and cuddle.'

This isn't just women being 'romantic'. Sexual excitement begins when some stimulus – most commonly a kiss or a touch, but it can even be a sound or smell – is registered by one or more of the senses. This interest and attraction is relayed to the brain, triggering a control centre called the hypothalamus. This orders another part of the brain, the pituitary gland, to send out a hormone which travels through the bloodstream to stimulate the ovaries and testicles into releasing more hormones – this makes you feel sexy. These hormones also trigger the hypothalamus into releasing more hormones. In other words, the sexier you feel, the sexier you feel.

Husbands who kiss and cuddle a lot are six times more likely to be rated excellent lovers than poor, and their wives are more likely to reach orgasm frequently.

Without a chance to build up the level of sex hormones through kissing and caressing, intercourse may be very uncomfortable for a woman. If anxiety, say, blocks his responses, a man may be unable to get and keep an erection.

Sensate focus exercises have been developed by sex therapists to help couples overcome just these problems.

These exercises, which I have explained in detail on pages 201 to 203, consist of exploring first your own and then your partner's body through touch, with the agreement not to have intercourse for a time. This encourages you both to focus on the pleasurable sensations you are feeling *now* instead of anticipating or worrying about intercourse, to learn to accept pleasure as well as give it.

47

The exercises can increase our sex drive; they help us tune in to our sexual responses and rediscover the delights of petting. Even people who have a good sex life find that they can enhance enjoyment – which is how you may be able to convince your partner they're worth trying. In fact, as we shall see, there is often plenty of room for improvement.

4 As You Like It

Some couples find increasing pleasure in their lovemaking over the years, while others are bored or disappointed after six months. Just as important as technique to a couple's lasting satisfaction are the many factors that affect sexual arousal – and these are what we concentrate on in this chapter.

Twenty-two per cent of wives said that their sexual relationship had always been good and 28 per cent said that it had steadily improved during their marriage.

Janet, 39, said, 'I don't find other men sexually attractive. We've built up our skill slowly and carefully through the years. What a waste to start again with another partner!'

'After we married it became less frequent,' said Polly, 26, 'but more relaxed, because we had more time together and one of us didn't have to get up to go home. We still don't make love nearly as often as when we were first married but we feel more satisfied when we do.'

Debbie, 32: 'Sex with a permanent partner should be interesting because there is so much variation available. It takes time to know how to approach these things; but if you are not adventurous it's like having egg and chips every day and you get bored with it after a few weeks.'

Fifteen per cent of wives say their sex life with their husband has steadily worsened. Many agreed with Charlotte, 26: 'We had a very good sex life before our marriage. We couldn't get enough of each other. As soon as we married it wasn't so good. We realized that some of the thrill had disappeared now it was legal and in the privacy of our own home.'

Boredom kills. It can damage even a very happy sexual relationship over years and years of making love together. *Twice as many wives are dissatisfied sexually as are unhappy with their marriage.*

Many married couples are still quite romantic. More than a third say 'I love you' every day, and a further quarter say it at least once a week. Only one in eight can't remember the last time or admits that she and her husband never say it any more.

However, if a couple make love just once a week for fifty years, they will tot up to a total of 2,600 times. How many variations on one theme can any two people dream up to prevent it going stale? 'Come Saturday, his only night off, he expects me to have sex,' said Shona, 24. 'I have lost all interest. It seems to be a ritual. Every Saturday night I know what to expect. It really turns me off.' 'It gets into such a mechanical routine of knowing exactly what is going to happen and when,' complained Lilian, after sixteen years together. Most couples in settled sexual relationships – unmarried ones, too – find that it's all too easy to let their sex life fall into a rut.

When

By far the largest group of married couples – 48 per cent – nearly always make love last thing in the evening, when they go to bed. The wives in these couples are more likely than other wives to be dissatisfied with their sex lives and to rate themselves and their husbands only average, passable or downright poor lovers.

The one in eight husbands who usually wakes up his wife during the night for sex gets a distinctly poor rating, and wanting to make love first thing in the morning is more likely to lead to a poor rating than a good one, though there's not much in it. Many men wake during the night or in the morning with an erection but it is less common for women to feel sexy when they've just woken – or been woken.

'He's quite happy to make love in the morning and sometimes wakes me up in the middle of the night, but I don't find it as satisfying,' said Elsie, 48. 'It's all right as a supplement but no good as a substitute. I get really cross and frustrated.'

More than one third of wives say that the time they make love often varies. These wives were far more likely to be completely satisfied with their sexual relationship and more likely to rate both their husbands and themselves as good lovers.

If a couple can't vary the time they make love – children and hours of work can make it tricky – then a wife is more likely to be satisfied if they regularly make love during the course of the evening rather than leaving it until their usual bedtime.

Tacking it on at the end of the day makes sex more likely to seem a chore. Tessa, 27: 'My husband uses sex for release rather than to enjoy making love to me.'

If you and your partner never start making love until you are tucked up in bed and both already weary, it's only to be expected that you may share some dreary sex. It can make a surprising difference to start cuddling on the sofa while you still have some energy left.

Sophie, 23, who said she and her husband 'seem to know instinctively when the other wants to make love', added, 'We may be sitting close together and begin kissing and cuddling and things lead on from there.' But for that to happen, you have to give it a chance, by being close and comfortable together to start with. It's harder to start showing affection if you are both marooned in armchairs on either side of the fire. That hearthrug can seem like a chasm.

It's the lack of kissing, cuddling and affectionate touching that probably makes most wives object so much to sex in the middle of the night. It's bad enough to be woken up, but to be woken up to what is, in effect, a straightforward act of intercourse with no effort to interest you first is bound to make you feel used.

Sandy, 28: 'If he wants sex, he wakes me up about one o'clock in the morning, takes what he wants and goes back to sleep. I just feel like a whore – there's no love in it.'

Denise, 46, is in bed when her husband gets home from his night shift. 'Sometimes he will kiss and cuddle me and we make love and it lasts an hour, but sometimes he just takes me quickly from behind and it lasts only a few minutes. He's satisfied but I'm not. I just feel used.'

Ninety-three per cent of married couples share a double bed. Four per cent have twin beds and 3 per cent have separate bedrooms. Having separate bedrooms doesn't necessarily mean that a couple have stopped having intercourse, though they are likely to have sex less often than couples sharing double beds.

But a double bed is little more than symbolic if you are rarely in it together. Shiftwork, for example, plays havoc with many couples' sex lives. Anne, 29, pointed out, 'Our sex life is almost non-existent. My husband's shifts get him up between 1.30 a.m. and 4.40 a.m., and he doesn't return home until up to 6.00 p.m. He then goes to bed at 8.00 to 8.30 p.m.' Anne and her husband have children which makes it hard for her to adjust her sleeping patterns to coincide with her husband's. But even without the pressure of children, most wives have their own work.

A surprisingly high proportion of couples rarely go to bed at the same time. Three out of ten wives say they only occasionally or never go to bed at the same time as their husbands. A wife who always goes to bed at the same time as her husband is much more likely to be completely satisfied with their sexual relationship, and a wife who rarely does so is more likely to be dissatisfied.

While external factors which make it difficult for a couple to go to bed together, or relax together beforehand, have a bad effect on their love life, sometimes it is *because* their sexual relationship is unsatisfactory that one or both partners avoid being awake at the same time in the same bed. They try to avoid sexual confrontation and the risk of being approached or rejected.

Kay, 41, 'Having made the move to go to bed, he reads on the loo for ages, has a shave, etc., by which time it is about 1.30 a.m. and all I want to do is go to sleep. I have to wake up by 7.30 a.m.' This can't exactly have escaped her husband's notice during seventeen years of marriage.

Where?

A couple who take pleasure in their sexual relationship are not only likely to vary the time they make love; they vary the place too.

The third of wives who always confine lovemaking to the bedroom are more likely to be unhappy with their love lives. Two thirds also make love in the living room and this is linked with being sexually more satisfied, but the most dramatic contrast is among those who make love in the bathroom – nearly a third of wives say they do and very few of these are dissatisfied!

Many wives crave more variety. 'I wish we could try somewhere else occasionally,' said Rosalind, 27. 'I've always wanted to do it outside, but my husband gets hay fever, or in the bath, but we only have a shower. He's talked about doing it there, but that's as far as he gets.'

The number of other couples who range further afield is surprising. It's not only courting couples behind the steamy windows of parked cars in side roads at night. One in eight married couples sometimes make love in the car, though Molly, 48, had reluctantly been put off: 'I won't drive out in the country and have sex in the car any more because I'm afraid of peeping toms.' One in sixteen couples sometimes make love in the countryside.

We are sensitive to our surroundings when we make love – Eileen, 36, gave as one of her reasons for having gone off making love that, 'I *hate* our bedroom. It looks like a second-hand shop and is permanently untidy in his half, with useless old record-players hanging about, but he doesn't care.' A pleasant setting helps, but even this we take for granted after a while. Variety is important in its own right. If our senses are refreshed by different timing and surroundings, we can react with renewed appreciation.

Julie, 23, has only been married two years but said, 'I know my husband's body inside out. I know how he makes love. I know his passions, likes and dislikes. It's not exciting any more. It's hard to get aroused by a body you've seen time and time again.'

The problem is more likely to be that *everything* in the way they make love has remained unchanged and they haven't discovered how to replace the thrill of the unknown.

Clare, 20: 'Sex was more exciting when we were courting, because it was more difficult to arrange and there was a feeling we were doing something naughty.'

Many couples deliberately set out to re-create the excitement of their early days together, and find it works. As already mentioned, some enjoy making love in the car or countryside.

Lara, 29, and her husband 'occasionally surprise each other with a weekend away at a hotel, where we can be pampered and pretend to be newly-weds. Unfortunately we can't afford to do this as often as we'd like.'

Why don't we have sex more often?

The most common change wives want for themselves is to be eager to make love more often. Sometimes it's simply a question of giving ourselves an opportunity to unfreeze some of our inhibitions. While clearly there are couples with very differing sex drives, there are many women who say they don't usually feel like sex, and so wouldn't make an approach to their husbands, until they have a few drinks. 'Saturdays are usually best,' said Denise, 'when we have both had a drink!'

A quarter of wives drink in order to get themselves 'in the mood'. These tend to be those who are not entirely happy about their sexual relationships.

Audrey, 46: 'While I enjoy sex to a certain extent, I feel I could quite happily live without it. I am most happy to please my husband because I really love him, but I never actually crave or long for sex. There is something slightly absurd about it all – the positions and sound effects. I cannot quite get into the spirit of things unless I have had a few drinks.'

Many women use other, more innocuous, stimuli to prepare them for lovemaking. Top of the list came wearing perfume, which more than half of wives do. Two out of five wear pretty nighties and a quarter put on clothes that make them feel specially attractive or they know have particular appeal for their partner. Roughly one in six put on make up, play music or cook a favourite meal.

It helps keep a relationship fresh if you show each other that you are still willing to take trouble. Nearly one in ten wives wishes she found her husband more attractive, a rather smaller proportion than those who wish their husband found them more attractive. If he comes to bed unshaved and in his vest to face you in your cream and curlers, it's not so easy to feel turned on by the prospect. By the way, we still seem to like to start our lovemaking wearing something to take off. Only 3 per cent of wives say that they go to bed naked to help them or their partner feel in the mood for love.

But the most expensive lingerie in the world doesn't help if it spends its life unused in the wardrobe. One in five wives does nothing to encourage lovemaking. We should keep reminding ourselves not to take our partner for granted, and giving him a dig if he seems to have stopped bothering to take trouble for us, but the problem usually lies deeper than just laziness. Before we can think of putting on the perfume and sexy undies, we need to feel at least open to the possibility of arousal.

Many men and women need some non-sexually-demanding loving to relax enough to feel sexual interest. Jo, 29, explained, 'My husband and I both have demanding careers but our jobs cause stress. Though this doesn't necessarily apply to him, I need to be completely relaxed and free from tiredness to be able to contemplate sex. Where has all the passion gone? Holidays are another matter – two weeks in the sun and we have sex two or three times a day. Unfortunately life is not one long holiday.'

Top of the list of reasons why wives who would like more sex aren't able to make love more often – given by more than half of them – is that their husband is too tired. (See Figure 6.)

Next most common is that they themselves are too tired. Almost as frequently the problem is that their husband 'doesn't feel like it that often or doesn't seem to'. When we asked wives

5%	Lack of privacy from parents, others
26%	Lack of opportunity because of children
44%	You are often too tired
52%	Your husband is often too tired
17%	You don't feel like it that often
42%	Your husband doesn't feel like it that often (or doesn't seem to)
20%	You find it hard to be responsive
11%	Your life is too busy
17%	Your husband's life is too busy
10%	Your husband is often away

Figure 6

whether their sex life was better or worse at different stages in their lives, the one factor that got the highest number of 'worse' votes was when their husband's job was very demanding.

Sheena, 41: 'I love my husband very much but feel we miss a lot of fulfilment together. It could be fantastic, I know, but laziness and tiredness now seem to be the norm. My husband was very sexually responsive and excited before we were married. I think what changed his attitude and need for sex was that his work became more demanding, plus there were family life and commitments – and the lure of the chase had gone.'

Diane, 48, said, 'I know my husband has a hard job. He's a painter and decorator so is always moving and climbing ladders etc., but he works like there's no tomorrow, and won't conserve his energy when he feels tired. If only he'd make love like there's no tomorrow!'

Not working can be just as bad. Moira, 22, said, 'While my husband was unemployed, our lovemaking slowly went from a few times a week to about once a month. The worry of being unemployed with two children under two and very little money made everything very unsatisfactory.

'We have never recovered completely from this traumatic time. We make love more often than when he was unemployed but less often than before he lost his job. Things were made worse because I was tired with worry and looking after the children.'

When we are under stress and tense – a likely situation for women at home with small children or those with high-powered jobs – this blocks our sexual responses. Most of us need to learn to unwind. Most of us are too strict with ourselves during our daily lives, we feel bad about spoiling ourselves. An excellent way to relax and enjoy lots of non-sexual (but very pleasant and sensual!) touching is massage – it's healthier than alcohol, too. Explaining massage properly is a book in itself. I've listed some publications which are easy to understand and widely available in the Help Directory. But if you want to start now, you can do so very simply, using baby oil. Make sure the room is very warm. It's enjoyable to massage all over the body and head; lightly massaging the face eases tension. You can use both firm and gentle strokes. The important safety rules are: always use firm strokes towards the heart, and avoid any direct pressure on the spine.

Massage helps you feel more in tune with your body and your partner's, but don't always expect to make love immediately after massage: this ruins the whole point – that it's an unpressured way to share sensation. However, if it does put both of you in the mood for love, use light feathery strokes at the end to caress the breasts and nipples and brush over the genitals – until the massage merges into lovemaking. If this happens, you will almost certainly find that it is extra-pleasurable because your whole body has already enjoyed so much attention.

Time for change

Apart from increased frequency, there are several other changes that both married and unmarried women would like to bring about in their lovemaking, as Figures 7 and 8 illustrate.

One of the most common changes sought by all women is that their partners should kiss and cuddle them more, should 'take more time in the beginning'.

Eileen, 36: 'I hate feeling like I do but cannot be ignored all day and then feel amorous. It isn't so much "not feeling like it" as not feeling like it at bedtime, having been put off during the evening. He listens so intently to the TV that he doesn't answer if I speak, or he tells me to shut up. By the time I go to bed, all I want to do is sleep.'

Linda, 29, said, 'I enjoy sex, feel I'm quite a sexy person and am gradually going off my husband sexually. I long for a loving,

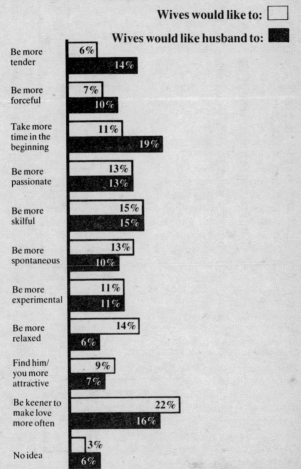

Figure 7

Changes wives would like in the way they and their husbands make love

Wives would like to: ☐
Wives would like husband to: ■

Be more tender — 6% / 14%

Be more forceful — 7% / 10%

Take more time in the beginning — 11% / 19%

Be more passionate — 13% / 13%

Be more skilful — 15% / 15%

Be more spontaneous — 13% / 10%

Be more experimental — 11% / 11%

Be more relaxed — 14% / 6%

Find him/you more attractive — 9% / 7%

Be keener to make love more often — 22% / 16%

No idea — 3% / 6%

Figure 8 Changes unmarried women would like in the way they and their partner make love

Unmarried women would like to: ☐

Unmarried women would like their partner to: ■

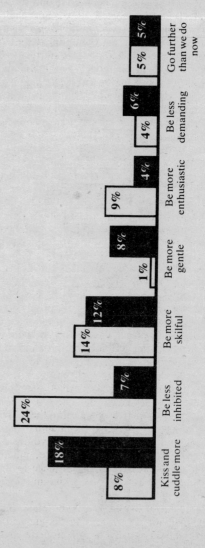

	Kiss and cuddle more	Be less inhibited	Be more skilful	Be more gentle	Be more enthusiastic	Be less demanding	Go further than we do now
Would like to	8%	24%	14%	1%	9%	4%	5%
Partner to	18%	7%	12%	8%	4%	6%	5%

sexual relationship but not to be bombarded by sex all the time. Even a goodbye kiss means a quiet grope. I would love him to want me first and sex second. He only measures my love by sex and feels utterly rejected if sex is not readily there.'

The main change unmarried women want for themselves is to be less inhibited. Instead of openly telling our partner that we want to make love and perhaps starting to caress him, we play demure Sleeping Beauty. We wait for him to make the first move with a kiss, and resent it like mad if he doesn't.

Some women feel more confident in their sexuality as they go through their twenties. Sheila commented, 'I read somewhere that a woman has a better sex life as she approaches 30, and for me, at least, that is true.'

But in 50 per cent of marriages it is still the husband who is expected to make the first move. 'I don't like to seem pushy,' explained Sarah, 29. 'I don't want my husband to think I'm loose.'

However, the wives who make the first move roughly as often as their husband are more likely to be satisfied with their sexual relationship, and both they and their husband are more likely to be happy about the frequency with which they make love.

A woman who never makes the first move can cause her partner to feel unwanted and bitter. Mandy, 28: 'My husband and I didn't have sex for about three weeks. In the end we had a blazing row. He told me he purposely didn't instigate making love because he wanted to see how long it took *me* to do or say something. I realized the situation bothered him immensely but I didn't feel I could discuss the problem. I didn't see that there was a problem. I just didn't want to make love. Therefore I ignored it, until we had our row.'

Mandy and her husband locked themselves into a miserable dead-end, but of course men are going to feel unwanted if we never show we love and desire them. If we don't feel like intercourse, we can still take the initiative in showing affection. If you tend to avoid that because you fear it will lead to more pressure on you to have intercourse, remember you can set the limits anywhere you like. But since loving contact can itself encourage arousal, having a kiss and a cuddle may stimulate our interest.

Four out of five of those who make the first move at least sometimes do so by starting kissing and cuddling. Our first move should usually be affectionate and inviting; but it is important to make it clear whether it's just a kiss and cuddle we want or whether we are feeling sexually interested. Because we are embarrassed by being sexually frank, some of us give indirect signals which can easily be misunderstood.

Joy, 42, said she was put off ever making the first move years ago. 'I suggested we went to bed and he carried on watching TV for ages. I felt cheap and nasty, rejected, and have never been able to make the first move since. He said afterwards he simply didn't realize.'

Pam, who's 40, would like to make love more often and believes that she is 'too highly sexed for my husband most of the time'. She explained, 'We go upstairs at the same time but I take a long time in the bathroom and when I come out he usually has his eyes shut. I always lie on my back if I want to make love. If I do this, instead of turning straight on to my left side to go to sleep, he knows I want to and sometimes is very keen, but I can lie waiting for up to an hour. I often have to touch him in order to get him to make love, though. I can't remember a time when I turned to go to sleep but he wanted to make love.'

Pam is giving her husband conflicting messages. She takes a long time, without explanation, in the bathroom, which suggests she is not eager to get to bed with him. She then lies waiting for him to make the first move, though she is conscious of wanting to have sex. The absence of any affectionate signs from her could in fact be making him feel threatened. It may seem to him as if she is actually saying, not 'I love and desire you,' but 'Go on, then, show me what a man you are.' Men are just as vulnerable as we are to feeling sexual failures.

'Very occasionally the feeling is mutual about wanting to make love,' Pam went on, 'but usually that is because I have made it pretty obvious during the evening that I want to.' When she does give him a clearer message, he feels wanted and sexually interested – and 'it can be almost perfect,' she said.

When women do make the first move, very few are turned down. Only 8 per cent of husbands refuse a sexual advance more than occasionally and generally they are keener for their wives to take the lead sexually than the women themselves are. While only 13 per cent of wives themselves like to take the sexual lead very frequently, 43 per cent believe that their husbands would like them to.

Shirley, 24, said, 'My main fantasy is of being more forward with my husband, or never being too embarrassed to ask for anything at any time in any room of our house. I like to fantasize about being more sexy during ordinary evenings at home and generally being more forceful.'

There are many women who would like to be more adventurous, to suggest more variety, but it is no use our expecting ourselves to be more forceful sexually if we do not learn to be more assertive in our everyday lives.

Sex is a highly charged and sensitive area, which makes it all the harder for us to be straightforward in asking for what we want. We have to learn through practising on simpler issues. This is of double benefit. Achieving desired changes in other areas of our lives will in itself usually have a beneficial effect on our sex lives. Many women don't feel like making love as often as they would like because they are unhappy and resentful about other unresolved problems in their relationships.

Judy, 38, complained, 'I'm expected to work too hard. If I have spent the evening cooking, cleaning and getting the children's things ready for the morning, I feel very weary. Meanwhile he has gone to bed with his paperback and is lying there all cosy and comfortable "waiting" for me. I feel too resentful to make love.'

Anita pointed out, 'Husbands generally not doing as much housework as they could leads to wives not giving as much in bed as they could – a subtle revenge!'

It's tempting to blame men, but part of the problem is that women find it hard to ask for change. We are raised to put ourselves second, to look after others, to be good wives and mothers, not to show anger. Kathy, 36, lamenting the fact that she so rarely feels inclined to wear all the sexy underwear her husband enjoys buying her, said, 'We get so wrapped up in being wives and mothers, we forget our own feelings, emotions and desires – in order not to complicate our relationships with our husbands. Sometimes our husbands don't want to listen; sometimes they don't have the time, or don't want to make the time, to listen.'

So resentments build up, egged on by the voice which says, 'But what about me? What about my needs, my turn to put my feet up, my turn to relax?' – and often spills over into our sex lives.

Many women find it impossible to enter into the spirit of sex if they haven't properly made up after a quarrel. Men more often see sex as a way of getting closer.

Sandy, 32, said, 'On the whole we have a happy and very

satisfying sex life. We have our ups and downs; on almost all occasions, this is due to other problems.

'Generally, if we have a row, I find the anger much more difficult to forget than my partner and will not have sex to make things up. I want the arguments resolved first.

'I found the initial period of moving into a flat together very trying. Many arguments arose which affected our sex life, mainly over the division of labour and the fact that, just because we had decided to move in together, I had not decided to become his maid, cleaner, cook as well. I resented him leaving me to take his shoes to the menders or his suits to be cleaned. I didn't when we lived separately. What got to me most was that, if I complained about something, his answer would be, "Tell me what to do and I'll do it." I saw no reason why I should take the responsibility of telling him what needed doing in his own home.'

Asking for change

Trying to resolve differences that arise from deep-seated attitudes can be very frustrating, as Judy found. 'Don't say that I should explain, go on strike, etc.' she said. 'I have tried it all. After an exhausting discussion I might get some help that night but next day we're back to square one.'

She probably says nothing until one day all her pent-up resentment boils over. So he helps that night, to keep the peace, but actually hasn't understood what it means to her nor how it reflects in her sexual responses – which certainly matter to him as well as to her.

If you are going to ask for a change, don't keep putting it off until anger gets in the way of calm discussion. Have clear in your mind what you want to achieve and what you want to say. Don't try to change your entire lifestyle and sex life at one go.

Choose your time and place carefully. Don't open the conversation just as your partner is going out or *Match of the Day* comes on.

Describe the behaviour, don't label the person. Say straightforwardly that his lack of involvement makes you feel angry and resentful, unloved and unsexy – for example. Then ask for what you want. Be specific – request that he takes on a particular job regularly, perhaps. If you face your partner with blanket demands that he be more considerate, less selfish, less lazy, he may not know where to start.

End on a positive note, making it clear that you're glad to have got it out into the open, because making love together is important to you.

Beware of red herrings. If Judy's husband keeps on about how he mows the lawn, for example, Judy should acknowledge it, but bring the discussion back to the point, not start competitively swapping lists of tasks. Steer clear of history, too. As soon as one of you says, 'You always . . .' you are no longer talking about the particular thing you want changed.

I realize that if you tell most men that you are practising becoming assertive, you will meet with teasing, irritation and suspicion. Whether you tell him is up to you. But, in fact, they have no need to be so defensive. Men confuse assertiveness with aggression; we are not talking about women becoming bullies who always get their own way.

Before asking for a change accept that, no matter how silly your feelings may appear to him or anyone else, you have a right to ask for what you want. Your wants are of equal value to anybody else's.

But they are not superior. You are asking, not demanding. A happy compromise may well mean you making changes, too.

Sandy added, 'After many discussions our attitudes have changed. He is more likely to do things without being told, but I have realized that I can't expect him to feel like doing housework just because I want it done at a particular time. If I feel angry because I am working and he is sitting with a book, I tell myself that I can just as easily leave the work and sit down.'

In fact, most men will find they prefer to negotiate as equals with a partner who knows what she wants and asks for it directly, rather than having to cope with hidden resentment, martyrdom, manipulation and often unconscious revenge.

We can practise this technique by requesting domestic changes and it works for sexual changes, too, such as asking for more kissing and cuddling before intercourse. Since we often find it hard to talk about sexual matters, having a calm framework for discussion can make it easier to set the ball rolling and stop you feeling so anxious.

Helena's experience shows the pitfalls of launching unpreparedly into discussion. 'Though we are dissatisfied with our sexual relationship, the problem is communication. I dislike the way he says, "I want to take you to bed," and expects me to be instantly aroused. I'd like to be wooed and romanced first! I tried to explain this. He replied that in the early days I was as eager as him, and never needed wooing, which is true, so we end up getting nowhere. He says he doesn't approach me sexually very often now because he doesn't know how to. He thinks I don't fancy him, though I assure him this isn't true.'

But Helena could have responded, 'I know I didn't need wooing to go to bed in the past, but I do need it now. I do fancy you but I do need some romancing before we make love.'

5 Who Needs Orgasm?
Faking and fulfilment

Female orgasm is still a fraught issue. A decade or two ago a flood of books and articles suggested that orgasm was every woman's right. This led to a fuller sex life for some but made many others worry themselves silly because they had never had an orgasm and didn't seem likely to. In the wake of that anxiety sex therapists and writers have repeatedly emphasized that orgasms really don't matter. What is important is whether you enjoy your sex life.

But *two out of five women, married and unmarried alike, still fake orgasm.*

'After ten years with my second husband,' said June, 43, 'I enjoy our sex life very much. We still fancy each other like crazy! Our relationship has always been affectionate and sex a natural part of it.

'My husband does not know that I fake. His ego is ten miles high! But as it is not that important to me and our general relationship is so good, what is the problem? If orgasm became an issue I would no longer enjoy sex. My husband is not inconsiderate. If he knew, he would worry that I was not happy. Life would become a quest for orgasms.'

Liz, 25, confirms June's fears: 'When I first met my husband-to-be I told him that I had never had an orgasm but that I really enjoyed sex anyway. Simon decided that he'd try everything to make me come and it ended up with me dreading sex because (a) he thought he was a failure and (b) I felt a failure.

'I then faked for the first time and it so thrilled him that afterwards our sex life was excellent again. Orgasm to me is not too important. I enjoy lovemaking for what it is – a sexy feeling and lots of kisses and cuddles. I don't regret faking. It has reassured Simon that we are a "normal" couple and given me peace and space to get what I want from sex.'

Women fake orgasms because it is so important to men.

Wives and unmarried women believe it is important to twice as many men as women that they should reach orgasm.

'He's obsessed with me having a bloody orgasm!' said Lyn, 21. 'He cannot conceive that I enjoy sex without it. To me it's just the icing on the cake, nice if it happens but not vital.'

The traditional male-dominated view of sex rates intercourse above all other contact and sees sex as excitement, erection and ejaculation. Ninety-seven per cent of husbands and 94 per cent of partners of unmarried women usually or always climax, the overwhelming majority of them in the vagina. Only tiny minorities usually climax through oral sex or manual stimulation.

If their partner doesn't also climax, preferably during intercourse, they feel they've failed. So, many women decide that it's easier to pretend.

Carrie, 24: 'When we first went out I faked orgasm. Now it's a problem. I fake less often but never admit it – the longer I have left it the harder it has become. Sometimes I nearly climax and fake it then. A few months ago I was depressed at work and became totally numb sexually. The fact that I was appearing for the first time not to have an orgasm upset him quite a lot – making it doubly hard to tell him.'

What's wrong with faking?

If orgasm isn't very important to you, it may seem easier and kinder simply to go on with the pretence. But it is not something to do unthinkingly. You are, after all, putting a lie right at the heart of your relationship. In effect you are telling yourself, 'My sexual responses are not right. My partner would be unhappy if he knew the truth about me. I must pretend to feel something I don't, be something I'm not.'

That feeling may be leaking into all sorts of other areas of your life, perhaps fed by lack of self-confidence in life generally.

If you stop faking, you and your partner can start to discuss the issue. Once you start talking about it, he may learn more about women's sexual responses, and accept that orgasm isn't as crucial to most women as it is to most men. It doesn't mean he is a failure. Women are *different*.

'At first my lack of orgasm worried us,' said Kim, 22. 'Gradually, by talking together, we accepted that making love doesn't have to be earth-moving every time.'

Among wives, only 15 per cent always reach orgasm when they make love and 43 per cent usually. This leaves 38 per cent who reach orgasm about half the time or occasionally and only 4 per cent who never do. Among unmarried women, it's a minority – 41 per cent – who usually or always reach orgasm. (See Figure 9.)

'For me, it's not a question of setting out to achieve orgasm,' said Rosy, 25. 'If I do, great. If I don't, I still enjoy it. It just indicates I was tired/sleepy when I started and not really bothered, but quite happy to lie back and enjoy being loved.' Feeling pressured to reach orgasm will prevent you enjoying the other pleasures of making love.

If you do wish you reached orgasm, there may be much to be gained by stopping faking.

'When my boyfriend and I started making love, I never had an orgasm,' said Pippa, 20. 'That worried me. Everything I had read told me that I really should have one. I didn't want to upset him so I faked them. Somehow he realized, and we talked and talked about sex – everything in detail. I stopped worrying and now I usually have an orgasm. If you have to fake it, maybe the real problem is you can't talk to each other.'

Figure 9

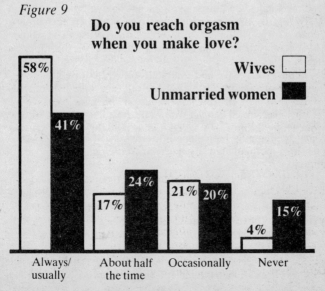

**Do you reach orgasm
when you make love?**

Wives ☐
Unmarried women ■

Always/ usually	About half the time	Occasionally	Never
58% / 41%	17% / 24%	21% / 20%	4% / 15%

Another common cause of faking is the inability to reach orgasm through intercourse. In fact, *only 42 per cent of wives and 24 per cent of unmarried women who reach orgasm usually do so through intercourse.* (See Figure 10.)

If you fake orgasm during intercourse when you could reach it another way, you are blocking your own pleasure and risking problems in your relationship.

Jackie, 31: 'He is a very exciting lover, but I was convinced that all women had multiple orgasms during intercourse, whereas I only had orgasms clitorally, i.e. with manual stimulation.

'I could not understand why I could not orgasm internally. It wasn't fair, so I faked it and sex was brilliant even without it.

'However, during a row I told him that they were all faked. His reaction was very destructive and it has caused many problems not just sexually, but because I lied about something so important.

'Recently, however, he has made a continued effort to satisfy me manually, which always works. We seem to be getting over this orgasm problem, which anyway never affected my attitude towards him, only towards myself. I felt inadequate.

'I have since "come out", so to speak, only to find that nearly all my friends are either faking or not having orgasms "internally" at all. We agree that it is easy during masturbation or manual stimulation, but not during intercourse. The whole – loving, masturbation and caressing combined – is the important thing.

'I only wish that I had come out sooner because now I feel I am one of millions instead of the odd one out. It is only my husband I have to convince because he believes every woman he has had sexual contact with in the past has had no difficulty in coming. I know they faked it and so do they!'

What causes orgasm?

It's amazing: with all that has been written about the female orgasm, researchers are still arguing about what it is and what causes it. There is a desire to find just one explanation that fits all women – one or two magic buttons that bring guaranteed response.

To see just how varied a response our pelvic area is capable of, it helps to understand its internal structure (see Figure 11).

Figure 10

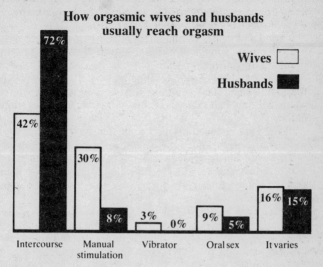

**How orgasmic wives and husbands
usually reach orgasm**

Wives ☐

Husbands ■

	Intercourse	Manual stimulation	Vibrator	Oral sex	It varies
Wives	42%	30%	3%	9%	16%
Husbands	72%	8%	0%	5%	15%

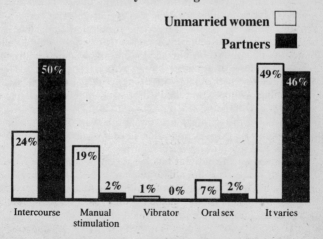

**How orgasmic unmarried women and their partners
usually reach orgasm**

Unmarried women ☐

Partners ■

	Intercourse	Manual stimulation	Vibrator	Oral sex	It varies
Unmarried women	24%	19%	1%	7%	49%
Partners	50%	2%	0%	2%	46%

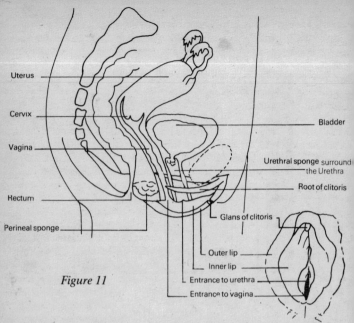

Uterus

Cervix

Vagina

Rectum

Perineal sponge

Figure 11

Bladder

Urethral sponge surround
the Urethra

Root of clitoris

Glans of clitoris

Outer lip

Inner lip

Entrance to urethra

Entrance to vagina

What we call the clitoris is in fact just the tip (or glans) of the clitoris. The far larger root runs beneath the surface and is also highly sensitive. Lying between the vagina and the urethra, through which we pass water, is the urethral sponge, like a cushion on the front wall of the vagina. It expands with blood during sexual arousal, as a penis does. Some women find firm pressure on this sponge very erotic. A book entitled *The G-Spot**, which drew popular attention to this area of sexual stimulation, also claimed that some women ejaculate, like men, through pressure on the 'G-spot'. Others believe it is either urine or the normal lubrication of the vagina. It could be that women with extra-strong pelvic floor muscles shoot out the lubricant as a result of powerful contractions during orgasm.

Many women worry that they urinate during orgasm. If this applies to you, rest assured that you are in good company. It may be a bit of a nuisance but nothing to be ashamed of. It will help you develop better control over your muscles if you do the pelvic-floor-muscle exercises described on page 75.

* *The G-Spot* by Ladas, Whipple and Perry (Corgi).

Between the vagina and the rectum there is another pad which fills with blood during sexual arousal – the perineal sponge. Firm pressure on this is very erotic for some women. Many enjoy stimulation of the anus and pressure against the lower wall of the vagina when making love.

And there's more! Supporting everything are the pelvic-floor muscles. They sweep across from the pubic bone at the front to the bone at the base of the spine, forming a figure 8 round the vagina and anus (see Figure 12).

The muscles are rich in nerve endings. Simply contracting and releasing them may make you aroused. To find them, put a finger inside your vagina and contract your muscles as if you wanted to stop the flow of urine. Those are the muscles nearest the outside; there are others out of reach inside.

These muscles and their network of nerves and blood vessels connect the clitoris, the vagina, bladder, uterus and anus. In most women the clitoris is the 'powerhouse' of sexual excitement and orgasm, but there's more to the clitoris than the glans we can see. When aroused, the entire clitoral system is about thirty times the size of the glans we see. It can be stimulated by

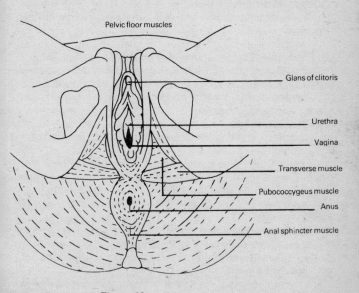

Figure 12

pressure on the pubic mound and the labia as well as by directly touching the glans – in fact, many women find the glans too sensitive to be touched directly or for long.

The clitoris sends waves of sexual pleasure through all the interconnected organs of the pelvic region, which can in turn register pleasure of their own through other stimulation. When all these different organs are drawn into the same harmonious pattern, the pelvic-floor muscles contract at 0.8-second intervals. That is orgasm!

You may feel your orgasm mainly in the clitoris or in the vagina or deeper inside your body or indeed all over your body. It may be overwhelming one day and quiet the next. It varies from woman to woman and in one woman from day to day. It is always the same physical reaction, the contracting of the muscles, but we experience it differently.

How important is orgasm?

Naomi, 21: 'It is only pure curiosity which makes me annoyed about my failure to reach orgasm. If so much had not been said about it, then I think I would be blissfully happy with our sex life. I always have the feeling that I must be missing out on something.'

A woman would have to wear mental blinkers not to be conscious that there is such a thing as female orgasm, but our letters told us again and again that too much importance is attached to it. If you are happy without an orgasm, then you may be more satisfied than a woman who has had one. Orgasm is not invariably pleasurable.

Marie, 21: 'I did have a very prolonged orgasm once and I felt so drained and depressed the next day that I'm not sure I want a repetition.'

Eve, 33: 'I don't have any difficulty reaching a climax, but when it happens it's such a miserable little whimper of a thing that I feel it wasn't worth the effort. I'm usually tired to start with and this only leaves me feeling more tired and highly irritated to boot.'

Even multi-orgasmic women may not enjoy the experience. 'From not knowing how to orgasm when I married,' said Peggy, 53, 'I became multi-orgasmic. My body responded but my head didn't like it.'

It's important not to get so anxious about reaching an orgasm that your very worry prevents it, or perhaps spoils an otherwise happy relationship. Nevertheless, many women feel physically unsatisfied without.

Beth, 30: 'I didn't know what I was missing. Since having had an orgasm I feel frustrated quite often now as I don't regularly reach a climax.'

'I have never reached orgasm with previous partners,' said Lorna, 24. 'But now that I have found the person I want to marry I do worry. I think there's something wrong with me and he thinks that maybe he's not doing things quite right.'

Reaching orgasm becomes more important to women once they are in a relationship they expect to last. *While only one third of unmarried women say it is important to them to reach orgasm, two thirds of wives say it is. However, a large number of wives have problems with orgasm. Only one in five never has difficulty; one in three has difficulty at least half the times she makes love.*

Orgasm seems to have little bearing on whether wives rate their marriage as happy but it is certainly linked to how they rate their sexual relationship and their husbands and them-selves as lovers. *Three quarters of those who are completely satisfied with their sexual relationship always or usually reach orgasm.*

Discovering what we like

Many women wish their men were more skilful and experi-mental lovers. But it's hard to tell them how they could 'improve'.

Mandy, 30: 'I would like to have the active sex life my husband dreams of but I wish it could happen as easily and effortlessly as in a trite film. Explaining destroys the mood.'

Betty, 42: 'Sometimes he asks me what I would like him to do but I am too embarrassed to tell him, even though we've been married for sixteen years.'

If we can tell our partners what brings pleasure, we give them a fair chance of being the skilful lover we dream of. We also increase our chances of being skilful lovers ourselves, which is something many women want to be.

Joanne, 21: 'Every time we make love is better than the last. I am also getting bolder and starting to initiate the lovemaking. Things that I found disgusting when I was a virgin and had never heavily petted I now see in a different light. Nothing is disgusting if it is done with love. I've learned how to love.'

What follows here is a voyage of discovery for women who have never experienced orgasm, who would like to reach it more easily and frequently, or who simply would like to know whether they could enjoy richer sensations.*

It's like turning the light on in your sexuality (which some couples will need to do quite literally. One in four still make love in the dark and these wives are much more likely to be dissatisfied with their sex lives.)

You need to set aside some time each day when you can be undisturbed, perhaps half an hour or so in the evening.

These exercises can be done by women alone as well as those with a partner. Lack of orgasm can trouble women who want to masturbate enjoyably and those whose partners are women as well as those with male partners. You can expect to take a few weeks to work gently through the exercises.

First give yourself time to relax. Lie down in a warm room. Let your breathing settle down for a couple of minutes. Then work your way through all the muscles on your body, tensing them as tight as you can and then relaxing. Curl your toes tight, and relax. Bend your feet back as hard as you can, and relax. Tense your calf muscles hard, harder and then relax . . . and so on, up through your body, to your fingertips, including your face.

Make friends with your body

Lisa, 22: 'I have tiny breasts. My husband swears they are his favourite part of me but I'm very self-conscious about them. I prefer to make love in darkness.

Melissa, 20: 'Our sex life is not as regular as we would like, largely because I am very overweight. My weight does not seem to affect how my husband feels about me sexually. He is very reassuring, but I feel very negative about myself.'

Stand naked in front of a full-length mirror. At first you may only see what you don't like. But keep looking. Notice what you do like. Maybe your eyes, your teeth, your elegant fingers. Work your way through your body saying, 'I like my . . .' or 'I like the way my . . .' Eventually when you look in the mirror your eye moves to the points you like instead of only seeing what you don't.

Explore your body through touch. When you have a bath,

* Adapted from the Redwood manual for women's sexuality courses by Anne Dickson.

74

take your time. Soap yourself all over, caress your body with firm and light strokes, discovering what feels good where. Dry yourself carefully and massage cream into your skin. Notice the different textures of the skin on the different parts of your body.

When this feels comfortable, get to know your body sexually. Sit with your feet well apart and your knees bent. Armed with a mirror, have a good slow look at your genitals.

Explore the feelings in your breasts, nipples and genitals. Touch and rub the clitoris and area around it, explore inside the vagina, around the anus. Don't worry what you ought to be feeling. Just discover what you do feel and what feels good. Try different firmness of touch and types of movement.

Unlock your pelvis

1. Stand with your feet 18 inches apart and heels flat on the ground. Press your fists into your back just above the waist. Breathe in and let your head fall back. Keep breathing, and hold as long as comfortable. When you lift your head, do so on an in-breath. On the out-breath let your head and top half of your body fall forwards like a rag doll so that your fingertips dangle to the ground. After a couple of minutes stand up and relax. Repeat a few times.

2. Lie on your back, arms by your side with palms to the floor, and draw up your knees so that your feet are flat on the ground. Push up your bottom and arch your back so they are off the ground. Hold and relax.

3. Lie on your back, palms down and legs flat. On an in-breath arch your back, keeping your bottom on the ground and letting your pelvis fall away in the direction of your feet. On an out-breath press your spine to the ground and pull your pelvis towards your head. Repeating these two movements as you breathe in and out rocks the pelvis to and fro.

4. Stand and move your hips in a circle like a hula dancer.

Try to do these pelvic-floor-muscle exercises daily to improve vaginal-muscle tone.

1. Find the pelvic floor as explained on page 71. Imagine that you have a drawstring pulling the vagina up towards the top of your head. Squeeze the muscles around the vagina for three

seconds, then relax for three seconds. Repeat ten times three times a day.

2. Try to flutter the vaginal muscles – it becomes easier with practice. Again, ten times, three times a day.

Self-pleasuring

A couple of weeks of body and genital massage and exploration will give you a clearer idea of what you like. Don't aim for orgasm. Just do whatever feels good.

When you have no partner or want to enjoy sex without your partner, masturbation is the natural way to do it. Your sexual pleasure is yours. Joyce, 42: 'When I masturbate I get one fantastic climax after another.'

When you know how your body responds and what you personally enjoy, you can help a partner share your sexual pleasure if you want to.

Annette, 25: 'I thought of sex as being something for the men. I worried if they thought I was doing it right. Through masturbating I learned what I like – it makes sex better for me and for my partner.'

Even if you're used to masturbating, paying some friendly attention to your sexuality may help to suggest new avenues of pleasure. You could also try a vibrator. Juliet, 21: 'Until recently the only way I could have orgasms was with a vibrator. Why should men have all the fun? Long live the vibrator – a girl's best friend!'

One day, think about what makes you angry or anxious in sex. What restrains you? What would happen if you let go? Would you shout and scream with ecstasy? When you have the house to yourself, give it a try – shout! Yell! Scream! Don't mind about being silly. See what it feels like. It's all right!

Starting to share

If you have a partner, you could now try the sensate focus exercises described on page 201 and begin to share some of your new knowledge of yourself.

Some couples enjoy masturbating together. Bridget, 29: 'I have never reached orgasm during intercourse. During a discussion on masturbation a couple of years back, I asked my husband if he'd like to watch me do it, and we've never looked back! He finds it a real turn on, and his attention to me while "indulging" makes the climax twice as good. I certainly don't feel guilty about it. It's added a new dimension to what was for me a very close, but *not* always satisfying, relationship.'

Women without a partner often find masturbation preferable to having sex with a man they don't really care for just for the physical release. Three out of five wives masturbate alone at least sometimes.

It's not always because they can't have sex with their husband. Sometimes it's nice to enjoy ourselves alone. We have no need to feel guilty about it; our partner shouldn't begrudge us, nor should we begrudge our partners, this right. It doesn't mean that there is something wrong. Muriel, 64: 'I can give myself an orgasm any time I want. That gives me a certain feeling of confidence. I've got quite smug about it. I can manipulate my clitoris in the bath and get my own satisfaction. I wouldn't advocate it instead of sexual inter-course, but it helps during a non-productive period to fill in the blanks.'

Four out of ten wives and – to their wives' knowledge – at least three out of ten husbands who are completely satisfied with their sexual relationship masturbate occasionally. If one of you is masturbating *continually* in preference to sex with your partner, of course it will make the other feel rejected. But many men and women enjoy masturbation *as well as* a happily shared sexual relationship.

The plan explained above really can help you discover what you enjoy. As a result of an article I wrote on similar lines in *Woman,* Anne, 27, found her married sex life transformed. 'My libido was zero and I'd never had an orgasm. It made me resentful towards my husband as orgasm was so easy for him. I read the *Woman* magazine article on women who had the same problem cured by self-exploration and tried this. It worked. My husband didn't know what hit him. I changed from a "drag" to a "lover" almost overnight.'

The exercises aren't magic, however. If difficulties in your relationship are blocking your orgasm, you will need to approach the problem in a different way.

Esther, 33: 'I used to ask him to tell me when he was coming so we could come together and it was usually great. In fact, I used to feel fantastic afterwards. I went all weak and felt as if I was floating. I used to come anything up to fifteen times depending on how long we did it, but the last time was usually the best. But I found out four weeks ago that my husband had an affair with my friend next door last year and I have not had an orgasm since. It is such a disappointment to feel nothing now.'

In such a situation, you may need the help of a marriage guidance counsellor – they help the unmarried, too. If you find it impossible to reach orgasm alone, or with your partner, when you can see no reason for it, ask your Marriage Guidance Council or GP about a referral for sex therapy. This will help most women and can also establish whether you are one of the rare women whose inability to have an orgasm is attributable to a physical cause, such as impaired blood flow into the pelvic region.

The exercises in this chapter won't make you reach orgasm at the same time as your partner. A few couples find this easy but most don't, and aiming single-mindedly for the goal of simultaneous climax can interfere with your enjoyment.

The same applies to reaching orgasm during intercourse. It may well be that, through your exploration of yourself, you will become more relaxed, more in tune with your sensations, more able to make helpful suggestions to your partner. It can help to have intercourse with you on top, or with your partner behind you, so he can easily stimulate the clitoris at the same time, for example. The pelvic-floor-muscle exercises can increase vaginal sensation, but worrying about that is counterproductive. When making love, it is not how you do it but whether you enjoy it that matters.

Your partner's problem?

Many women take considerable time and stimulation to build up to their peak of sexual arousal.

Fifty-four per cent of wives said their husband sometimes climaxes too soon, and 16 per cent that this often or always happens.

Angela said, 'He only lasts twenty thrusts. It's all over too soon. I fake half the time as I don't want to upset him. Other times he realizes I haven't come and says sorry. I have asked him whether he tries to pace himself and he said no, he is scared of losing it. But I live in hope.'

Some men overcome this by giving the woman a lot of stimulation before intercourse, but many women find this doesn't work for them. The change from fingers or tongue to penis breaks into their build-up.

Some men worry that their penis is too small for their partner to climax during intercourse.

Celia, 20: 'My vagina is rather big and I can't feel my husband sometimes. He blames himself for being small.'

Moira, 37: 'They say length makes no difference to a woman's satisfaction, but my husband has a large penis and this does make orgasm easier for me. After each thrust he can withdraw further and so rub it against my clitoris.'

On the other hand, Sue said, 'How can you tell a man that, far from being every woman's fantasy, being bigger than normal is a problem? My husband is well endowed and sex is so uncomfortable I try to avoid it. My lover was if anything smaller than average and I could enjoy the whole act.'

Penis size is a factor in some women's enjoyment; but, being visible and obvious, the penis is blamed for many sexual dissatisfactions which are nothing to do with it.

No penis can ever be too thick comfortably to enter the vagina of a fully sexually aroused and relaxed woman. The vagina is extremely elastic. However, an unusually long penis may bump against the cervix. Some women find this exciting but for others it is uncomfortable. This can usually be sorted out by changing the position so that penetration isn't so deep.

A smaller penis should cause no insoluble problems. If the woman doesn't think she can feel enough during intercourse, it could be because she isn't fully aroused. It is other stimulation that is needed, rather than a bigger penis. It can also help if she does the pelvic-floor muscle exercises to improve muscle tone.

It is rarely direct pressure of the penis on the glans of the clitoris which causes orgasm during intercourse. The thrusting causes pressure on the pubic mound and labia which can stimulate the entire clitoral system, and this can be achieved without any penetration at all.

In general, penis size doesn't matter as much to women as men think, and in any case they vary in whether they prefer larger or smaller ones.

A little of what you fancy

For any of your newfound knowledge to help you, you have to be able to communicate it to your partner. *Only one third of wives often talk openly to their husbands about sex or their sexual feelings, and one third had held back from making a request while making love which would have brought them greater pleasure.* Wives who often talk openly about sex are far more likely to be completely satisfied with their sexual relationship than those who don't.

Maggie, 23, always has difficulty reaching orgasm and is not at all satisfied with their sexual relationship: 'I am too embarrassed to talk during lovemaking. I find it extremely difficult to say "that feels nice" or "please do this". Sometimes I try to show him by moving his hands but more often I just keep quiet. This is stupid. My husband is always asking me what I want him to do, and never holds back such a request himself!'

Barbara, 32: 'I hold back through a sort of fear. What would he think? Do I really want him to or is it just a whim? Would he be shocked? Would he refuse? Would it spoil what we were enjoying at that moment?'

The most common unspoken requests were for manual stimulation, oral sex, anal sex, and for words either of appreciation and affection or more basic ones.

Jane, 22: 'I would like my husband to tell me how much he enjoys my body and to actually say words instead of the usual sexual groaning.'

Madeleine, 29, said, 'I would occasionally like my husband to perform oral sex on me, but refrain from asking because I know he doesn't like the idea. I do it to him.'

Lindsay, 21: 'Once or twice just recently I have enjoyed accidental stimulation of my anal area by my husband's penis. I would like to try anal intercourse but I think it is rather perverted and somehow not decent. I think my husband would too, so I daren't suggest it. Also I think it would hurt and I'm not sure if it is dangerous or would damage either of us physically.'

In fact, most husbands are willing to consider such requests. Only 8 per cent of husbands ever do anything during lovemaking which their wife believes makes them uneasy (oral sex comes top of the list), and that's only occasionally. Only 7 per cent of husbands ever refuse such requests from their wife.

If husbands are uneasy about oral sex it should help reassure them, and you, to know that the inside of a healthy vagina contains fewer bacteria than the mouth. All that is needed for hygiene is to wash the genital area – not inside the vagina – with mild soap and plenty of water before making love.

Many couples enjoy anal sex. For the woman it increases stimulation of the perineal sponge which lies between the vagina and anus. Your partner needs to be very gentle because the anal tissues aren't as elastic as the vagina, nor is there any natural lubrication, so it helps to use a safe substitute such as KY Jelly. Since the bacteria which live naturally in the rectum can cause infection in the vagina, you should wash between touching the anus and the vagina.

At the time of writing anal sex is technically illegal between heterosexual couples, though not between adult consenting homosexual couples. It is hard to see what is wrong with it as long as you both enjoy it, and you follow the simple precautions I've mentioned. There are moves to change the law, which is obviously unenforceable.

As well as the women who enjoy, or would like to have the chance to enjoy, anal sex, there are some who do it to please their partner.

Sian, 32: 'To prove how much I love my husband, especially after a row, I participate. Don't think I'm a masochist. Once he's inside, and with the right muscle control, it doesn't hurt. I just want to give him pleasure.'

More than a third of wives regularly agree to things that they don't enjoy and which make them feel uneasy. In one in ten cases this is anal sex and in nearly one in two oral sex.

Penny, 22: 'I don't like my husband to ejaculate in my mouth as I do not like the taste of sperm. He does know, but we still do it as it turns him on more.'

You may put up with discomfort in order to be loving and unselfish, or simply keeps the peace. If it's only occasional, it's unlikely to cause problems; but doing something that you don't like is not going to make you an eager and responsive lover.

There are no rights and wrongs about different ways of enjoying our bodies. What is important is that we should feel free to express our feelings so that sex is a mutually pleasurable experience.

Experiments

Many more wives than husbands – nearly a quarter – regularly refuse to try a different position or new technique, though not always openly. Ingrid, 23: 'When he suggests a new position or experimenting in some way, I pretend I haven't heard.'

It's worth asking yourself whether there is any sound reason for not trying it. Do you really think it distasteful – if so, of course you should not feel pressured to try it – or could your

81

reluctance be the result of inhibitions you haven't re-examined for years?

Diane, 28: 'We talk about the new position or technique and, if we feel right and relaxed about it, then we try it out. For example, we now use a vibrator. At first I thought it was common and dirty to use one. Now we find it a natural part of our lovemaking.'

Dawn, 29, said, 'Our sex life has always been excellent and very open, both of us wanting to learn how the other feels. We try many different things. There is never any embarrassment, and if one of us doesn't want to try something then we don't do it. It is never forced, but always approached with good humour by both of us. I want to know what he finds sensual and he asks the same of me. So we seem to find many different ways of reaching orgasm.'

Many women commented that it 'spoiled spontaneity' or that their husband said 'it put him off' if they tried to say what they wanted at the time. It can help to make brief, positive suggestions – not 'Don't do that' but 'Please do more of that beautiful thing you were doing before'. To help yourselves learn to talk specifically about what you enjoy, start outside the bedroom. You could both separately list three things that you would like to try – who knows, you may come up with the same three! Talk together about your lists, your feelings about each other's requests.

Then both put down just one thing that makes you feel uneasy when making love. It doesn't have to be a sexual technique. It could be that you wish he would wash his feet before he comes to bed, or that he would kiss and cuddle you more beforehand.

This will give you a clearer idea of new avenues you would both like to explore. You don't have to rush off and try them immediately – though talking like this can be arousing – but neither of you will forget, and may well feel less self-conscious about putting them into practice at a later date.

6 Real and Fantasy Lovers

Sexual dreams and 'acting out'

The most important organ of sexual pleasure is not the vagina, nor even the clitoris, but the brain. We feel aroused and experience sexual pleasure not just because the right part of our body has been touched in the right way. Our brain must accept and act on the messages it receives from the senses and trigger off our sexual responses.

If we are anxious, angry or miserable, all the caressing in the world may leave us cold. But it can work in reverse, too. Even without stimulation from outside, simply thinking sexy thoughts, fantasizing, can make our skin tingle and our vagina lubricate, though many women are embarrassed by their imaginings.

'I am too embarrassed to describe my favourite fantasy even anonymously,' said a wife married for fifteen years, 'but it concerns Alex Higgins and a snooker table. Another fantasy concerns being held by one or more men while another forces me to have sex with him, and/or being forced to watch someone else being forced to have sex (sometimes all men). I would like to point out that I am perfectly normal, respectable, ordinary and very clean. I am not at all disgusting, perverted or abnormal, and no one would dream that I think these things sometimes. It is only to achieve orgasm that I think them, not at other times. It takes so long for my husband to give me orgasm otherwise that I am forced to think them. But I feel extremely guilty at having such thoughts.'

Just over 50 per cent of wives fantasize when making love, rather less than half of them regularly. Wives who say they are completely satisfied with their sexual relationship tend to fantasize less often than those who are unsatisfied.

Nevertheless, *wives who rate their husbands as passable to excellent lovers are more likely to fantasize occasionally than those who say their husbands are poor lovers.* And *wives who rate themselves as good lovers are more likely to use fantasy than those who rate themselves as poor lovers.* Fantasy is a valuable and powerful sexual aid to help us free ourselves from our inhibitions. Many women specifically find it helps them reach orgasm on occasions when they otherwise wouldn't.

Penny's favourite fantasy: 'My husband and I have been filming rare animals in the jungle. Just as we come out into the clearing we spot a lion and lioness mating, and as he thrusts in and out, you can see that his penis is really huge.

'When I look over to my husband, he has undressed and his penis is now very swollen and erect. He undresses me and slips his penis into my vagina; as he does this, I begin to orgasm.

'When we have finished making love and again look in the direction of the lions, they are now standing watching us.'

Women's most common fantasies

40%	A man you know/former or present lover
20%	Different or exotic location
8%	Film/TV/rock star
8%	Rape/violence
8%	Being watched/filmed watching others in public
8%	Sex with several men
4%	Man of a different colour
4%	Complete stranger
4%	Husband and another couple/woman/man
4%	Another woman

Figure 13

Dream lover

Two out of five fantasies involve another man known to the wife (see Figure 13). 'I fantasize about someone I've seen and thought sexy, such as my husband's friends and acquaintances at work,' said Mandy, 28. 'I imagine them touching me for the first time all over and then making love to me. I try to recapture the excitement and novelty that you lose by being with the same partner all the time, although I would never leave my husband or be unfaithful to him in reality.'

Fiona, 32, fantasizes 'that I am a stripper in a club with tassles on my nipples and a python which wraps itself round my body in a sexual fashion. All the time this is happening I am thinking about being with my husband and his best friend (who was our best man and whom I have fancied for years) on a fur rug in front of a large open fire; we are smothering each other with warm coconut oil and looking at our glistening bodies in the light of the fire.'

This type of fantasy is a way of introducing variety into our sex life that would be hard to arrange ordinarily or would positively threaten our relationship if we acted it out.

Joanne's fantasy is of a friend's husband. 'It is possible to love two people at once. About 18 months ago this man and I had the chance to explain our feelings to one another. But I really do love my husband and he me. We also have four children between us; that is why we promised *never* to do anything about it. So my release is to fantasize about him and the sort of life we would have together. He is so very, very sexy (a lot like Bryan Ferry). My favourite fantasy is living with him in a beautiful sunny place; we have an apartment overlooking the sea with a beautiful private bay. We spend all our time swimming and sunbathing, just spending our time together alone.'

Often the fantasy lover is a former lover whose faults are now blurred by rose-coloured spectacles. Rather than the man himself, the fantasy often seems to symbolize the more romantic wooing that the wife enjoyed before she became a wife and taken for granted – one wife actually commented that her husband was her fantasy until she married him!

Esther, 47, says her fantasy is based on a former relationship: 'The ESP between us was unique. In my fantasy I'm desired with a passion by an attractive man who is smart, intelligent, suave, sophisticated, dresses with a flair and has a quiet assurance. He has a down-to-earth, yet charming manner, considerate of all people's feelings.

'He makes love with such gentle passion that it becomes an experience rather than a quick roll in the hay. Starting with the old romantic idea of looking at the woman longingly, quiet undertones persist through the evening, with knowledge of the inevitable outcome. It is romantic, erotic, passionate and gentle.

'Of course, I am looking my best. I'm slim in the right places, fit, healthy, glowing, suntanned, dressed beautifully in silk, with subtle yet very expensive jewellery, perfume, and am scintillating company and a satisfactory partner in bed.

'We find we have in common so many things like choice of books, poems, poets, interests. Our lovemaking is uninhibited without going to extremes, and fulfilling and not over after reaching the first orgasm. We do it again in the shower, after drinking champagne.'

Many wives' dream lovers compensate for what they see as particular deficiencies in their husbands.

Andrea said, 'When we were courting he was always giving me a quick kiss or a cuddle and we used to spend hours in bed talking, or just lying and enjoying each other. Now I feel I'm just a chattel and he pays me once a month with a bit of affection.

'I fantasize about a faceless man treating me like a sexy lady and giving me lots of affection.'

Sadie's fantasy 'is with a man who has been a ladies' man and is an expert in the art of love. He is mature-looking, a Sacha Distel type, with perfect manners. He takes me out to a beautiful restaurant, we talk and touch hands, then we go back to his beautiful apartment and have a few drinks. Then he slowly and carefully undresses me, saying lovely things to me while he is doing so, then he carries me to bed and makes love to me for virtually most of the night. He is tender and passionate and at the same time someone who will see to my needs and make sure I am ready before he is.'

Are you surprised to learn that Sadie says her husband's premature ejaculation is a problem?

Beverley said, 'Fondling of my breasts prior to sex is important in my fantasy. I'm embarrassed at asking my husband to play with my breasts before we make love.'

Wives who never talk openly to their husband about sex or sexual problems are more likely to fantasize very regularly. All sorts of criticisms were made of husbands, often comparing them disparagingly with perfect dream lovers, sometimes with real ones.

'I only fantasize to the extent that I imagine and wish I had a great lover by my side,' said Sian. 'One who tries to satisfy me instead of just reaching ejaculation by treating my body as an instrument.'

Ingrid's problem is: 'My husband is not a clean person and his job as a chef makes him smell. For a year I have asked him to bath once a day but he will not. My fantasy is for him to smell nice and to consider my feelings when making love.'

'He has no idea in bed,' said Diane, 42. 'He never touches my breasts and there is no foreplay. He touches me roughly, often leans on me and nearly flattens me. I have tried to talk with him, but he has a big ego and gets offended very easy. When we have been away on holiday I have tried to introduce variety into our lovemaking (nothing kinky) but in the morning he has asked me if I was drunk the night before. This makes me feel bad and I have ceased to try anything new.'

'Sometimes he won't bathe or brush his teeth for a couple of days,' complained Carolyn, 37. 'He smokes as well. He expects me to do all sorts of things and wonders why I find them distasteful.'

Bridget, 50, says of her husband: 'If he is feeling very randy, he talks a lot and uses obscene words. They reduce what should be beautiful to something dirty, tasteless, crude.'

'I have to pretend my husband is someone else to make it bearable,' explained Betty, 38. 'The only problem in our marriage is that physically I just don't fancy my husband any more. He is a kind, generous man and would be devastated if he knew I had a lover. He thinks I am frigid and don't like sex, but my lover only has to look at me and I melt.

'We were married for fifteen years before I was unfaithful. From the beginning of our marriage my husband has made love in a way that made me feel it was purely for his sexual satisfaction and not because he particularly wanted me. I have discussed this with him but he naturally denies it.'

All these women probably think that they have made their feelings plain to their partner. Some certainly will have and for various reasons he is unwilling to change. However, often, when we have something we find difficult or embarrassing to say, or are afraid that what we are saying will hurt, we don't actually get across our meaning. If we could manage to explain clearly, we might encourage our real lover to behave more like our fantasy one.

Desert island dreams

Another common fantasy, enjoyed by 20 per cent, is to imagine we are making love in some sort of exotic location. A sun-drenched beach seems the most common, often bringing back happy holiday memories.

Kerry, 25, said her favourite fantasy is 'to be making love with my husband on a beautiful deserted beach in a small Spanish fishing village where we spent one of our sexiest holidays. We lie, sun-bronzed, on the shoreline and the waves lap over us. It's based on facts – reliving a truly romantic and happy holiday. Long live the siesta!'

Many wives feel the need for relief from humdrum chores of family life, from the role of wife and mother.

Sue, 38, said, 'I like to imagine I'm an exotic Eastern queen lying in luxury on a satin-covered divan, surrounded by slaves whose task is to give me pleasure, one feeding me delicious morsels of fruit, others stroking and caressing me, and another sucking me off.'

'I suppose my fantasy is much the same as numerous other women's,' said Lisa, 32. 'The person making love to me is a rich, very attractive man. We're in a luxurious room with plush furniture. He's gentle and thoughtful but also very insistent. During these fantasies, I have to push all thoughts of my two small children right to the back of my mind. In my fantasy, I'm completely independent, with no husband or children. The minute my mind wanders and I think of the children, the fantasy ends.

'I can't fit me, as housewife and mother, into a fantasy. I have to be someone completely different. If I fantasize "as myself" that I'm with this fantastic guy I always feel guilty. I have to switch myself off and become some non-existent person.'

'I sometimes wish someone would make a pass at me, and see me as a woman and not a mother and housewife,' said Lois. 'It might make me feel wanted.'

More than 50 per cent of wives find that their thoughts stray on to day-to-day worries or the children while making love.

I'm afraid we can't assertively request that the ironing, washing and small children should disappear. But we can recognize that, by becoming obsessed with household chores, we are stifling some part of ourselves. The result can be depression – we just give up expecting pleasure and become unable to experience it when it does occur – or anger. If a woman does not feel desirable, it can make her vulnerable to the first man who pays her a compliment.

If we have these sorts of colourful fantasies, we should perhaps pay more heed to them. We don't have to take them literally, but consider what is within our scope that will make us feel a woman in our own right again. It may simply be a question of organizing a babysitter to make sure we go out together as a couple once a week, the way we used to do before we had a home and family to worry about. You might decide that you want to follow up some interest of your own, take a nightclass, join a sports club – write a book! It doesn't matter what it is, as long as you are sure that you are doing it for *you.*

Husbands also have fantasies of escaping from the responsibilities of family life. Some couples share their fantasies. Melissa, 22: 'We imagine going away for a weekend and being romantic in a very quiet country town, walking around and making love in fields of long grass.'

Julia, 27, said, 'I just wish that we had a bit more money and our bedroom looked a bit more luxurious than it is. My husband is my fantasy, and on the nights when our lovemaking is really good we tell each other what we need, like silk sheets, mirrors on the ceiling.'

A starring role

One in twelve wives fantasizes that she is making love with a favourite film or rock star, or sportsman.

Some couples act out sexual fantasies. 'My favourite fantasy is being made love to by my favourite snooker star, Alex Higgins,' said Cheryl, 28 (he seems to be popular). 'My husband encourages this, even to the extent of making a snooker cue. He thinks anything that turns me on is great. He also picks out clothes for me to wear that Alex would like, with my husband's favourite black underwear underneath.' 'My favourite fantasy is that I'm making love to Tom Jones on a water bed.' 'After a James Bond film I am always aroused and I pretend my husband is 007.'

My husband and I play out our fantasies together,' said Sally, 24. 'Mine are to be tied up and made helpless. My husband's are to serve and be dominated by a beautiful, wicked lady who does not allow him sexual satisfaction.

'We play various games, sometimes using props, sometimes just speaking, giving imaginative descriptions to each other while performing manual stimulation. During these games I never think of any man but my husband. Our games and fantasies give us a great pleasure and lots of laughs, and we are very open with each other.'

'I hope you don't think this really stupid,' said Moira, 31. 'It takes place in the Dark Ages. I am an adventurous female war leader and my husband is the leader of an enemy tribe. It involves lots of chases, swordfights, etc. I am bold and resourceful. When he captures me, I stand up to him. Eventually we end up together very romantically. We remain as equals throughout and continue to have adventures together. Over the years we have developed the plot and added characters in real life – like overcoming shyness or going to the dentist. I think: I mustn't be cowardly. She wouldn't be!'

However, some women find that, if they share their fantasy, it loses its power. They need to keep this inner life private.

Revealing your dreams can feel like surrendering a hostage. Di, 33: 'Once my husband and I did get close enough to discuss fantasies. He was extremely eager to hear mine, which I told him, not feeling 100 per cent comfortable. He then informed me that he never had any and that his imagination just could not stretch like mine. I really thought we were getting somewhere, and was very disappointed. I cannot believe that a man doesn't have fantasies, especially one who against his will doesn't have a very active sex life.'

There does seem a tendency, too, for men to see fantasies as something which you literally want to happen, while women often have fantasies which they definitely don't want to happen in reality.

'My favourite fantasy,' said Viv, 29, 'concerns my husband being seduced by, or seducing, another woman. This turns me on a lot, and yet, if it really happened, I'd be horrified and would consider leaving him! All my fantasies would be unacceptable, even disgusting, to me in real life, and yet they excite me considerably during sexual intercourse.

'This does not cause me concern or guilt, as I realize there is no chance of fantasy becoming fact, or that I'd confuse the two. I also like to fantasize about sex between two women, or two men.

'My husband knows nothing about my fantasizing. I would like us to share fantasies – that is, pretend to be different people in different situations. The nearest we have come to that is when he pretends to pick me up in a pub or somewhere, and we come home and have sex. I'd like it to go further – for example, pretending he's a schoolteacher and I'm a young pupil he seduces – but find I can't suggest these things. I think that's because he might take it as unspoken criticism; in other words, he might feel I'm not satisfied with him as a lover and need to be turned on by other means.'

Threesomes and foursomes

One drawback to sharing your fantasy may be that your partner will want to act it out. Michaela, 34, said, 'My favourite fantasy, funnily enough, is imagining another woman present (though I've tried it in past relationships and hated it). I can't tell my husband this fantasy as, also from past experience, I know: "Tell your man your fantasy and he's immediately demanding you turn it into reality." Fantasy and reality, to me anyway, are worlds apart. I make up pretend fantasies when he asks me to.'

Annette agreed. 'My favourite fantasy is of my husband making love to another woman. The three of us are under the influence of drink. I pretend to fall asleep and my husband makes advances towards the other woman and ends up making love to her while trying to keep this a secret from me. We are usually all in the same bed. When I realize my husband is making love to her I am really turned on. If this took place in reality, I would divorce him.'

Often we use this sort of fantasy to concentrate our minds on what is actually happening to us, our own lovemaking. We 'see' what is happening as well as experience it. Some couples, however, do act out this type of fantasy, by having sex with more than one partner at a time.

Juliet, 33: 'Four-in-a-bed has only happened once, fairly recently, after seven years' marriage. They were friends of my husband, not close ones but from some years ago, before I met him. He had slept with the wife, in the same bed as the husband (and enjoyed it!).

'I liked the change, as did he. We had both had lots of love affairs before marriage and enjoyed almost all of them. Both of us like sex; we don't want to have it away behind the other's back but do miss the variety and freedom of choice. I would rather have the experience with my husband. We're very much in love and have never had any problems, sexual or otherwise. I'm not bored with him either. I enjoyed seeing him with another lady, he enjoyed seeing me with another man (no jealousy – though there would be if it were on the side), and the lady and I felt very close throughout. I wouldn't mind trying it again some time!

'Marriage hasn't stopped me fancying other men. I don't want any other emotional involvement and neither does my husband. I'm also curious about sex between women. Raving sex maniac? No, loving wife and mother, with a responsible job, and respected member of the community – but would I still be if my sexual life were made public?'

Juliet and her husband are not alone in sharing sex with another couple. We heard from several other wives who had joined in willingly. Lorraine asked, 'If there are any more like me, I hope you will be honest and publish the facts, as I would like to know if I am on my own with these feelings that women should have sexual freedom.'

The great danger with acting out this type of fantasy is that real people aren't as well behaved as those in fantasies. When we feel the need of fantasies, we can take them out, dust them down, use them pleasurably – and put them away again till next time. Real people have feelings, and since sex for the overwhelming majority of us is closely bound up with our feelings, we can find ourselves emotionally entangled – and the hurt goes on when the sex has stopped.

'My husband and I swapped partners with another couple,' said Jan, 24. 'We never did anything behind each other's backs as we were always in the same houses. We all got on well. But my lover and I got emotionally involved, and found it was getting too serious and out of hand. It caused a lot of upset and heartbreak. We never discuss this subject as we pretend we have forgotten, but I feel we are all embarrassed.'

Erica, 28: 'We discovered that two couples who were close friends of ours were sharing each other sexually. I was told this by one of the husbands in a blatant attempt to get me into bed with him. He told me that his marriage was entirely satisfactory and the "sharing" would not work otherwise. However, we later discovered that his marriage was extremely rocky and he felt betrayed.

'We tried a similar situation with the two of them. My husband was very unsure about the whole thing to start with. I encouraged him because I found it exciting. However, the roles were then reversed, as he enjoyed the relationship with the other woman and I got very upset and did not want the situation to continue. This led to ill-feeling, particularly between myself and the wife. She saw me as leading on her husband and then backing down, while she was very attracted to my husband and wanted the relationship to continue. We

92

now have very little contact with this couple. I would not recommend it to others. It can cause harm and hostility.'

'I can't do anything about it'

About 30 per cent of women's fantasies involve situations which they know very well they don't want to happen in real life: 'I dream of being gang-banged by Aston Villa football club!'

They include scenes of rape, bondage, group sex, being watched having sex.

Fantasies about being watched or touched by many men (and often women, too) probably help us focus our attention on our sexual responses, make them almost 'larger than life'. This will encourage the brain to respond even more enthusiastically to the signals of arousal it is receiving and so send out hormones which increase the excitement in our genital organs.

The descriptions of some of these fantasies are explicit and may make some people uncomfortable. I have included them because they were written by perfectly ordinary women, many of whom asked for reassurance that they were normal. If you find you react very strongly, it can help you understand your own sexual attitudes to reflect on why this is.

'My favourite fantasy,' said Alex, 31, 'is that about a dozen men undress me and then measure me to see if I'm suitable to serve in their "cocktail" bar (and to have sex with their clients). I have to stand still while they remove each bit of my clothing slowly and carefully and then measure each part of my body, even down to minute details like how big my nipples are and what the length and width of my vagina are.

'When I'm measured and approved, two or three of the men wash me and then I start serving in the cocktail bar. All I wear is a tray tied around my neck which rests under and supports my breasts. The purpose of the tray is to prevent me seeing what people put in me. Clients are allowed and encouraged to touch me as they want. A group of six men come in together and want to have sex with me. I take off the tray and we go into another room. They tie me down to the bed tightly so that I can't move, but not so tightly that it hurts. Each of them has sex with me and then they start putting all sorts of different things on and in me, like ice cubes, cream (which they lick off).

'Then one of the men produces a type of cream which they

93

put on my nipples and in my vagina. Then they sit back to watch as the cream brings me very slowly to an orgasm; because I'm tied down, I can't do anything about it and I just keep coming. After what seems like an eternity they finally release me and I go back to work in the bar until the next time.'

Ellen: 'I am lying naked on a table in the kitchen. My arms are being held above my head and I can't move them much. The man who is holding them is dressed in a suit. He fondles and kisses my breasts and murmurs that I'm beautiful. Another man is standing at the end of the table holding my legs open and is thrusting into me strongly. Sometimes he crouches down and uses his tongue and mouth on my genitals. He is also dressed, except that his trousers are down about his hips; his dress is jeans and denim jacket. He never says anything but stares at me intently when he is thrusting into me. I don't know either of these men (i.e., I don't know them in real life) and I do not feel threatened by them (it is not a rape). They think I'm wonderful and they can't get enough of me.

'The one in the denim jacket is what is known as a "bit of rough". The man in the suit is not as important as the other one; his face can change each time I have the fantasy. There are other people in the next room and I am anticipating one of them discovering us and joining in and others staying to watch. They never do, but I find the idea exciting!'

Gentle rape

Fantasies about rape certainly do not indicate that women secretly long to be overpowered and taken by force. Ten per cent of wives say they would like their husband to be a more forceful lover sometimes (see Figure 7) but they don't want completely to lose control of the situation. They can only enjoy acting out such a fantasy if they are absolutely confident that he will stop the moment they give a signal that they've had enough. The fantasies bear no relation to the reality of rape.

'My favourite fantasy,' said Gwen, 39, 'is being raped *very gently* [my italics] by a number of men all at once. Being kissed in intimate places and intercourse and oral sex all happening together. I am tied by my hands and feet, straddled, so that I cannot stop them. I hasten to add that the reality would horrify me.'

Monica, 35, explained, 'In my fantasies I am usually in a

94

situation where I have no choice about partaking in sex (usually physically restrained). Several men or women make love to me. I protest but this is ignored or laughed at, and they continue despite my protests. I usually climax and feel no guilt at all, as I was "forced" into the situation. The venue is totally different from my usual environment, either extremely lavish apartments or sleazy bars – never ordinary places – with the participants matching the surroundings.'

While we don't want such fantasies acted out in real life, and they are nothing to feel ashamed of, it's worth thinking what this shows of our image of our own sexuality. I have sometimes had such fantasies and wondered what this reflected about my innermost feelings if part of me had to be mentally subjected to force in order to accept sexual pleasure. Are these images which we would really want to have chosen for ourselves?

Another type of fantasy suggests that inside many a timid housewife there is a big, strong, sexy woman longing to get out. Not only is this inner woman more sexually confident than we are – she usually has a better figure, too!

Kitty, 42, said her fantasy was of 'Several anonymous men making love to me with others looking on, in the great outdoors. This to me means I am selfish, possessive and a show-off, and want to tell all that at my age I can still pull in the men, am a fantastic lover with a good healthy body (whereas in fact I have three stomachs and am two stone overweight!).'

'My most common fantasies are concerned with exhibitionism,' said Anne, 26. 'Me being a stripper, making love in public, etc. In fact, I am a very shy person and could never do any of these things.'

Clare, 21, said, 'I suppose my favourite fantasy is that I'm the sexiest woman in the world and it gives me a great feeling of *power*.'

'I like to imagine my husband being tied to a chair unable to move; I enter dressed sexily and he is reduced to a state of highly frustrated excitement,' said Shona, 22. 'Or else I like to recall scenes from blue movies we have seen on video.'

Erotica or pornography

Fantasy – enjoyed by 50 per cent of wives – is the most popular, cheapest and probably most effective sex aid. Alternatively, one in eight wives possesses a vibrator; one in twelve dresses up in special sexy underwear or other clothes – 'He loves me wearing my old school uniform'; one in three, like Shona, enjoys reading or seeing erotic material. There is a wide divergence of opinion, however, about what constitutes legitimate erotic material and what is unacceptable pornography.

Sales of romantic fiction suggest that the attitude of Kay, 37, is common: 'When I fantasize it is often about a romantic book or a film on television. You imagine yourself in that setting. These thoughts often help me to have an orgasm.'

Many women strongly dislike pornographic magazines and videos. 'I believe that girlie magazines are a cause of resentment, both to the men who read them and actually believe the alleged readers' contributions, and to the women who tolerate them and feel demoralized,' said Shirley, 29.

'Could we have a campaign for equal rights about all the films that show nude women but *never* nude men?' asked Judy, 18. 'Most of the time it is not necessary; it is sexually biased against women. If we must see nude scenes, could we please see men as well as women?'

Coral, 27: 'Let's have more equality. We are constantly being bombarded with young, attractive, naked women on TV, making real women feel inadequate. Perhaps the boot should be put on the other foot. Let's see more naked men on TV who are slim, attractive, etc., and not the fat slobs we see now. They *reflect* the typical beer-bellied male, making him feel he is perfectly acceptable. If women's genitals are displayed, then so should men's be.'

Eileen, 37: 'Sex is thrown at people today in videos and books and it makes them expect more from their partners. They don't understand that they are just watching an act and when the photo session is finished the actors just get dressed – it's like any other everyday job. I bet all those sexy men in pictures are no good in bed.'

Unrealistic expectations aroused by pornography cause problems between some couples.

'My husband bought a video machine and at first borrowed "skin flicks" which I quite enjoyed,' said Wendy, 41, 'but the films have got bluer and bluer. Now he borrows hard porn from sex shops which I am expected to watch. If I find it off-putting, I have to leave the room and he blames me and says I'm not sexy enough. This must be happening to other wives, too. Can't something be done? He can become very bad-tempered when I don't join in masturbating to these films. I find it a bit degrading.'

In the end, like all issues affecting a shared sex life, it is a question of mutual respect and negotiation. Some women, after all, do enjoy material which others find offensive. 'I enjoy reading girlie magazines, and during our lovemaking I often imagine I'm in some of the situations described in the various letters. I find this really turns me on a lot,' said Brenda, 32.

But Wendy ended her account with the comment: 'On more than one occasion I have been hit across the face for not joining in.' If you are being subjected to pressure to watch material you find offensive, to join in sexual activities you do not enjoy, then the problems involved go far beyond the public availability of pornography or even your sex life. What is at stake is more likely to be whether you want to continue in a relationship in which your views and preferences generally are given far from equal weight, and whether your partner is willing to change his attitude.

7 The Fertility Trap
Contraception, menstrual cycles and the menopause

In the sixties the pill ushered in a new era in the way women regarded their sex lives. Pregnancy became a separate issue from intercourse. The pill gave women freedom to enjoy sex without fear of repercussions – until then, a male prerogative.

Dorothy, 47, reminds us of how it used to be: 'After our first baby we used withdrawal. I was always scared of getting pregnant but didn't like to complain in case it caused a row.

'After our second child I was fitted with a cap. I hated the clinic. We had to roll our stockings down and wait in a queue and answer a lot of questions. My husband was at it morning, noon and night, even came home in the dinner hour, but I told the lady doctor we only did it once a week. I hated the cap – it was so messy.

'After the third baby I went on the pill. Oh, the bliss! Now I knew how men felt – no worry.'

Phyllis, now 51, remembered what a difference it made to her married life. 'I love my husband with my body and my mind but we had four sons because he wouldn't use contraception and always "blamed me" until the marvel of the pill. I was on it for eleven years. It was fantastic. Lovemaking became fabulous for him and me, no holds barred. Then I got blood pressure, so I was sterilized.'

The cloud on the horizon of this new world of unfettered sexuality was that the pill might bring health hazards all of its own – and, in recent years, choosing contraception has increasingly become a question of weighing up relative risks.

Some feared that the pill would lead to a decline in the nation's morals. But *more than four out of five unmarried women believe that if contraception is hard to obtain it leads to more pregnancies, not less sex.*

Gwen, 24: 'You can't be too young to use contraception, you can be too young to get pregnant. Contraception doesn't hurry people into sex – most people will wait until they are ready emotionally, if they are given enough space and ease of communication to help them decide for themselves.'

Risking it

Many women still have sex without using contraception, even when they do not want to get pregnant. *Seven out of ten unmarried women say that they have had intercourse without them or their partner using a method of contraception.* Figure 14 shows the reasons given by 16-to-18 year-olds.

Why did you have sex without using contraceptions?

Women aged 16–18

23%	I was carried away
40%	We decided to risk it
10%	I decided to risk it
14%	I thought it was the safe time of the month
1%	I wanted to get pregnant
9%	My boyfriend said it would be OK
1%	I never gave it a thought
1%	I was forced

Figure 14

In four out of ten cases these women say that they and their partner jointly decided to risk it; one out of ten say that their boyfriend had told them it would be all right. This means that in at least half the cases the man knew that the girl was unprotected.

Many young women find it extremely hard to refuse intercourse on the grounds that they are unprotected. 'I just let him do whatever he wanted,' said Liz. 'I didn't dare mention the question of contraception.'

'One thing led to another,' said Carrie, 18. 'He said, "Do you want to have sex with me?" By then he had started undressing me. I wasn't using any contraception nor was he, but he didn't ask so I didn't bother saying anything.'

Kim's boyfriend is Roman Catholic. 'I would very much like to use contraception,' she said, 'but he won't talk about it. When I say I would like to go on the pill, he just goes very quiet and says it will be all right. I really would like to go on the pill but I won't until he agrees. I would not go behind his back.'

Many of these young women, and those who say 'I was carried away' or 'I decided to risk it', have a blind optimism that they are not running any real risk, that it can't happen to them.

Di was 16 the first time she had intercourse. 'Thinking it was the done thing, I went to bed with him and we had very satisfying sex. He asked me if I was on the pill, and I said I was, even though I wasn't, because I didn't want to scare him off.'

Jillian, 17, said, 'We got in the back seat of the car and as we had sex he said to me, "What if you get pregnant?" I replied, "It's too late to think about that now!"'

The younger a girl is, the more worried she may be about her family discovering that she is using contraception and, therefore, the more nervous she is about seeking advice.

While one in ten 19-to-21-year-olds regularly take a chance when having intercourse, twice as high a proportion of 16-to-18-year-olds do so.

'It was a typical case of everyone at school talking about sex and my wanting to know what it was like,' said Madelaine. 'Contraception or the idea I might get pregnant never entered my head.'

'On the one occasion I had sex without using any form of contraception, I became pregnant,' said Eve.

'Although my boyfriend and I have now been going out together for nearly a year,' said Lois, who's 16, 'we only use the withdrawal method or sheath. If my family found out I was on the pill, they would be horrified, and I wouldn't like to speak to a doctor about sex.'

Not just a woman's worry

Increasingly, men feel they should share responsibility for birth control. Among younger couples, where the man is aged 16 to 18, nearly two thirds feel jointly responsible – see Figure 15.

'I am on the pill but my boyfriend feels responsible, too. He sometimes reminds me if I don't take the pill until a few hours later than usual,' said Kerry, 23.

Bridget, 22: 'I'm the one who has to take the pill every night, and I'm the one who's going to get pregnant. But I wish my partner would not assume it is my responsibility. I wish he'd acknowledge that I am doing it for both of us.'

Who feels more responsible for contraception?

	Couples in which man is aged 16–18	Man aged 19–25	Man aged 26–40
Woman feels more responsible	26%	40%	47%
Man feels more responsible	12%	4%	4%
Feel jointly responsible	62%	56%	49%

Figure 15

The results of disagreement over the method of family planning can be harrowing. Eileen, 44: 'When my doctor said I had to come off the pill because of my age, my lover wasn't very pleased. We used a sheath for two years but he couldn't climax wearing one. One night he got very frustrated, threw it out and made love to me unprotected. The result was I found myself pregnant at the age of 43, for the first time in my life. I had an abortion.

'I went back on the mini-pill but this stopped my periods and gave me chest pains so I came off it. I have tried to persuade him to have a vasectomy but he won't, and he has suggested I get sterilized. I have refused since it's much easier for him. So we have reverted to the sheath. His cowardly, self-centred attitude doesn't help our lovemaking. Sometimes I hate him!'

Many women told us of their unhappiness about having an abortion, even if it was the only realistic decision in the circumstances. Abortion is a complicated issue beyond the scope of our surveys, but the stories women volunteered about abortions suggested that it is something they do not take lightly – nor do they generally regard it as an alternative to contraception, even if some of them were victims of their own muddled thinking.

Cheryl, 17: 'We didn't use contraception. I didn't tell my boyfriend but either subconsciously or consciously I didn't want to go on the pill until I felt I could have sex. I was scared I would have too much pain and not be able to have sex, and I thought that, if I was "unprotected" and it got too painful, I could use the excuse, "Stop, it's not safe." However, unfortu-

101

nately, it was not too painful, we had sex and I got pregnant. I have since had an abortion which I feel will mentally scar me for life.'

Moira's boyfriend finished their two-year relationship the night she phoned with the intention of telling him she was having his baby. 'After what we had said to each other, I couldn't bring myself to tell him. I didn't want him to think I was trying to hang on to something that wasn't there any more.

'I had an abortion. Although I wanted that baby more than anything else, I knew I wouldn't be able to cope with it. How could I bring a child into the world and make it suffer because of me? Even now, living where I do, there is a stigma attached to unmarried mothers. There are only two people who know about my baby. I didn't even tell my mum. I just took myself off to a private clinic and killed the one good thing that could have come out of my love for him. My baby should have been born this month and, although I'm thinking about it most of the time, I still can't really bring myself to hate Mike. I've promised myself that I'll never get involved again because I don't ever want to feel this kind of hurt.'

Many women need to talk through their feelings after abortion, and I've listed where to seek advice in the Help Directory.

Wendy, 21, wanted more women to know they can get help to prevent the need for an abortion. 'I thought I knew everything but my man friend is sterile so I don't use contraception. A few week ago at a wedding party I bumped into an old flame; he came home with me – it's the old story. I was horrified the next morning, which was Sunday. I decided to go and see my GP on the Monday to inquire about morning-after pills. She wasn't there, so I had to go on the Tuesday. She is the best person I know of where contraception is concerned. She didn't have any morning-after pills with her and said it might be too late anyway.' (While morning-after pills are usually effective up to seventy-two hours after intercourse, they are best taken within forty-eight hours.) 'She suggested an IUD. Apparently, if you insert a coil within five days it prevents pregnancy. It worked. I had never read of this anywhere. Please, please print that fact. It would save such a lot of worry to women who take the occasional risk.'

Ignorance and anxieties – the pill

One in five unmarried women said they feel they don't know enough about contraception and, while three-quarters of those using contraception were taking the pill, many expressed reservations.

Sadie, 20: 'There is not enough information about contraception. Most of us don't know how the pill works. The new facts coming out about it make me even more worried.'

There are those who use no contraception rather than trust the pill. Melanie, 16, said, 'My relationship won't last long – he's only 17. I certainly don't want to be tied down at my age, but I should be more responsible about contraception. If I go on the pill now I might be on it for another ten years. It's a rotten excuse, I know, but I worry about the dangers.'

Lindsey, 21: 'I am unhappy about using the pill, and have had problems with it, bad headaches and tiredness. Doctors cannot supply any figures on the extent of the risk except to say that it is less dangerous than pregnancy. The alternatives are not pill *vs* pregnancy, they are pill *vs* less effective but medically safer methods. When they say the pill is less risky than pregnancy, do they mean risk of death or what? It's not only death from breast cancer that's worrying me. It's losing a breast as well.'

The combined pill contains oestrogen and progestogen (manufactured progesterone) and prevents ovulation; it also affects the lining of the womb so that it will not be able to receive an egg, and prevents fertile mucus (see page 107). The progestogen-only mini-pill affects just the lining of the womb and mucus. While the combined pill may cause a small, increased risk of cancer of the cervix in some women, pill-scare stories often make the headlines before they have been substantiated and it now looks very doubtful that it causes any real increased risk of breast cancer. While it can increase the likelihood of thrombosis in women who are older, smoke or are overweight, doctors are well informed about which women are most threatened and can miniminize the risks.

The pill is not only safer than pregnancy but has beneficial effects as well as preventing pregnancy. It seems to have some protective effect against cancer of the ovary, of the uterus, some pelvic infections and rheumatoid arthritis, possibly even ulcers. It often has a good effect on problems connected with the menstrual cycle such as premenstrual tension and painful or heavy periods. It prevents fibroids and endometriosis.

Pyridoxine (vitamin B6) has been found safely to relieve the side-effects some women suffer on the pill, such as headaches and depression.

Full information exists about every method of birth control – and several new alternatives are becoming available – though we may need persistence to find it. Sometimes we may simply need to be firmer when asking for information from the doctor. However, family planning specialists will have more up-to-date detailed knowledge than your GP unless he is particularly interested in the subject. Keep asking questions until you understand. (See Help Directory for further information).

No perfect method

Young unmarried women are not alone in taking chances. One in seven fertile married women (not intending to get pregnant) takes a chance at least sometimes, one in fourteen regularly. More than a third of abortions are performed on married women.

We asked married women how much the various methods of birth control inhibited their sexual pleasure; their answers are shown in Figure 16.

Far and away the least popular method is withdrawal: 'He always has to stop when it gets nice.' 'It's far from satisfying emotionally.' Its drawbacks are not only aesthetic: 'The withdrawal method resulted in a baby,' said Carolyn. Even the most controlled man may unknowingly leak some semen before ejaculation.

Reactions to other methods were very individual. 'We use the sheath and find that on the few occasions we do make love it's a bother and ruins what spontaneous reaction we do have,' complained Marjorie, 27.

Bernice, 26, found, 'I wasn't happy on the pill because when he ejaculated I found it terribly messy. It revolted me. I managed to persuade my husband to use a sheath and I am now a lot happier – I think he is, too.'

It was reassuring to see that vasectomy and sterilization, given that they must be considered irreversible, were so trouble-free.

Amy, 34, has been sterilized and said, 'My husband and I now enjoy a full sex life without any pregnancy worries at all.

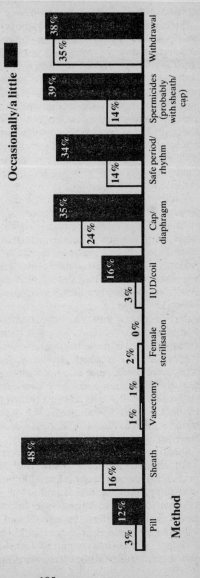

Figure 16

How much does your method of family planning interfere with your enjoyment of sex?

☐ Considerably
■ Occasionally/a little

Pill — 3% / 12%
Sheath — 16% / 48%
Vasectomy — 1% / 1%
Female sterilisation — 2% / 0%
IUD/coil — 3% / 16%
Cap/diaphragm — 24% / 35%
Safe period/rhythm — 14% / 34%
Spermicides (probably with sheath/cap) — 14% / 39%
Withdrawal — 35% / 38%

Method

Neither of us realized just how much we subconsciously worried about it until after the op.'

'Since my husband had a vasectomy everything has been fine,' said Vera, 49. 'That was about twenty years ago. It's wonderful how it's made all the difference in the world, nothing to worry about, no unwanted pregnancies.'

While vasectomy and female sterilization are very safe operations and have no physical effect on sexual responsiveness – men's fear that vasectomy will lead to impotence has no medical basis – they can affect our feelings. Barbara: 'If I had realized what a drastic effect sterilization would have on me, I would not have had it done. I have lost all interest in sex now. It is meaningless to make love when I can no longer bear children.' No one should ever pressure a partner into vasectomy or sterilization.

While couples vary greatly in their reactions to individual methods of birth control, many are not entirely happy with any of them. The perfect method of birth control, with no side-effects, safe to use for decades, which interferes in no way with making love, has yet to be invented.

Maggie, 29: 'Family planning interfered all the time with our lovemaking. I have tried the pill after each child with the same results: continuous headaches and loss of interest in sex, due to a very dry vagina causing acute soreness. The cap used to make me feel dirty and took away the spontaneity. I hated removing it. Spermicides caused a lot of irritation in both of us. The sheath resulted in no sensation for either of us.'

Jane, 33: 'After nearly twelve years of marriage we very rarely have sex because I do not wish to get pregnant again. We have three children and I had a miscarriage before the third. My husband will not have a vasectomy. I can't take the pill and my doctor doesn't recommend the coil as I have trouble with period pain. That leaves the sheath, which I hate and mistrust, so we are at stalemate.'

Sometimes the problems are very serious.

Angela, 21: 'My dear gentle husband doesn't know how much sex hurts me because I wouldn't dream of telling him.

'I can't go on the pill because I get migraine and don't absorb it properly. After we started using first a diaphragm and then a sheath with pessaries, the pain began. I am allergic to the cream and my FPA doctor came to the conclusion I am allergic to rubber. I have been treated for thrush, etc. My GP suggests I have a child to desensitize the vagina but I don't want a baby yet. Despite the pain I can feel pleasure, but orgasms can't break through the pain barrier and I feel as if making love for, say, half an hour is abusing my body.'

Some felt that difficult cases were not always very sympathetically received. 'Doctors and family planning clinics seem reluctant to help people such as myself who are unsuitable for nearly every form of contraception,' said Sandy, 24.

Many want more knowledge. 'I don't understand as much about contraception as I would like,' said Lisa, 22. 'While I respect the doctors' expertise, I wish they would endeavour to enlighten those patients who wish to learn a little more about their bodies and reactions, if only to allay silly, out-of-perspective fears.'

Get in tune with your rhythms

It can help us to make more informed choices about contraception if we learn to read our bodies so we know when we are fertile (though this does not apply if you are on the pill, which 'suspends' the natural cycle). Some women feel an ache or stabbing pain at the time of ovulation, for example; some find their breasts become more sensitive, some notice a feeling of fullness in the genitals, some suffer from abdominal bloating. Some notice changes in the oiliness of the hair or skin and the clarity of the complexion.

Before ovulation the mucus at the cervix, the neck of the womb, becomes thin, slippery, clear and stretchy, rather like egg white. This fertile-type mucus, which allows sperm to swim easily up through the cervix, flows until ovulation, and at this time the vagina feels slippery and wet. After ovulation it becomes thick and sticky for a day or two and then there are normally dry days until the next period. This mucus passes out through the vagina and you can check it. You may notice it on your pants, or you can wipe a tissue across the mouth of the vagina before passing water.

You can also check your cervix, which alters during the cycle. Slip a finger or two inside your vagina. Early and late in the cycle the cervix is lower in the vagina and it feels firm, like the tip of a nose. The opening – called the os – is closed and feels a bit like a dimple, though it will be more irregular if you have had a baby. During the fertile phase the cervix rises about an inch and as ovulation approaches it feels softer and the os begins to open and feels slippery with mucus.

You can pinpoint ovulation more accurately, in conjunction with these other methods of reading your body, by checking your temperature first thing every morning. There is a rise in temperature at or after ovulation caused by the rise of progesterone in the system. After three days of raised temperatures the fertile phase is over. This temperature rise is usually only points of a degree, and is more easily measured with a special fertility thermometer.

A couple having problems with birth control might find the combination of intercourse with no contraception during infertile time and a barrier method when fertile preferable to always using a method with which they are unhappy. The explanation about how to pinpoint fertile periods given above is far from full enough to be used as a basis for birth control; it is just to help you understand your body better and feel in tune with its rhythms. If you want to try 'natural' birth control – of which more accurate and sophisticated versions are replacing the old calendar and rhythm methods – you must get full information from your family planning clinic. Further sources of detailed information are listed in the Help Directory.

Infertility – nobody's 'fault'

At least one in ten couples suffer fertility problems. Desperately trying to conceive can have a detrimental effect on your whole relationship. Diane, 32: 'We attended a fertility clinic for about six years. I found that I became numb and preoccupied with getting pregnant. Some of the tests we did required us to make love at certain times and sometimes to order. This kills all spontaneity and is very boring. It affected both my love-making and my health. Once we decided to adopt, things got better. We are still waiting to adopt but our sex life has steadily improved and I now feel as good as when we were first married.'

It can be hard for couples not to start blaming each other. In one third of cases it is the wife who is infertile, in one third the husband, and in the other one third both have problems.

Alex, 29: 'My husband used to say it was my fault and I used to say it was him. After the first twelve months of our trying, the GP said that this period was not long enough to merit tests. He told me that there was nothing obviously preventing my getting pregnant and that we should go home and try for another six months; if nothing happened, we should both return and they would start conducting tests. Well, it was only another three months before I fell.'

There are only a few days in your cycle during which you are likely to conceive, so couples who are wondering why they have not started a family yet may simply not be hitting upon the right days.

Sexy cycles

Women's moods and feelings of sexiness can vary greatly with their menstrual cycle.

Sue, 32: 'My menstrual cycle has an immense effect on my love life. Just before, during and immediately after my period I don't want any kind of sex. But by the time two weeks have elapsed I enjoy sex very much. For between five and ten days I have the urge for sex several times a day.

'The week before my period is due this gradually eases off to once a day or every other day, although it is still enjoyable, but immediately around the period I lose interest in sex very dramatically to the point where, if my partner approaches me, I feel used and totally uninterested.

'On the whole my partner is understanding. He enjoys my good times and good-humouredly puts up with my bad times.'

Some women feel most desire around ovulation, when oestrogen levels are highest. Others feel sexiest when oestrogen levels are very low – around the time of menstruation.

'We tend to make love three or four nights in a row just after my period (hormones rule!) and then not bother for a week or two,' said Andrea, 27. 'Two of my friends are the same so perhaps this is quite common. Two or three hours' loss of sleep each night for four days does nothing for the bags under the eyes!'

It could well be that Andrea feels sexier during a period but that, like many people, she and her husband abstain from intercourse at that time. Some religious faiths ban intercourse during a period and all over the world there are age-old myths about menstruating women being 'unclean'.

Few couples these days believe, consciously at least, that there is any risk attached and are more likely to say they avoid intercourse at this time because it is messy.

Some couples make love in other ways apart from intercourse during periods. Some women – and some men, too – masturbate alone for sexual relief. Many women have mixed feelings about masturbating at such times. Joan, 37: 'During the middle of my menstrual cycle for three or four days I want sex all the time, and I often masturbate. My husband doesn't know I do and it is the only thing I have never been able to mention to him. I wish I could manage without it.'

But if she enjoys the sexual relief why on earth should she try to manage without it?

If the question of intercourse during a period causes serious problems between you and your partner, this is almost certainly a reflection of other difficulties in your relationship. It may be a focus for general discontent about the frequency and quality of your lovemaking.

If you are feeling pressured, then you may look on menstruation as a welcome respite. Avril, 43: 'When I had my periods I used to get five days of peace. Now I've had a hysterectomy I've got no excuse any more!'

Premenstrual tension

'The day my period begins,' explained Juliet, 22. 'I feel very sexy and this can continue all the day through. It is not the most convenient time to feel this way.

'I do not think my period spoils our physical relationship unless it is a particularly heavy one. We enjoy making love at this time -- but that is if we survive my premenstrual tension on loving terms.

'I am healthy, fit and happy, but for one or two days before my period I cannot deal with the slightest let-down or disappointment. The silliest things upset me, like missing a television programme I wanted to watch or being late for something. With that I have water retention, which gives me a bloated stomach and tender breasts. I generally feel like a heavy ragdoll that nobody wants. This is totally unlike me, as I am usually easy-going and laugh at most things, but when I feel fragile at the onset of my period I am not very good company. I am moody and I don't feel like conversation, which creates unnecessary hurt feelings all round.'

Many women commented either that they suffered from premenstrual tension, or that their libido was at rock bottom just before a period, or both. Some women mentioned this as a time when they cannot reach orgasm.

'Men need to be educated about PMT,' said Annette, 29. 'At those times I could no more have sex than fly to the moon.'

PMT can make us more vulnerable to the stresses and strains of everyday life; what normally would be a ripple becomes a tidal wave submerging us. Equally, other worries can make us more liable to notice the effects of PMT. To tell whether PMT is playing some part in your mood changes, keep a daily record for three months or so, noting your periods, mark down days of bleeding, and any other relevant information – your mood, powers of concentration, whether you feel sexy, energetic, any aches or bloatedness.

After three months you will see if any pattern is emerging. It is usually a lot easier to cope with sudden changes of mood if you have some idea what has caused them and can warn your partner.

Loraine, 34: 'The tension during the last two weeks of the month makes me feel that I just don't want to be bothered to make any effort to enjoy even a close relationship. It helps tremendously to have a loving and understanding husband who is prepared to put more into winning me round.'

If your PMT is really troublesome, then almost certainly there is treatment to help you, and the chart you have kept will be of great help to your doctor in deciding what this might best be. Many women find vitamin B6 (pyridoxine) or evening primrose oil (Efamol) relieve their symptoms with no side-effects.

Sources of information are listed in the Help Directory.

The menopause

For some, the menopause means a blessed relief from PMT and contraception. Others will miss their cyclical sexy 'highs' and suffer from their loss of fertility. Though the menopause has had an almost universally bad press, recently a more balanced view has begun to emerge.

One basic fear is that it means the end of your life as a sexual woman. Ninety-nine per cent of women have stopped menstruating by the age of 56, but *three in six women aged 55-plus still make love once a week or more, two in six less frequently; just one in six never.*

Roughly one third of wives over 55 would like to make love more often, and a slightly larger proportion in the 45-to-54 age group – these figures are not far off the average for women of all ages. Their husbands are rather more likely to be content with the frequency of lovemaking than the younger man, though many of them would still like to make love more often. In answer to the question 'How satisfied are you with your sexual relationship?' women around or past the age of the menopause were slightly – though certainly not dramatically – more likely to be dissatisfied, but they are also slightly more likely to rate their husband as only a poor or passable lover and to wish that he was more skilful. Overall, there is nothing in the statistics to suggest that the menopause brings about a radical and widespread disruption of couples' sex lives.

However, it clearly does cause problems for some. Among wives over 55, one in six says the menopause did or still does cause sexual difficulties. As several wives pointed out, it tends to coincide with a particularly stressful time of life – even though the symptoms themselves may not be so terrible.

Brenda, 44, explained, 'Eighteen months ago we hit a bad patch. My father and my mother-in-law both died, my husband was made redundant and there were other problems in the family. All this has caused a great deal of emotional stress and worry, and both my husband and myself have suffered all manner of complaints – loss of sleep, anxiety, indigestion, pains in the chest and so on.

'As a consequence our sex life has suffered, in that we are too tired or unable to respond. I have felt like something quite dead and as if I might as well be a piece of wood, and he has had difficulty in maintaining an erection on occasions, but we both know the cause of the trouble and feel sure time will put things right.

'I have, however, begun the symptoms of the menopause: hot flushes and sweats, scanty irregular one-day periods, and dryness of the vagina, and this is not helping. I hope we are right in thinking time will improve things, as we both feel very sad that such a lovely part of our lives, which has given us a great deal of pleasure over the years, is under strain. I am seriously considering seeing my doctor about hormone-replacement therapy for the menopausal symptoms, in the hope that I will feel better and some of my sensual feelings will return.'

At the menopause the ovaries slow down production of oestrogen and progesterone. This may happen in a smooth, even decline, with periods getting lighter and lighter until they stop altogether, or it may happen suddenly. Most commonly, it happens in fits and starts, with periods varying in their spacing, heaviness and duration as hormone levels fluctuate.

While the only symptom of the menopause certain to be shared by all women is the cessation of periods, there are other common changes which take place at this time which may affect your sex life. Progesterone is thought to help you feel calm and contented, so a sudden lack of it might cause anxiety and irritation – as with PMT – making you feel less like sex, or at least in need of a more tender approach.

Lower levels of oestrogen may cause the walls of the vagina to shrink and to seem drier as the lubricating reaction to sexual stimulus slows down. This means that it is especially important that you and your partner allow plenty of time for caressing and foreplay before intercourse, in order to allow for natural lubrication.

Brenda added, 'We have found that if we make love less often and plan quietness and an early night and give it our full concentration, we can still enjoy kissing and cuddling – and intercourse if it happens, though neither of us will worry if it doesn't.'

Some women find the changes in the vagina give pleasurably increased sensation. In other women, however, they can cause pain and itching. This can lead to a chicken and egg situation. Because sex has been uncomfortable, you worry that it will be uncomfortable again, which slows down your sexual responses – including lubrication – still further, so it's more uncomfortable. Then you start avoiding sex, and because sex is less frequent the vagina becomes even less able to respond.

Additional lubrication for the vagina, such as KY Jelly, which is safe, colourless and odourless, can help. You can have an oestrogen cream prescribed to soften and thicken the vaginal tissues.

You may find you have to be persistent. Not all women meet with very sympathetic treatment.

Eleanor, 52: 'Intercourse was impossible. When I summoned up courage to tell my GP he practically laughed at me. "What do you expect at your age? There's nothing wrong with you, it's all in your mind." As the pain I was suffering was quite real, I abandoned all efforts to please my husband.

'Six months ago I saw a private consultant. The condition was put right by a course of hormones prescribed by a caring doctor – at a cost. What was described as "imagination" by my GP was a real trouble caused by age and dryness.'

Hormone-replacement therapy (HRT) may help, but hormones are not, as many people seem to think, aphrodisiacs.

They can help make sex more comfortable and therefore pleasanter, but they cannot create an interest in sex which isn't already there, particularly if it has been absent for many years.

While lack of oestrogen can bring about loss of sex drive – especially until your body has adjusted to its new hormone levels following the menopause – even after the menopause small quantities of oestrogen continue to be manufactured. If you are given HRT when shortage of oestrogen is not your problem, it could increase the risk of other health problems such as thrombosis. Just as with the pill, there are various groups who are thought to be a bad risk for oestrogen treatment. Women taking HRT need to be carefully monitored, and oestrogen is not a magic cure-all.

The understanding, sympathy, talking, kissing and cuddling that Brenda is sharing with her husband is likely to be the best treatment she could have to ease her passage through the menopause and to help them both recover from the stress of the last year or two. Certainly HRT alone wouldn't be enough.

Many women find this a vulnerable time, and what makes all the difference is how close and confiding a relationship you have with your partner.

Coral, 48: 'The children were growing up and needing their mother less, and my husband was immersed in work.

'I lost a lot of confidence in myself and eventually had two affairs. My husband must have realized I was slipping away from him. He started to be very warm and affectionate again and finally convinced me he loved and needed me, which was all I had ever wanted. We are now very happy and will never take each other for granted again.'

Men too can experience a midlife crisis. Their self-confidence can feel threatened by signs of ageing, by slowing of sex drive, by younger, more energetic men rising up the promotion ladder at work.

But there is no need for the menopause to spell the end of enjoyable sex. While one in ten wives stops making love round about the time of the menopause, this is more likely to be because one or both partners was never really happy with the quality of sex they shared rather than that the symptoms of the menopause alone made it intolerable. Wives over 55 are more likely than younger women to have been troubled by their husband's lack of interest in sex and the quality of his love making.

If sex has always played an important part in your relationship, there is no reason to suppose it will not continue to do so after the menopause, especially now that you are free of worries about contraception. Women who undergo hysterectomy – the removal of the womb – obviously face many of the implications of the menopause in an acute form; this is a very common operation (if you have undergone or may undergo a hysterectomy, see Help Directory for further information). Yet Elsie could cheerfully write, 'I thought you might like to hear from a happy 60-year-old (married 38 years). Our sex life has been much better since my hysterectomy at 40. Family planning failed very early in our marriage at a difficult time – giving rise to twins – so we always had slight problems in the early days. Not any more though!'

8 Is Motherhood Bad For Sex?

Pregnancy, childbirth and the early days

The image of a dear little baby cooing in a cradle is very alluring to many of us. A hidden wish to conceive lies behind some of the occasions on which teenagers don't use contraception.

Jay: 'We hardly ever used contraceptives; neither of us worried about it. We were in love and the thought of a baby was a childish romantic notion. I gave birth shortly before my eighteenth birthday.'

Some women who feel unloved and insecure believe that a baby will give them love and perhaps cement an ailing relationship. Denise, 18: 'I loved that man. I thought that if we finished at least I would have my son to remind me of him every time I looked at him. In some ways I'm glad I had a baby because it means someone else is dependent on me, but I should have waited. Although I have some freedom, I would like a lot more.'

Kathy's husband was violent towards her. 'Sex with him was a disaster. I honestly used to feel revolted. Yet while I was married I tried for a baby for three years without success. I was daft enough to think it would make things better.'

For many women the drive to conceive is closely linked to their sexuality. Pam, 38: 'My fantasies during lovemaking are specifically to replace the excitement which I believe contraception takes away. I always imagine myself being made pregnant. Only in this way am I able to reach orgasm. My husband does all he can, but it is the added mental stimulation which is the completing factor. If I am in a position where I might possibly be made pregnant (if my husband starts lovemaking without his sheath), then I reach orgasm very quickly. If this cannot be the actual situation, then I have to imagine it.

116

'I believe in contraception. I would probably have died by now without it, because I have problems with childbirth. But all contraception has the same effect: the coil, the cap, anything. As long as I know I am "safe", I won't have an orgasm.'

This link between fertility and sexuality is more than just psychological. Some women seem to feel at their sexiest around the time of ovulation. Pam: 'For those three or four days in the month I want sex all the time.' Even women who from their accounts don't seem aware that this was the time of peak fertility commented, like Janet, 37, 'No matter how much I love him my desire is basically emotional not physical. I can only approach this great physical feeling – the way he feels all the time – for two or three days in the middle of my cycle.'

Many women experience waves of broodiness; even those who start their twenties believing they do not want children may change their minds by the time they're 30.

Nicky is 30 now. 'I was 24 when I married. From the beginning I knew my husband didn't want children. I believed I didn't either. In the past two years I have needed to become a mother. I am now convinced that it is an immensely fulfilling experience for a woman.

'I would not stop taking the pill without telling him. My husband says he doesn't believe in paternal instinct and would be most unwilling to give it a try. It takes two to make a baby and it definitely takes two to provide a loving, stable home where a child would know how much it had been wanted and how it had been created out of love.'

Most of us expect a child to be 'a close bond, a proof of our love for one another'. Having a baby and bringing it up can be deeply satisfying. It is frequently also a testing time for relationships and sometimes disrupts a couple's sex life far more seriously than they expected. Our survey showed that, if there are already stresses and strains between partners, having a baby is more likely to drive them apart than bring them together.

Fifty per cent of wives with children under 3 say that having babies had a bad effect on their sex life; and wives who have not had children or whose children have left home are more likely to rate their marriage as very happy than those who have children living with them.

Pregnancy

Pregnancy can be good for sex. *One fifth of wives who have children under 3, whose memories should be fresh, say that their sex lives were better than average during pregnancy.*

During pregnancy the placenta, where the baby's umbilical cord joins the womb, becomes a virtual hormone factory, producing large amounts of progesterone and oestrogen. These help some women feel blissfully calm and sexy. 'My pregnancy was one of the happiest and most voluptuous times of my life,' remembered Anne, 27. Some feel more seductive because at long last they may be a 38D rather than 34A. Jan, 26: 'During pregnancies and nursing my babies I look for sex more, owing to the increased inches on my bust.'

Just under two fifths say that their sex lives were average during pregnancy, but rather more than two-fifths say it was worse.

Most frequently it is their changing shape which women mention as being the reason why they stopped feeling sexy during pregnancy. 'Before the baby was born, I felt either too tired or too much of an elephant to make love,' said Tessa, 26. 'I am seven months pregnant,' said Sophie, 24, 'and I am finding making love very uncomfortable, and I feel unattractive although my husband says he thinks I'm still very sexy.'

However, there are other common problems. Jo, 29: 'After previous miscarriages and a threatened miscarriage in my successful pregnancy, sex was not recommended. Although my husband said, "There are other ways," I just never felt very sexy. I was too worried.'

Hannah, 26: 'I was five months pregnant when my husband stopped making love to me. Until this time he demonstrably adored me and his withdrawal of love was terrifying. We talked about it and he said he just felt there was someone inside me.'

If a mother-to-be or her partner stops wanting to make love during pregnancy, it helps if they can talk together about what lies behind it and still kiss and cuddle. If nothing else, this closeness gives them a chance to reassure each other that they do still love one another, that pregnancy is only temporary. If one or other refuses all sexual contact, there's no doubt that it puts a very real strain on a relationship. Several women said, like Majorie, 29, 'When I had our first baby my husband had two or three affairs, one-night flings, which I didn't find out about till years later.'

If pregnancy ends in miscarriage or stillbirth, it can have a shattering effect on a couple, especially if they nurse their grief privately rather than sharing it. Amy, 26: 'Our baby daughter was stillborn. I have never completely recovered from this awful, harrowing experience, and we became alienated from one another, at a time when I needed love more than ever.'

Childbirth

One in five of all wives troubled by sexual difficulties say these are or were connected with childbirth.

Elaine, 27: 'After our baby was born three months ago, the physical and mental changes came as quite a shock to us. None of the books emphasizes this.

'I had severe anaemia, which led to extreme tiredness and depression, and the scar from a large episiotomy made sex painful.

'The emotional upheaval of bringing a new baby home tired us out. We were both glad just to get to sleep. Fortunately, although my husband wanted to make love, he was more concerned with my emotional and physical well-being and was prepared to wait until I felt ready. My GP was also a great help. At least he made me understand that I wasn't a freak.'

Pregnancy and childbirth subject the womb, cervix (neck of the womb) and vagina to a buffeting which can cause loss of interest in intercourse until the system has settled down. A difficult birth puts some women off sex for a long time.

Gemma, 24: 'After a rough time having my third child, it was six months before I would let my husband even touch me. After having a bad time and gynaecologists probing about, you lose your dignity and the feeling of privacy, which you usually share only with your husband.

'My husband used to get really frustrated and ask why I didn't want to make love or be touched. It was very hard to get him to understand but I could not really expect him to. You have to experience it at first hand.'

Above all, women complained about the effects of epi-siotomy – the cut often made in the vagina to prevent tearing during delivery. 'I had a very painful episiotomy scar after my first baby,' said Val, 28. 'I got no help from doctors over this. They thought the problem was emotional but I'm quite sure it was physical. I was feeling sexy, my vagina was wet, but the scar hurt. After about six months it gradually got better.

'The doctors at the family planning clinic admitted I'd been sewn up too tight but just told me to go back to my own doctor.'

Gina: 'Before my first child was born I reached orgasm quite often and easily when having intercourse. About eighteen months after the birth, I realized I had not had one at all in that time. At first I thought it was perhaps because my husband had adopted a position "further away" during the last few months of pregnancy so as not to squash the baby. It was not until another year had passed that I realized it was caused by the episiotomy. I can only liken it to cutting through the elasticated waist of pyjama bottoms and then making a careless repair – they stitched up the waistband material but did not repair the broken elastic.

'I had another episiotomy at the birth of my second child, but it hardly mattered by then; the damage had been done. I was horrified to read that an episiotomy is the only operation which does *not* require the agreement of the patient. I did not have a difficult or long labour and in fact would imagine that my notes would read like a textbook, and yet I was cut on both occasions. Now I feel outraged that it caused me, unnecessarily, total loss of orgasmic pleasure.

'With hindsight, I should have refused an episiotomy unless absolutely necessary for the baby's safety, and then only on a doctor's insistence, with a second or third opinion.

'I have come to accept the fact that I won't have an orgasm like I used to, but I feel very angry at my fate. Episiotomy is a barbaric practice.'

Many of those who wrote to us emphasized the lack of information about what to expect and the lack of control over what is happening to them during and after childbirth. Episiotomy without the woman's consent is an example of this.

In fact, routine episiotomy is being questioned within the medical profession and it may be a 'fashion' which is passing. Some doctors defend it as often essential to ease birth for mother and baby. But a mother-to-be can make it clear to the medical staff that she wishes to avoid episiotomy if at all possible. If an episiotomy is performed, having it stitched up quickly aids swift healing; the stitches should not be too tight – they must allow for the swelling of the tissues. If pain persists, it may be that the stitches haven't fallen out properly or there is an infection. Looking with a mirror may identify the problem, which should be reported to your GP or gynaecologist.

You can save many worries if you persist in asking questions. I know from personal experience how difficult it can be to get hospital staff to see you as an adult with a mind of your own. That's why I think it is so helpful to have your partner with you, particularly if you have any doubts about the procedure being followed.

After childbirth some women find that, while they used to reach orgasm during intercourse, they can no longer do so – or even that they can't reach orgasm at all. Perhaps one touch or position that used to be pleasurable is no longer. If we experiment, however, we will usually find alternative ways of satisfying ourselves.

After the birth

If there are no particular physical difficulties, once the baby's born many couples expect to resume their sex life after only a brief interval – in fact, they are encouraged to have intercourse before the six-week post-natal check-up. 'After childbirth we just wait the normal time it takes to recover; until then, I give my husband oral sex,' said Helena, 29.

Thirteen per cent find a positive improvement after childbirth.

'I have always enjoyed sex,' said Jackie, 31, 'but only reached orgasm after having my little girl.' Rita, 38: 'In early marriage, although willing to try different positions for intercourse with my husband, I found all but the missionary position most uncomfortable. I don't know if it's because after having children things became more supple, but I have no difficulty with any position now.'

As we have seen, however, *50 per cent say their sex life is worse.*

'The baby is now eight months old and I still have no interest in sex,' said Ruth, 32. 'I know it is a silly problem but I just can't seem to snap out of it. I feel guilty because the baby is all I want and I seem to have fallen out of love with my husband. I just don't fancy him any more. I wish it was all back to normal because I do love him deep down.'

Libby, 36: 'I found it impossible to have intercourse for several months after childbirth for emotional reasons. I was in despair. More open discussion of the topic would have been a help.'

It is common for mothers not to feel like sex for several

121

weeks after the birth, no matter how close and loving the couple. Trying to manage intercourse before the six-week post-natal check-up in hospital, for example, may seem like an ordeal. It may be partly because they felt so fulfilled by giving birth, which is very much part of women's sexual experience, that many women simply don't feel the need of sex for a while.

Some mothers can enjoy kissing and cuddling when they don't feel ready for intercourse, and this obviously helps them and their partner feel loved and wanted, but some find they don't want even to be touched. This is a strain, but it's not something mothers can 'snap out of' – nor does it mean that they don't love their husbands. If women try to rush into intercourse when they don't feel ready, lubrication is impaired and the muscles around the vagina may be tense, with the result that intercourse is uncomfortable. This may make them dread the next time, and establish a vicious circle.

Also, new mothers often feel exhausted. 'I wish that children didn't make you feel too tired to make love,' sighed Isabel.

Nearly two thirds of wives who have children under 3 and would like to make love more are prevented from doing so by tiredness.

Meg, 33: 'I have lost my sex drive since I had my son. I feel tired from looking after the baby all day. Half the time I just have sex for the sake of it because it's easier to get it over and done with than to argue about the fact I never want it. After the argument I always feel selfish and have sex anyway.'

A difficult new role

Heather, 27, had been home from hospital with her baby son for just four days when she noticed her husband was acting strangely. 'My husband had felt it was the right time for a baby. We both had good careers but I was prepared to give it all up for motherhood. I had an uncomplicated pregnancy but I was unhappy in hospital after the birth, depressed and homesick. My husband appeared to be over the moon with his son and as soon as I returned home I felt fine.

'Soon, however, I knew something was wrong but he wouldn't admit it. I was desperately unhappy, and when our son was five weeks old he admitted to me that he was seeing someone else. I was devastated and had to stop breast-feeding as I wasn't eating.'

It was only after Heather had gone to stay with a sister abroad that he stopped seeing the other woman.

'He begged forgiveness. When the baby was three months old we returned. My husband met us at the airport with a bouquet of flowers. We talked a lot and the root of it all had been the baby.

'My husband was jealous. He couldn't bear me to breast-feed him. Another problem was the lack of sex. We had talked about these things while I was pregnant; he assured me he was not worried, that he loved me and knew it would only be for a short while. One can never be certain . . . I'm sure this tale is very common, although at the time I felt I was the loneliest person in the world.'

When she has a child a woman may give up her job to become a full-time dependent wife and mother. Even if she is happy, as well as coping with a new baby she must make vast adjustments in her own way of life, at a time when she is already likely to feel weak. Her husband may find it difficult to understand. Unless unemployed, he probably still goes out to work; his life hasn't changed so much. She may feel lonely during the day and then in the evening discover she can't really share her feelings with her husband.

Most couples cope. But if there are any doubts about your feelings for one another – buried resentments, previous dissatisfaction with your sex life – these stresses will seek out those doubts and they may show up in bed.

Equally, you may be worried by the responsibilities of becoming parents, about money, lack of freedom, lack of help with the baby; you may be unable to go out together in the evenings. You can't revitalize your sex life without first coming to terms with such problems. Some manage to work through them together, but if a couple finds it difficult to be patient and loving with one another, or if they haven't resumed their love life after six months, they might benefit from outside advice (see Help Directory). Don't lose heart: this testing time can strengthen your relationship in the end.

Christine said, 'Our best-ever sex was after the birth of our first – from when she was a year old. I think the pressure of having children brought problems to the surface and, when we'd sorted them out with help from Marriage Guidance, our marriage and sex life was very good.'

Post-natal depression

Sometimes depression is at the root of sexual problems. About one in ten mothers suffer from fairly serious post-natal depression and one in four from a milder form.

Sandy, 38: 'After the baby I had very bad post-natal depression. During this period my husband had an affair. I feel sad that when I needed him he turned to another woman instead of trying to talk to me, or consulting professional help, about his need for lovemaking.'

Women often try to soldier on through post-natal depression but it is important to see your doctor, who can offer advice and may also test and treat for deficiencies such as anaemia, which could be affecting your feelings and energy levels.

If you are not happy about your contraception, you can sort this out with the doctor, too. You can't look forward to making love if you are worried about getting pregnant again. And it is a risk. Fran, 28: 'I had two pregnancies in two years and a miscarriage. We had started talking about a vasectomy but I didn't want to push him into it. We were using the sheath around the fertile period. This worked until I was run down and so sleeping like a log. One morning my husband woke up randy and took what he wanted before I'd even had a chance to open my eyes properly. Of course, he didn't think about using a sheath. He blamed himself for the pregnancy but took it out on me. He completely rejected me from the second month on.'

Children in the home

Nearly three out of five wives with children under 5 who would like to make love more often say that their problem is lack of opportunity due to the children.

Laurie, 29: 'Now our son is 19 months old, we are much more understanding of each other and our sex life has improved, but on occasion he still wakes up and demands attention as we start to make love: sometimes the beginning is also the end. I think we would like to make love more often but it is relatively infrequently that we both have the energy and inclination at the same time!'

'We used to make love nearly every day and it was always pretty good,' said Sarah, 28. 'It's only since the birth of the children that our sex life has deteriorated, through lack of opportunity: the little one is always in our bed and the other one is constantly waking up.'

Andrea, 27: 'Our child has an inbuilt sense of when my husband and I feel like sex and immediately starts to cry. Guaranteed to cool our ardour!'

At least younger children usually go to bed before their parents. Not so teenagers. 'I should emphasize the inhibiting effect of teenagers and young adults in the house,' said Muriel, 48. 'They are still studying so do not often go out in the evenings; they are awake at adult bedtime but young and inexperienced enough to be embarrassed by parents' sex. My daughter keeps hinting complaints.'

Irene, 42: 'We would probably make love in different places but our sons and daughter are always around – they're all three unemployed.'

Of course, it's difficult to make love during the day while teenagers are at home. However, for parents who feel embarrassed about making love at night, in their own room, it might be worth trying to work out why. Does it harm teenagers to know that their parents love each other, and express their love for one another physically and regularly? Isn't it a good example to show that good loving is linked with strong, caring, lasting relationships?

Embarrassment at being overheard by the children may stem from our fear of being overheard by our own parents when we were young. If the children seem disapproving, this may simply be because they can tell this is what is expected of them. Children pick up their deepest attitudes from parents. If we seem comfortable with our sexuality, it will help children to feel comfortable with their own.

Many of us, however, find it hard to be both mothers and fully sexual beings, with our own needs, desires and dreams.

Rosy has been married for sixteen years. 'I was so busy being a housewife and mother I didn't bother about sex much. As the children grew up, I started working and *being a woman again*. I wanted more. I didn't know much about sex, though my husband thought he did. Instead of finding another man, I started experimenting with masturbation. This was the first time I climaxed in fifteen years of marriage. It took a long time to tell my husband. He knew something was wrong and was glad I hadn't turned to other men. I now climax regularly as a result of my husband's stimulation.'

Rosy's words should remind mothers how important it is not to lose touch with the woman inside. This won't be achieved at the expense of your children. They will benefit from having a mother who accepts her own sexuality and rejoices in it.

9 Why Do Women Have Affairs?

Two sides of the eternal triangle

Sexual fidelity – 'forsaking all others' – is still one of the basic pledges in our marriage vows, but it is a hard promise to keep. No matter how honourable our intentions, we can't guarantee that we will never meet another person to whom we will be sexually attracted. It's unlikely that we won't.

Moira, 39: 'It was very much a physical attraction and lasted for five months. I experienced the feelings of my youth, of "falling in love" again. There was always this conflict between what I had in my home – no worries, a kind and responsible husband, a happy family life – and a very strong physical need and desire for someone who could offer more than that.

'When I realized how far I was prepared to go, I backed off. After much heartache, I put my energies back into my marriage.'

Many women aren't so strong-willed, or perhaps haven't a marriage that can command such loyalty. Affairs are surprisingly common. *Three out of ten wives have had at least one affair since they married. Half of these have had two or more lovers. One in ten wives is having an affair at this moment.*

'I am a 41-year-old social worker, used to dealing with other people's problems. About six months ago I was discussing a particular case with my principal and as I leant over his desk he accidentally brushed my nipple with his arm. Had we been in darkness, I'm sure that the electric sparks could have been seen! I have never in my life experienced such a surge of physical longing for a man and it was quite obvious that he felt the same.

'I arranged to "work late" the next evening and we drove out into the country and made love in the back of his car. I didn't have an orgasm but reached heights of sexual passion which I had never imagined possible. Neither of us understands what

127

has happened. He is far less attractive than my husband but he makes me feel so very sexy. This affair will have to end very shortly. Now that I know I am not really frigid, I don't know how I can adjust to my husband's lovemaking in the future.'

Why an affair?

It is often thought that, if you don't sow any wild oats before meeting the man you eventually marry, you will always be wondering whether the grass is greener and so be more tempted to stray. 'My husband is the only man ever to have touched me or made love to me. I simply wonder what it would be like with another man.' 'I was a virgin when I met my husband but I strongly believe we would have a more fulfilling sex life (or I would!) if I had had other partners before my marriage.'

Three out of ten wives wish they had had more sexual experience. 'There's a saying, "Why go out for a hamburger when you've got steak at home?" but first one has to know the difference between steak and hamburger.'

Statistically, however, whether wives had any previous lovers has no bearing on their sexual satisfaction, nor on whether they rate their husband as a good lover.

Lack of sexual experience appears to lessen self-confidence – a wife who has had no other lovers before marriage is more likely to rate herself, and to believe her husband rates her, a poor lover – but she is slightly *less* likely to have an affair than a woman who did have other lovers before marriage. Like Jan, 42, she may 'sometimes feel it would be nice just to have the experience with someone else but would never risk breaking up my marriage. More than likely I'd be eaten up with guilt afterwards.'

Yet one in five of those who are very happily married and the same proportion of those who are completely satisfied with their sexual relationship has had an affair; roughly half of these women have had more than one. The lover often provides a dimension that is missing in the relationship with the husband.

Liza, 38: 'My affair is with a rich, dynamic company director who thinks I'm the best fuck in the world! He's exciting and buys me super presents and we have dinners and lunches which I love. I feel sophisticated and he's my secret, but my husband is a far better lover. We wouldn't dream of hurting our partners and really we're just very good friends with sexual overtones.

128

I'm a little in love with him but I would be horrified at the thought of him being my husband. It's a lovely, uncomplicated, lustful relationship and I can't imagine him not being there in the background.'

Beverley, 44, said, 'My extra-marital relationships have been satisfying, exciting and emotionally rewarding to me but that doesn't mean they are preferable to marriage.'

Taking a lover may coincide with a low point in a generally happy marriage. Nicky, 27: 'My affair happened when our relationship was going through a bad stage after we had been married five years. I wanted a house of our own where we would be able to begin a family if and when we so wanted. My husband was content to carry on as we were and would not save money at all. I began to feel he did not care for me, so when a man I met through work made it clear he was attracted to me, and the feeling was mutual, we began a brief affair. He was good-looking, attentive to me and a gentle lover, but still not as good as my husband.

'In a way my lover showed me that what I had got in my marriage was worth saving. After a couple of months we agreed it was no use continuing the affair. My husband never found out about it. Meanwhile the regular arguments with my husband were beginning to bear fruit and we started to save. Our love life improved again – though it never suffered a great deal – and continued the upward trend it has been on since our marriage. Now we are closer than ever.'

A wife is far more likely to take a risk if she is generally dissatisfied with her sexual relationship with her husband and rates him as a poor lover. *Nearly half the wives who are not at all satisfied sexually with their husband have affairs.*

'I never enjoyed sex with my husband,' said Erica, 41. 'There was no foreplay or kind words; it was just a twice-a-week duty that took about five or ten minutes. The first time I experienced an orgasm I was 35 years old. I thought I was going crazy. It was with my lover and the most wonderful experience. He was very caring and understanding and we could both be open with each other.'

Diane, 46: 'My husband has always been prudish. He didn't French-kiss and never touched my genitals or kissed my breasts, much less anything else. He became increasingly less interested in sex, and after twenty years of marriage, when I was 40, it dwindled away altogether. As I had never climaxed with him but only through masturbation, I didn't miss it. In

129

fact, I was quite relieved, as his lovemaking had been fruitless and clumsy.

'For a couple of years I put up with it, but I am attractive and easily get lovers who excite me and with whom I have orgasms. He has never known about these as I am very discreet. Some last for years, others are one-night stands. I have tried all sorts of things he wouldn't dream of.

'In spite of it all, we are good friends, enjoy a cuddle and are happily married. I accept him as he is and recognize that he can't fulfil all my needs.'

But it is not just sex that women look for in affairs. An unhappy marriage makes a woman more likely to have an affair than being dissatisfied sexually. *Three out of five wives who are not at all happy with their marriage have had affairs.*

Joanne, 27: 'My affairs have been triggered by someone being there and willing at the periods in my life when I felt my husband didn't feel anything for me and treated me like a piece of furniture.'

Juliet, 43, said, 'Most of my women friends feel the lack of tender, loving care. We are all in our early forties and would like to be encouraged and praised a little more. When your looks begin to fade, you like to be told you are still attractive. When we cook for dinner parties, we would like to be appreciated. I can take two hours to get ready to go out with my husband and he doesn't even comment on my appearance. Several of my friends would – like me – take a lover if they could. Usually it is not that they want sex elsewhere, just affection.'

The forties is the peak decade for wives to have affairs.

If husbands won't listen and refuse to change when their wives tell them they are unhappy, either sexually or because they feel taken for granted in their marriage and in need of more affection, they are pushing them closer to the brink of having an affair.

Clare, 28, said, 'I had not felt so much for any man before my husband. I respect him and find him physically attractive. However, he's very abusive if I grumble about his lack of kissing and touching *not* during lovemaking. My lover is a way to get back at my husband's cruel words and lack of interest in me – even though I can't tell him, because he would end our marriage, since he thinks I should just grin and bear it!'

Viv, 36, said, 'My affair started when I was extremely unhappy. I tried to tell my husband that I felt like an unpaid housekeeper as he was uninterested in sex or anything to do with the home or family, but he wouldn't talk about it.'

Eve, 43, said, 'I have tried very hard to accept my husband as he is because he says he doesn't wish to change even though he knows I feel the lack of warmth. My lover is extremely warm, kind and humorous, and very affectionate. I think, if my husband was asked, he would say he is very fond of me – but he won't talk to me about feelings, which my lover does. On the surface I am outgoing and happy. Underneath I am miserable wondering how long I can keep up this pretence.'

Many husbands who have had affairs might also protest that their complaints to their wives fell on deaf ears, and some husbands whose wives have had affairs could justifiably point out that the women never told them what was wrong in a way that would have given them a chance to put it right.

Marjorie, 47, said, 'My husband considered himself a good lover but I often faked orgasm and felt frustrated. He used to try to find my clitoris but never seemed quite to manage it and after a time gave up trying.

'We have a neighbour, a womanizer but a good sort. He used to try and kiss me and flirt with me, and one day he grabbed me and forced me to accept his kisses. I tried to stop him but my senses responded so strongly that I felt physically weak. When it happened, I had an orgasm like nothing I'd known before.

'Several times after that we made love standing in the kitchen against the door, and once we even had a strip session on the bed. He knew how to please a woman and I must confess I enjoyed it, but I felt so guilty, betraying my husband who trusted me. I had to stop it so I kept the door locked.

'I know I did wrong but I'm glad I found out how good sex can be. I often feel desire for his body but will not ever allow it to happen again. I love my husband, who is a good man. He still thinks he's a marvellous lover and I wouldn't upset him by telling him my true feelings, but my thoughts often stray back.'

A wife who never talks openly with her husband about sexual feelings and problems is twice as likely to have an affair as those who often talk freely. It's another sad symptom of the Sleeping Beauty syndrome. If our husband doesn't bring us sexual satisfaction, instead of discovering what will please us and showing him, we have an affair with another man who we hope will know what to do without our having to take any responsibility. *Wives who consider themselves excellent lovers are less likely to have an affair than those who consider themselves only average.*

What do you get out of an affair?

Figure 17 shows the benefits wives consider they get from affairs as compared with those they get from marriage.*

Sixty per cent find an affair more exciting than marriage.

Valerie, 29, said, 'My sex life with my husband has gradually worsened over the years and now I find it very boring. I think almost all wives go through this stage. My lover is more exciting, loving and much better in every other way. Maybe it's the idea of being so secretive that makes it thrilling – I can't explain.'

Figure 17

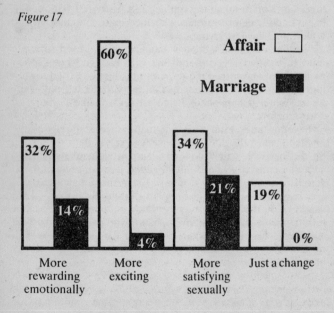

* Percentages don't add up to 100 because we asked wives only to mark those they felt applied in their case.

Sheena, 26, met her lover at a sales convention. 'I felt like a teenager again – the atmosphere, drinking and discos were all so exciting. Afterwards I lived in a complete dream world. He was in my thoughts every second of the day. We couldn't bear being apart. I lied at home and we went away to the coast. Making love was a whole new experience. It was so open and different. He talked and said sensual things and I began doing the same.

'I didn't worry about my marriage much. I love my husband dearly, but I pushed it to the back of my mind. After a few months the guilt started to grow. Even writing this down now I feel terribly cruel to my husband. He has no idea and loves me very much. When my affair began to cool, it was very hard for me to come to terms with it and build up feelings for my husband again.

'I am basically happy and wish time after time that I had never entered into this. It's such a battle with my conscience. Also, sex with my lover was so different and exciting – it will never be the same with my husband. I realize, though, that I was living in a fantasy world.'

Of course, much of the thrill of an affair arises from the very fact that it *is* an affair. Many women commented that their relationship with their lover would not survive if they were married to him. 'At the end of the day,' said Nina, 'you just end up washing someone else's dirty socks!'

The excitement may anyway be short-lived, and an affair can prove far more of a dead-end than marriage. 'I was physically attracted to him immediately,' said Rene. 'It was pure sex on his part; I fell in love. I ended up getting a divorce and now, thirty years on, he is still only interested in sex; for want of anything better, I have settled for an unrewarding relationship. The magic has worn off. I still finds him physically irresistible, but *love*?'

One in three wives having an affair finds it more rewarding emotionally than marriage, compared with just one in seven who says her marriage is more rewarding.

'My feelings for my friend are so strong and intense they are almost frightening,' said Lisa, 29. 'He is very romantic and tells me he loves me all the time. My husband doesn't show any feelings.'

'Sex was not the most important aspect of my affair,' said Sylvia, 43. 'Mutual admiration, companionship, friendship, being happy in each other's company, all played a greater part.

Our relationship was very loving and involved a lot of kissing and cuddling.'

Fran, 26, is having an affair with a man twenty years older than her. 'He is not a devastatingly handsome man in the Paul Newman mould. His lovemaking experience was very limited, but he is extremely kind, patient, very loving, and he does not take me for granted.'

Whether an affair will be more satisfying sexually than marriage is far less clear cut. *One in three wives does find her affair more sexually satisfying, but one in five finds it less satisfying, than her marriage.*

Lesley said, 'I am addicted to my lover because he is everything I could dream of in a sexual way. If only my husband had my lover's desire for me . . .'

Gwen, 39: 'My second affair opened my eyes to the fact that, handled properly, I could respond. I always had an orgasm and was warm and responsive. It took me a long time to lie back and enjoy being made love to. I lost the pressure of having to prove myself, accepted that I was normal and found for the first time ever that I couldn't get enough. Unfortunately, you can't live on sex alone. My present marriage is basically happy with three smashing children and a fairly considerate husband. We just don't click sexually but keep trying occasionally.'

But Charlotte found, 'At the final count-up, no one satisfied me like my husband.'

Monica, 42, said, 'It was disastrous. I felt almost nothing sexually while we were in bed and I had pinned my hopes on feeling great, because my lover was and still is the great passion of my life. I was very much in love with him but I don't think the sexual side of our life would or could be any good.'

For one in five wives the main benefit of an affair is that it provides 'a change'. Anne, 29: 'I did it because I felt like it. I don't regret what I did and my husband will never know because I do love him. It was boredom being a housewife, I suppose. Although I know I'm attractive enough – my husband does tell me – I needed to hear it from somebody different. It was purely a sexual experience which we both enjoyed. With no hard feelings, both affairs died a natural death.'

Eileen, 48: 'I need extra-marital stimulation. I love what I do. Though I hate deceiving my husband, he is not my whole life. I am me, so what I think and feel is the real me. We all have imperfections. Marriage is too rigid for most of us. Some break out, others have headaches, get fat, live mundane lives.

My husband is a good person, I have some love for him, but I love me more.'

Debbie is 23 and has had four lovers since she married. 'The first was a one-off occasion with the man who came to service the washing machine. It all started by him finding my "exotic" undies in the machine; he started to chat me up and finished making love to me against the kitchen table.

'The affair I have at the moment is with the husband of a friend down the road. Usually we meet about once a week and he takes me to the country, but it is rather awkward as I have a small child, so sometimes he will visit me at home. We haven't any special feelings for each other; we just seem to have a wonderful understanding sexually.'

How do affairs affect marriage?

Some affairs break up marriages, or at least coincide with the break-up of a marriage. Of course, one or both of those involved may have been looking – consciously or unconsciously – for another partner rather than just an affair, which is by implication a limited relationship. How affairs affect the marriages of couples who stay together is shown in Figure 18.

One in four wives who has had an affair says that it has improved her sexual relationship with her husband, one in five that it improved their emotional relationship.

Judy, 28: 'I know that my affair improved my relationship with my husband. He does not know of the affair but I know I am more alive than I was before I met this other man.'

Some wives find that risking their marriage with an affair gives them, and their husband if he knows of it, the jolt needed to make them put more effort into their marriage.

Janet, 27, said, 'My short affair made me sit up and think just how lucky I am. It wasn't at all what I had expected. I suppose I thought it would be like a fairy tale. I think it did me good; it brought me back to reality.'

Anita, 31, said, 'I decided to leave, but my husband made me see that we had a relationship worth holding on to. I realized that I love him very much, and that the only way to make a relationship work is to put oneself totally into it, which I hadn't been doing. Our emotional relationship has improved 100 per cent; our sexual relationship has improved quite a bit. The great outcome of this affair is that we can talk about anything now.'

There are a few couples who tolerate or even encourage affairs as a way of preventing their life together going stale. 'Neither of us is monogamous,' said Kathy, 31. 'I think it inevitable that the sex in a long-lasting relationship will go through highs and lows. Having another lover occasionally renews our sexual interest in each other. I am completely honest with him.'

More commonly, though, the 'improvement' seems to be that an affair enables a wife to stay with an otherwise intolerable husband.

Lorraine, a mother aged 31, said, 'My marriage only survives because of my lover. Life is not so frustrating sexually and mentally. If I had not met this man, who I have no intention of settling with, I would definitely have left my husband.'

Polly, 49, said, 'My lover of ten years is a safety valve for me. My husband and I have just had our silver wedding and I told my lover he should be the guest of honour as I don't think we would have made it without him.'

Denise, 32, said, 'My lover and I have truly loved each other for nine years. I stay with my husband only to avoid hurting him and to keep the children and their father together. Although I am still fond of him, it is more a sisterly feeling.'

One third of wives who have had an affair believed that it had had no effect one way or another on their marriage. This was usually in cases where their husband didn't know about the affair(s). 'I wouldn't want my husband to know. It would hurt him too badly and destroy our basically happy marriage,' said Kay, 39.

One in seven said it worsened the sexual relationship and one in four that it worsened her emotional relationship with her husband.

As we have already seen, an affair sometimes makes a wife realize what she has been missing – 'I always thought things could be better but it wasn't until I met someone else that I found just how wonderful sex could be' – but the more frequent cause of worsening relationships is the husband's discovery of the affair.

And this is a drawback of affairs. Often it is not until all has come out into the open that we discover just how serious our partner's reaction may be, how long we are going to have to live with the aftermath, how it's going to affect our children.

Joy, 41: 'For a year my husband has tortured me mentally over the terrible thing I have done – i.e. sleeping with another man.'

'It was about twenty-three years ago, with my boss who used to give me a lift to the office,' said Audrey. 'It has blighted our lives and, worse, our children's. I have never been forgiven and am still constantly reminded of it and accused of "carrying on". Maybe at 50 that should be a compliment, but it is upsetting.'

'I nearly lost my dear husband over my affairs,' said Jo, 'and he is the only one who really cares for me.'

Wives' views of husband's affairs

Nearly seven out of ten wives believed that their husband hadn't had any affairs. Of the rest, roughly half knew that he had had an affair and half didn't know whether he had or not. For how the discovery of a husband's affair affected the marriage as compared with the effects of wives' affairs, see Figure 18, but do remember that all references to the effects of husbands' affairs relate to those cases *where the wives had found out about them.*

Figure 18

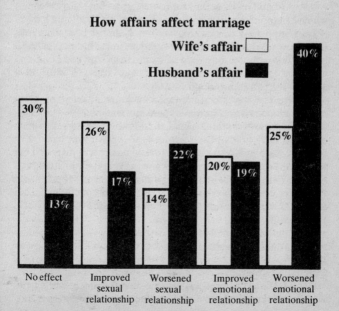

How affairs affect marriage

Wife's affair ☐
Husband's affair ■

No effect	Improved sexual relationship	Worsened sexual relationship	Improved emotional relationship	Worsened emotional relationship
30% / 13%	26% / 17%	14% / 22%	20% / 19%	25% / 40%

137

Wives are far less likely to feel that their husband's affair has no effect on the marriage, and far more likely to think it worsened the sexual and emotional relationship than their own affair.

Some wives are devastated to discover their husband has been having an affair.

Helena, 36: 'It took me two years to trust him again and the affair has ruined our sex life. He feels I should be able to understand the affair was in no way threatening to our marriage. He says it was to give the other woman love and comfort from someone she knew well when she needed it (her marriage had broken up). I still can't understand it and I don't think I ever will. We are left with the shell of what was such a lovely, joyful, happy marriage and it is so, so sad.'

Some wives react by wanting to have or having an affair of their own. 'My first reaction was to get drunk and find a man,' said Polly, 29. 'Then I wanted to show my husband up, shoplift or smash things. Luckily I could talk to him and after weekends away together and lots of talking we are back to square one, except that I will never completely trust him again and I feel very sad that in him I lost the best friend I ever had.'

'My husband had an affair for four years which I suspected but which he emphatically denied,' said Tessa, 42. 'I felt much more sexy. I suppose I was competing but I almost had a nervous breakdown. When he finally admitted his unfaithfulness, I had a brief affair with a young man at work. It did my ego good and was very exciting. My husband does not know. I still find it difficult to trust him though.'

Quite a few wives commented that knowing their husband might be having an affair made them more responsive sexually – 'I fought with everything I had to keep him, even sex, which quite honestly holds little for me. Now I have him back, I've "gone off" sex again. Although I love him dearly, I just can't get turned on' – but others find that knowing that their husband has had sex with another woman can make even his touch seem repulsive. 'I couldn't bear my husband to touch me,' said Sheena, 23, 'and I couldn't bring myself to get into bed with him. I slept on the sofa.'

Most of the thoughts we have seen here of wives having affairs would probably be echoed by husbands having affairs. Most of the hurt and outrage in reaction of wives to husbands' affairs would probably also be felt by husbands learning of wives' affairs. But one notable difference that emerged from what wives told us is that husbands are likely to be less tolerant.

Linda, 26: 'Although both my husband and myself have had a fair number of lovers, during arguments he calls me names like whore, although nothing could be further from the truth. Yet he sees himself as one of the lads. Men seem to want women to be sexual beings but, when they are, they resent it. Perhaps they fear being compared with other men.'

'My husband has had quite a few affairs and when I found out I had one just to spite him,' said Elaine, 31. 'This put an enormous strain on our marriage for a year, as he claimed my one affair was worse than his seven. Some days I feel very bitter. If we row, my affair is thrown up, which I hate.'

The timing of the husbands' affairs sometimes seemed extra cruel. 'I was about eight months pregnant.' 'My husband had an affair when I had become depressed after coming off the pill.' 'My husband's affair was carried out when I was forbidden by my doctor to have intercourse during a difficult pregnancy following a miscarriage,' said Phyllis, 51.

However, Phyllis herself showed that sometimes there could be another view of the situation. 'My own affair was with a close friend. His wife had just had their third child and turned her whole attention to it and the other two. He felt as if he'd been used as a stud to provide the required number of children and that she just regarded him as a good provider, the one who paid the bills.'

Are affairs worth it?

Some think they are. There are couples who manage to survive 'open marriage' and live together to tell the tale. There are those who feel they can only survive their marriage while they can have an affair, too. Often they tell themselves they are only staying for the good of their spouse and their children, but chances are that there is a large part of them that wants to stay in their marriage, too.

There are even those who manage to welcome their spouse's affair. Heather, 43: 'My husband's affair was the best thing that ever happened to me. It made me stop and reassess my whole married life. I forgave my husband on the understanding he would never see this girl again, as I felt I could forgive him, but I couldn't share him. He made the break and we began to rebuild our marriage.

'It wasn't easy. In fact, it would have been easier to split up, but we decided we had something worth fighting for.'

139

Talking to each other, listening and being willing to change is a way to keep a marriage together. It's talking and listening that help us through the crisis caused by an affair, too; only in this way can we identify what's lacking in our relationship that led one or both to go looking outside.

An affair which is revealed to or discovered by our partner is more likely to damage our marriage than benefit it.

An affair almost certainly will seem more exciting but it's short-lived excitement. It can be a mistake to think that the lover is more exciting than our husband. It may just be he has an exciting role to play. Could our dull husband be someone else's exciting lover?

There are people in poor marriages who think that the risk of an affair is worthwhile because they feel they have so little to lose. Fiona, 32: 'I married for the wrong reasons – security, to leave home, have babies – not for love. The original reasons no longer apply so how about looking for the love and companionship before it's too late? I can't find it with my husband so shall have to find it elsewhere.'

But if we value our marriage at all, it helps to take off the blinkers of fantasy and infatuation before starting an affair. Away from the children, the leaking washing machine, the overgrown lawn, the back room which needs a coat of paint, we nearly all find it easier to behave like seductive, sensual lovers. Even those of us who don't feel our marriage is in trouble could be lulled into a false sense of security by the very solidity of the institution of marriage. If you fear this situation, try a few pre-emptive strikes. When did you last try it in the back of a car, meet in a hotel room, go away for a dirty weekend?

How happy is a mistress?

In our survey of unmarried women, one in eight of those in sexual relationships was having an affair with a married man. Is it candlelight dinners and red roses all the way?

Lara, 30, would rather be a mistress than a wife. 'My man is happily married and looks after both our needs, though his wife doesn't know about me. I've been a wife and know what it's like to share a husband – no thanks! Being a mistress is much more romantic and exciting, though I do respect her position as the family backbone and hard worker.'

Some women welcome the role of mistress simply because the man already belongs to someone else. Sophy's fiancé left

140

her for another girl. 'My friends tried fixing up dates for me but as far as I was concerned all men should have been shot. Since we split up three years ago I still can't bear the thought of a steady relationship with someone. I don't think I could go through the heartache again. At the moment I am having an affair with a married man. I feel safe with him because I don't have any commitments.'

Others are less enthusiastic. Alice, 20: 'Even now, a year later, I still miss my boyfriend. I'm dreading Christmas. I'm now seeing another man, but he will have to spend Christmas with his wife and family where he belongs. I knew what I was getting into when I got involved with him, but the need for someone to hold me and make me feel wanted again was too great to resist. I have a good relationship with him. I see him at weekends and I know that our affair is also livening up his marriage. Nothing can come of it, but I'm not thinking about that just yet.'

Most mistresses who keep up the relationship for any length of time do not seem to relish the role, and either admit they would rather be wives or talk rather wistfully of the fact that this is impossible. They feel they are being treated as second best.

'I never asked him to leave his family, though in years to come I hoped he might.' 'I still don't know where I stand with him. I hurt inside just thinking about him. If this is love, I hope I never fall in love with anyone again. It hurts too much.' 'I don't want to be a mistress for the rest of my life, but neither do I want anyone else.'

Pam, a widow: 'He admits to being happily married but needs sex outside his marriage. I agreed because at my age – in my forties – it is very difficult to meet unattached men of my age group. I am silly for putting up with him but I am lonely and he gives me something to think about.'

'I once left him because he was married,' said Shona, 24. 'After a few years I wanted more from the relationship. We subsequently got back together. Since then he has talked about leaving his wife but so far has not done so despite many protests.'

Such a stalemate can persist for years, leading in the end to a sense of a wasted life. Sarah is in her sixties. 'I had known him and his wife for some years before we fell in love. She was kind to me but never missed an opportunity of making him look small in front of others. She told me once never to marry, as sex was revolting and men did nothing but make a woman's life hell.

'He never once complained about his wife but, as we were working closely together, we eventually found we couldn't live without each other. I supported him in seeking promotion and eventually he reached a top position in public life. He never left home for me and so I had to be satisfied with evenings and occasional weekends. This I found hard to take as the years went by.

'I had an idea his wife might have known about us but she never said anything and didn't seem to care. In fact, she enjoyed his being away on occasions. In a way I lost him before he died because, as he progressed in business, he became obsessed with work and his final promotion took him to the south of England. By then I had begun to feel used, having missed chances of marriage by remaining loyal to him, and at times I almost feel hatred towards him.'

Some of the saddest cases are those involving an invalid wife – or invalid husband, for we also heard from wives having affairs who felt they could not leave their partner but nor could they lead a sexless existence.

Hannah, 48, said, 'My man's wife has rheumatoid arthritis from which she will never recover. I am divorced. We have no hope of ever being together. He is full of guilt and pity for his wife. It is an impossible situation. There is no answer. She relies on him entirely; there's a half-grown family. A physical relationship with her is impossible. I have kept him happy for six years, desperately longing for him to leave, but how can he? There's virtually no money on his side or mine. There can never be anyone else for me or for him. The vicar told me, "When one door closes, another opens." I could have punched him. With two marriages and many men behind me, do you think I can say goodbye to the man I was made for?'

If a wife suspects there's a mistress but doesn't protest it may be because she would rather maintain the status quo; she may even welcome the sexual pressure being taken off her. The risk that such a wife runs is that her husband will decide to 'make an honest woman' of his mistress, will decide that he wants love, sexual pleasure and family life within one relationship. The risk the mistress runs who wants to become a wife – as, it seems, so many do – is that he will never make the break.

That's the tough decision facing the mistress who is genuinely in love and wants to become a wife. Does she believe him when he says that he will leave as soon as the children are older, or the mortgage smaller, or ⁚ . . ? Chances are she shouldn't. If a man is going to reject his wife now he's met a new woman it will probably happen reasonably speedily if it's going to happen at all. Once he has settled down into a routine where he has both his mistress and his wife and children, it will be difficult for him to give up either.

And there is even the risk that, if he does leave his wife, he will not join his mistress. He may see her *as* a mistress rather than as a wife, or he may have been relishing the affair itself more than her as a person.

Wendy, 42: 'I thought it was a holiday quickie but I saw a lot of him, over weekends sailing. It was intensely romantic. He left his wife and made noises for a while about us living together but I think he eventually came to see that he managed very well on his own. It was best before he left his wife. He changed in many ways, as though a lot of his pleasure had been in cheating his wife! He said the magic escaped. Nothing escaped for me, my feelings were much the same, but he withdrew from me.'

A mistress who does not expect, or want, to become her man's full-time woman is more likely to be happy, like Val: 'I now don't want him to leave his wife. He'd never cope with the trauma of divorce and he'd never be rid of his guilty feeling. As far as I'm concerned, I have a loving and fulfilling relationship as things are. I see him every day, we have holidays together, and I can keep my independence. He did move in with me for a couple of weeks some time ago and I felt trapped.'

10 Women Who Love Women
Lesbianism and bisexuality

*A*mong the unmarried women who replied to our survey, almost all of whom have or have had relationships with men, nearly one in ten has made love with another woman. Only one in ten of these was having such a relationship now (not surprising in view of the fact that this question was near the end of a long heterosexually oriented questionnaire). Nonetheless three out of ten of this number said their last such relationship had taken place between the ages of 17 and 21, and more than another one in ten after the age of 21.

How many married women are also having sexual relationships with other women is a question I can't answer from our survey. When drafting the questions for the survey on wives, the first of the two, I drastically underestimated how common this was likely to be. It shows how we can trip up on our own assumptions even when we wouldn't think we were prejudiced!

Had I put the question to married women, it is likely that the figures would have been even higher than those for unmarried. 'From my experience as a member of Friend [a gay counselling and befriending group],' wrote a social researcher, 'it is clear that there are more married lesbians than single ones. Probably about 60 per cent are married. Many married lesbians lead a completely double life – much to the surprise of their husbands, if they ever find out. Married lesbians may be less visible, but probably make up the majority.'

Once we raised the subject in *Woman* magazine when reporting back our initial findings, we did receive many letters from married women who either have or would like to have a relationship with a woman.

A lonely love

Finding yourself sexually attracted towards other women can

make you feel very lonely as you realize that admitting this to others may bring disapproval.

Christine, 19: 'About three years ago I had a sexual relationship with my best friend. She was very beautiful and understanding. We knew each other's needs. I have never regretted this relationship but I have always wanted to talk to someone. I cannot talk to my friends as I don't think they would approve and I would lose their friendship. You finally gave me the nerve to write. You will never know how much it means to me.'

Isabel: 'For the past twelve years I have lived alone. I married at 20 but it was a disaster, and for eight years I had a relationship with a lady friend I confided in. We never went out socially in case anybody recognized us. In most gay clubs and pubs a lot of straight people go along just for curiosity to jeer and make fun, and watch the "queers" dancing together, so we couldn't take the chance of mixing with our "own". I would never "confess" to my parents because it would hurt them deeply and they could never understand. We don't hate men but for various reasons can't have sex with them.

'People have been conditioned to think homosexuality is wrong. We are not monsters who corrupt others. Lesbians would never harm a child. How often do you hear of *women* sexually assaulting young girls?

'If there was more education about the reasons for homosexuality, perhaps there would be more tolerance. Then maybe people like me wouldn't feel so desperately lonely, living alone, frightened to go out, hiding myself away, and doomed to be regarded as "peculiar" because I'm not married nor do I have children. The loneliness is unbearable at times. Even though I have a good job to keep me busy, I go home to an empty house and watch TV.

'Although there are butch women who dress like men, we are not all like that. Many of us are decent law-abiding citizens who are no threat to society.'

Many women who wrote about loving other women were keen to dissociate themselves from the lesbians they see in the news. Yet liking short hair and trousers isn't a threat to law and order. Dawn, 25: 'Women who dress comfortably like I do (I wear baggy trousers and jumpers, no bra – what's the point? – plus Doc Marten boots) get ridiculed, abused, socially censored. I was once beaten up by nine men for dressing like a man. Is violence more normal than wearing baggy trousers?'

Pictures in the news are almost always chosen by men, who may feel threatened by the idea of 'lesbians'. News editors have been known to tell photographers, 'Shoot the ugly ones.'

In fact, most of the women who wrote to us about their homosexuality also have or have had relationships with men. Many are married. They often feel worried and lonely.

Jeannette is 38: 'I have been married for sixteen years and have two children. My family know nothing about this. The first time I ever went to bed with a woman, at the age of 35, I knew it was what I had been waiting for.

'My next-door neighbour's husband left home. She didn't want to be left on her own at night and my husband was away at the time. She used to sit in my house, late at night and start to cry. I can't just watch someone cry without offering some comfort, but it developed into more than that.

'I worshipped her, I would have done anything for her. I've never in my life known any feeling like it. She didn't look on it in the same way. I was there when she needed someone and that's all it meant. She is now married. I went through absolute torture.

'My husband came back home, everything was back to normal, except inside me. Two years have gone by since then and I still have an overwhelming need for a woman's love, but there's nothing I can do.

'I want to stay married, I want to keep my family as it is, but I need more. I know a lot of women but I can hardly ask any of them to go to bed with me, can I?'

Libby, 32, is married with one child. She has been having an affair with a woman for seven years. 'We are very close and have been through thick and thin together. If circumstances were different, we probably would be living together but we consider that everyone else would be horrified.

'I am sure that neither of us is completely gay. We both fancy men. Don't get us wrong, we are not butch.

'What does the relationship mean to me? I feel peaceful, secure, happy, loved, cared for, and I have someone who appreciates my love. But I know my life really is in a mess.'

Just a phase?

For some, making love with a woman is or was part of the exploration of their sexuality. They have formed or want to form their main relationships with men.

Gina, 21: 'From an early age I was involved in "experiments" with other girls. Once I was with a friend in her front room. Her parents came back unexpectedly and caught us.

'Since then I haven't had any close contact with anyone of my own sex. Not that I haven't wanted to, though. I frequently yearn to be with one special friend and hold her in my arms and tell her how I feel. I'm sure if I did I would lose her as a friend.

'I'm very happily engaged. My fiancé knows how I feel about my friend and he accepts this. I don't think I could ever leave him to go in for a lesbian life as I love him very much. It's just that I yearn for more sometimes.'

Experiments can start young. Trisha, 17, mentioned 'childhood experimentation, aged 8 to 12. I would think that was perfectly normal.'

But many parents don't see it as normal at all. Donna, 16: 'I have been having a relationship with a girl at my convent school for a year. She had a similar relationship about three years ago; it was purely physical and neither took it too seriously, until they were caught by the other girl's parents, who blew the whole thing out of proportion. Drastic measures were taken. She had to change schools.

'I love her and she loves me. At the moment I have no desire for the petty boyfriends other girls in my class have, but I am still very attracted towards men, as is my friend. I have merely become more choosy. When "Mr Right" comes along, I will recognize him immediately and not have silly infatuations like most other women.

'I won't go for the popular signs of masculinity but for a deep meaningful relationship that will last.

'It doesn't worry me that I am in love with a member of my own sex. I can fall in love with a man just as easily. I suppose you would call me a bisexual but I am not attracted to other women at all.

'My parents go to mass every Sunday and are quite devout. They have no idea. We always keep one ear open, so to speak, whenever we are indulging in anything physical.'

Carrie, 21, is sure that making love with a woman has enriched her relationship with her boyfriend. 'She and I were 17 at the time and virgins. Our lovemaking was a way of exploring, experiencing and understanding our own sexual fantasies. There was a lot of role-playing involved.

'It ended when she fell in love with a man. I felt a certain amount of rejection. But the experiences my partner and I shared help me to understand myself and my body.

'This aided my boyfriend and me when we first made love, and still does. I know instinctively what turns him on and I can help him to turn me on in ways that he would not think of.'

Feeling 'safer'

Some have lesbian relationships because they are nervous of men or specifically as a reaction to a bad experience, but then go on to develop further relationships with men.

Lisa, 28: 'After a series of highly unsatisfactory relationships with men, I was celibate for two years, after which I decided I was a lesbian and had a number of equally unsatisfactory relationships with women. During this time I met my fiancé; because I thought I was a lesbian, we did not have sex until we fell in love.'

Lilian, 44: 'When I was 8 an acquaintance of my father's used to stand close to me and feel under my clothes. I thought it was one of the things we had to put up with from adults, like being chucked under the chin. When I started going out with boys, I found I was frightened of men coming close to me and smiling. I didn't want physical contact, and dropped them if they attempted to get physical.

'When I left home I suddenly fell for one of my flatmates, totally unexpectedly. She'd already had affairs with men, and our affair taught me much about myself sexually.'

Lilian is now having an affair with a married man. 'My regret is that I found heterosexual love so late – not until I was 37. Now it is too late for me to marry and have children. Looking back, the only way I could have progressed towards sex at all was by having an affair with a woman, because women didn't threaten me like men did, and then with a man who didn't threaten me because he was married, and therefore safe.'

Pippa, 23: 'A friend and I got very drunk the day her divorce came through. We started a we-don't-need-men conversation, and ended up in bed. We kissed and caressed each other for a short while before going to sleep. The next morning we were both worried about each other's reaction. In fact, we just giggled. We are still good friends but have never wanted to repeat the experience. At the time it was natural. I have not been attracted to her since but do not regret what we did.'

Lyn, 20: 'When I was 14 my boyfriend, who was 18, told me

148

to prove I loved him by making love to him. I was very shy, because I didn't know exactly how to, apart from undoing his trousers and touching his penis. Instead of showing me, he laughed at me, and said, "You're doing your job wrong." I really felt bad.

'Next day a very close friend said that the same had happened to her. We were in her bedroom and she put her arm around me. We started kissing, then I reached up her skirt. It was fantastic, although I was thinking about my boyfriend. I was making love. It didn't really matter to me that it was with a female; we were both being satisfied, we stayed in bed all afternoon.

'I turned lesbian at that time because I knew what girls had and how to touch them properly. I'm not a lesbian now but I hide my body when lads make love to me. I still cannot touch them without feeling shy and guilty. I often think of being with other females – at least with a female you know roughly what they like, and vice versa.

'I believe that a lot of girls think the way I do but are so scared of the embarrassment. I would never tell anyone the way I feel – because I'm ashamed, I suppose.'

'Am I really a lesbian?'

Women who make love with other women are often very concerned about labels. They ask themselves, 'Does this mean I am a lesbian?' 'Am I bisexual?' They say, 'I was a lesbian then but I'm not now,' as if they were crucially different at the time.

Very few people have absolutely no capacity to feel aroused by their own sex. Many women who consider themselves completely heterosexual enjoy looking at erotic pictures of women, for example. We are all on a sliding scale, and some are more likely to respond to our own sex than others.

Fear of being abnormal or perverted can block this response. Those who react angrily to the idea of homosexual love may find that beneath this worry they themselves are attracted to the same sex.

Some women choose to define themselves as 'lesbians' as a political stance. They feel like a beleaguered minority, and they take pride in identifying themselves with other women who are involved in the same struggle. In general, though, our sexuality is private. It isn't relevant – except through social pressures – to our performance in other areas of our lives, so it doesn't describe us as people. Yet the general prejudice against homosexuality is such that women writing to us even just about *wanting* to make love with another woman kept apologizing; they felt the need to seek approval and to assure us that they were decent and respectable.

Our sexuality is a part of ourselves. But you as a person don't change from one being into another according to whether you are sharing sex with a man or a woman. You are you and the blend that makes up the sexual identity of each one of us too subtly varying for crude categorisations into heterosexual, homosexual or bisexual.

Social disapproval

People with homosexual inclinations often find themselves making all sorts of compromises to try to balance their sexual needs with society's expectations. Many are held back by fear of general disapproval.

Avril: 'I haven't made love with another woman but I've always wanted to. I get a lot of pleasure from naked ladies' bodies but they are always in pictures.'

Sue: 'I enjoy sex with my boyfriend but I would really like to experience sex with another woman. My boyfriend knows this but doesn't object. I often masturbate to "girlie" magazines.'

Rosy, 21: 'I'm engaged. We lead a very active sex life using manual stimulation, oral sex and our own various techniques. I would like to make love with another woman, but I'm afraid what my friends will think. I am a perfectly honest person, a hard-working nurse, and I'm glad to have expressed my feelings to someone.'

Amy, 25: 'I have never had the opportunity of a sexual relationship with a woman, but 'the feelings I have for women are strong enough for me to make the jump from fantasy to reality if the chance arose.

'I live happily with my boyfriend and think of myself as mainly heterosexual. I began to feel sexual attraction for other girls at 13, and didn't worry about it – I was aware that most people go through a phase like this and just enjoyed my fantasies and real-life close friendships.

'Now I'm 25 it seems it isn't just a phase – I can't see it ever completely disappearing. So why this attraction?

'Firstly, I think it sad that we are restricted to showing sexual love only to the opposite sex. It's always seemed natural to me for a woman to be curious about and attracted to a body like her own.

'Also it is refreshing to get away from the tired old rules and habits of male/female partnerships. There is a fantastic feeling of equality, freedom, in attraction to a woman. You know they don't have the stereotyped expectations of you that a man often has. I often feel more confident of my appeal to women than to men.

'This equality has a more disturbing aspect though, because it leaves no hiding place for some of your fears and weaknesses. For example, if a woman friend is doing better than you at her job, or is socially more popular, you may feel inadequate – whereas, if it were your husband, you could perhaps comfortably convince yourself that the difference is because he's a man, so it doesn't matter so much.

'There is also, for me, an exhilaration in the defiance of social mores, but it's a minor factor.

'Neither I nor the women I fancy are at all "butch". The very fact we are attracted to women means that we tend to reject masculine values, and are feminine and attracted to feminine women – that is, a *woman's* definition of femininity, not a man's. The kind of woman I find attractive wears neither a boiler suit nor three layers of make-up, but is intelligent, characterful, unconventionally attractive, full of life.

'I'm not attracted to obviously straight women; I'm never attracted to anyone who I know couldn't possibly be interested in me.

'I really do think many, many more women than admit it feel like this. I've known women you'd have thought were as straight as ninepins fall head over heels for one particular girl.

'I still feel no guilt within myself about it, although I'd curl up and die if my parents or certain of my friends knew – no matter how I explained, I know things would never be the same.

'I don't worry about what my boyfriend would think because a woman is not such a threat to him as a man. I don't feel the guilt which accompanies my occasional thoughts of other men. As far as my boyfriend's concerned, I wouldn't agonize for long before starting a relationship with a woman, but another man would mean something was seriously wrong with our relationship. I think a woman is a relatively harmless way to channel the restlessness which affects almost every couple at some time.'

Enjoying men and women

Anyone, man or woman, used just as a 'channel' for restlessness by one of a couple risks getting hurt, but some women enjoy sex with men and women, and in some cases their partners know and are happy about it.

Irene, 31: 'My lovers have been female. My husband knows about them and has met them on occasions. I get most satisfaction with him but I also get satisfaction with my girlfriends.'

Naomi, 24, has been with the same boyfriend for five years but had a sexual relationship with another girl two years ago. 'Sexually it was by far the most sensuous experience I have ever had. She was very experienced, very tender, and it was quite different from making love with a man. Given half the chance, I would definitely do it again.

'The physical side was great and emotionally it was also very good and easy to handle. We were best friends and it was like extending the friendship without running into the jealousy which can happen in heterosexual relationships – we both had boyfriends but we were away from them at the time.

'I told my boyfriend. Because it was another girl, he didn't regard it as infidelity and was basically very curious about the whole incident. In a funny way, I think he envied me.'

Jillian, 29: 'Both of my affairs have been with women, and before I married most of my lovers were women. I married because I love my husband and wanted children but I can never see myself being completely faithful as I do prefer making love to women.

'I would feel guilty about sex with another man, but do not about my lesbian relationships. My husband knew I slept with women when we first met but he thinks I have "grown out of all that". He is ten years older than me and I just know that one day in the future I will finally have a permanent female lover, which is what I want. In the meantime, nobody gets hurt and I stay happy.'

Any marriage where the woman prefers making love with another woman is obviously under particular pressure. Some women who are in this situation didn't choose it at all. They married, often young, perhaps realizing that they didn't enjoy sex with their husband very much but exploring no further. Later they discovered that they enjoy it far more with a woman.

Carol, 32: 'I was surprised to find that nearly 10 per cent of women in reply to your survey had made love with another woman. I was also relieved to find out I am not odd in having had such a relationship. I am 32, married since 21, and have two young children. I made love to a colleague one night only (unfortunately) after she came round for a meal and stayed the night. My husband was away on business at the time.

'We did not know that we each had bisexual tendencies as we are quite attractive, not butch-looking or fraily feminine. Both of us have had a fair experience of men. We made love spontaneously with a little wine, which undoubtedly helped break down inhibitions. I can honestly say it was the most exciting moment in my whole life. I mean exciting both sexually and mentally. I had my first climax without masturbating. I have never had an orgasm with any man and have now resigned myself to the fact that I never will. I would pay a man a thousand pounds if he could guarantee an orgasm just so I could die knowing what it is like during intercourse.

'My friend got such a thrill bringing me to a climax that she kept doing it time and time again. Naturally, I did not want her to stop. I felt a beautiful warm feeling when we kissed and cuddled. It was much more real than can ever be possible with any man.

'We found it impossible to work together after that night. All the time I was longing to grab hold of her. Soon afterwards, my husband's job took us to another part of the country, which solved the problem.

'I live in the past sexually and think of that night when I am making love with my husband. I married my husband because I love him, but not sexually. We have both had affairs but I would love to meet another housewife to have a relationship with while the children are at school, though I know it would not be the same as my first experience. I would not want it to be, as that was too precious. The problem is knowing how to recognize another lesbian.'

For women with children, the dilemma can be agonizing. Lorna, 29: 'I married, pregnant, at 20. Sex with my husband was nothing. I just presumed that was how it was for everyone, though when I read books and saw films I thought that surely I must be missing something. I began to feel a little resentful towards men because they always seemed to enjoy themselves, though my husband was never bothered about sex.

'It was one night during my first affair with a girl rather younger than me that it happened – I had my first orgasm. This probably sounds wrong to you, but I didn't feel as guilty about sleeping with a woman as I did with a man.

'I am now having an affair with another woman. We have been together eighteen months. My husband doesn't know. In the past he has questioned me but I have always denied anything.

'You see, I have an eight-year-old son whom I truly worship and could never leave. This is the only reason I am still with my husband. He is a very good man, I am not running him down at all. It's just that we have nothing in common. I know deep down I cannot go on living this double life, but while my child is so young I will not do anything legally. Friends who have been through all this before have told me I must deny my affair if I wish to keep my child. I have read that in most cases the husband wins the child if the women is having an affair with another woman. However, things are slowly changing and some judges give the woman the child.

'My husband likes my girl – why should he not, as he doesn't know? My son loves her. We all get on really well, but today I am more confused about my future than ever.'

We heard from one woman who intended some time in the future to have children by AID and share them with another woman; others have already done this – but few feel it is a realistic option. Many seem to resolve the dilemma by telling themselves that they are bisexual, even if they know they prefer making love with a woman. If they can tolerate sex with a husband, they can also have children and social acceptability.

If the wife does leave her husband to live with another woman, it can cut her off from friends and family.

Maggie, 29: 'After leaving my husband I felt extremely guilty. I had lost my marriage, my in-laws, my own family's approval (though my father has since accepted me much more) and the approval of society in general. The relationship I have now is fulfilling in every way but I still get feelings of guilt and think that I should be doing "the right thing!"'

154

Coming out

While in the long run 'coming out' usually gives women who prefer lesbian relationships greater peace of mind and the strength and comfort of meeting other women who share their feelings, they can face many pressures and prejudices.

Barbara, 27: 'I know several lesbians who were subjected to harassment and punishment as teenagers. Many young lesbians are told they are sick and pressured into seeing doctors and psychotherapists to be "cured". This kind of "treatment" leaves terrible, sometimes disabling scars.

'For years I fell in love with women but had sex with men; this brought me so little pleasure that I became quite disillusioned with sex in general. When I came close to sleeping with certain women, they were always as nervous of it as I was, and it never happened.

'Six years ago I met a woman who had had previous homosexual relationships, with women in the States. The attraction between us worried me. I left the area and began to work as a psychiatric auxiliary nurse, close to breakdown. I was miserable and sick of a life that seemed to be nothing but continual, fruitless struggles with men.

'About a year later I slept with this woman. I felt great about it. We both saw it as an extension of our friendship rather than a grand passion.

'The new-found relaxation was short-lived. My fragile self-esteem was completely knocked by my closest friend of the time. One night she asked me to stay at her place, but found it necessary to add that she didn't want to have sex with me.

'Since the thought had never crossed my mind and I wasn't in the least attracted to her, I was very shocked. I felt as if I had been cast in the role of predatory dyke and that disgusted me. I submerged my sexuality yet again.'

It was nearly two years later that Barbara 'fell in love and began to sleep with a woman who was my lover for two years and remains a very close friend. At last, you may think, I had found happiness as a self-accepting lesbian but unfortunately it wasn't that simple.

'Although I said to myself, "Lots of my best friends are gay and I'm liberated enough to sleep with women," coming to terms with actually being a lesbian was still hard. The word itself still had the power to conjure up all these images of predatory monsters that I thought I had overcome years before. I was scared people would think I was a danger to their children, that my family would freak out, that I would be sacked, etc. Some of these were groundless fears, but others are quite realistic reflections of the prejudice lesbians encounter.'

Some women who come out do find tolerance and understanding. Angelia, 28: 'I have been living with the woman I love for four years. We are blissfully happy together. Not only are we lovers, we are also good friends. We can communicate with each other and we respect and trust each other.

'Our friends, both heterosexual and homosexual, admire our relationship. Both sets of parents treat us as a couple, which we appreciate. We are both professional people who enjoy a great deal of respect from colleagues. We are just as happy together as a satisfied heterosexual couple.

'We both tried to conform during our teenage years, having several heterosexual relationships which only brought about confusion and unhappiness until we each finally came to accept ourselves.'

Lois, 21: 'I have defined myself as lesbian for the last two years. I am a black woman. My family came here from the West Indies. I enjoy being a lesbian. I am emotionally and sexually more oriented towards women. I feel more at ease and "myself" with women – I don't have to pretend. My early childhood experiences were with other girls. I experimented with men in my teens; I used to say I was bisexual but then began to feel that wasn't strictly true. I can have sex with men still; I go through the mechanics – "Lie back and think of Africa" – but I agree with the saying "Women do it better".

'Being a lesbian is more than who you sleep with. It is recognizing your emotional, physical and spiritual self. It's about being a woman, identifying with other women. I don't see myself competing against other women for the favours of men. Women are my friends, my "sisters".'

As we have seen, some women who call themselves lesbians do not consider themselves feminists. However, many who have come out are so appalled by society's attitude towards them that they struggle to change it.

Barbara, again: 'I can't write this without being political. The women's movement has been the support that allowed me to come to terms with my own sexuality. I'm not shy or unconfident, yet it has been quite a struggle for me to come out. The message of society has always been negative about lesbianism and this is no accident. It is rubbish to think we are free to choose lesbianism when it is made so difficult for us to see lesbianism as a possible, even positive, choice. Lesbians threaten male dominance in a number of ways, and don't men know it! The attitude to lesbianism in a society is a very good measure of how oppressed women are within that society. Until it is as easy to choose lesbianism as heterosexual relationships, women will not be free. Until women have access to housing, work, social spaces, the media on our own terms, it will never be easy to be a lesbian.'

I myself must admit to feeling irritated on occasion by the way lesbian feminists seem almost to have taken over the women's movement, so that women who wanted to make a go of getting on with men on more equal terms, wanted marriage and children, to work comfortably alongside men, felt alienated from it. Successful women often seem to feel obliged to preface anything they have to say with 'I'm not a feminist but . . .' before they go on to affirm their belief in many feminist ideals, because of the man-hating tag that the women's movement has acquired. Of course, many lesbians don't hate men; they just don't want to go to bed with them. And if I had to put up with the same abuse and scorn that they have to over my choice of sexual mate, then I hope I'd have their courage to make a fuss about it.

What do you enjoy about making love with other women?

Jayne, 25: 'I feel valued in a way that I never felt with any man and I have learned to value myself more. There is far more real caring for me *as I am* and not me composed of all the different parts *he* wanted to know about. The potential for honesty is so much greater, since women have been through similar experiences and problems all their lives.

'Heterosexual sex is in comparison a greedy act. "How many times did I really enjoy *all* of it?" I asked myself recently. Oh, I enjoyed the build-up, the touching, but that was simply a prelude to the real thing, which was penetration. Lesbian sex is

157

far more arousing, since I know I'm going to enjoy the whole experience and I don't have to submit to anything.

'There isn't a point of no return, when you know you're going to have to go through with being fucked. You can go to orgasm, if you want to, or not, depending. There's as much joy in giving as in receiving, and that's something men cannot understand, because, for men, sex equals penetration. I have orgasms more frequently with lesbian sex and they are more total, too.'

Lindsay, 19: 'I was always worried that I wouldn't be good enough with a boy and therefore I couldn't relax while having sex. With my girlfriend it seemed so natural. There was no roughness, and it wasn't hurried. We could just express our love and affection for each other in a gentle and caring way. I didn't feel I had to prove anything in the way I did with boys.

'I don't dislike men but I think I am a little scared of them. I find that women are much more gentle and men are mostly hard – I say "mostly" because I know there are some gentle men in the world, but I feel I will always be happier with a woman. My relationships with men (well, boys) finished about eighteen months ago, when I realized I couldn't pretend to myself any longer.'

Melanie: 'I found that with men their main aim is to have sex and for me it was always more important to have someone hug me, cuddle me, touch and stroke me. With my friend, sex isn't the main part of our relationship.

'It's really lovely lying in each other's arms. It's a bit like being a baby again, feeling the warmth and softness of your mother's skin. Her touch is so soft, something I've never felt with a man, and we can tell each other what we like without feeling stupid or demanding. It's a bit like stroking or touching your own body; I sometimes get mixed up and I find I'm stroking my own arm or something.

'I feel so whole with her and neither of us has to dominate all the time. We each have our strengths and weaknesses and we can support each other when we need to. Women are sensitive to each other's feelings (most of the time) in a way that no man can ever be – well, not the ones I've known.

'I never realized how easy orgasms were until I met my friend. I think that half the men I've known didn't even know that my clitoris existed!

'I now know more about myself and my body than I've ever known, and I know that I can never stop learning and growing with her. I have never felt so close to anyone before. Sex is an expression of this and not something separate.'

11 Women Alone
Pleasures and problems of the unattached over-25s

'**P**eople think that, if you are 28 and single, and have no boyfriends, you must be gay or nuts.' 'The moment our marriage broke up, the married women I knew treated me as a social leper.' 'I am a freak in this day and age – a 47-year-old virgin who isn't a man-hater, just terribly shy.'

Once you are over 25 or 30, you find that social life tends to be conducted in couples. But there are six million unmarried women over 25 in Great Britain today. They may be single, willingly or unwillingly, widowed, divorced or separated. They feel left out.

Sylvia, 43, divorced: 'Where are all the attractive, intelligent, humorous men? At home with their attractive, intelligent wives? Surely the ratio of men to women can't be that low! I could write a lot about women's loneliness. It grieves me to see so much potential love going to waste. Living is a lonely business. Companionship and loving feelings make it so much easier.'

Fifty per cent of women over the age of 25 who haven't got a special man friend want one.

Jay, 31: 'I'm independent. I have my own flat and hate having to ask anyone for help. But deep down, I'm sorry to say, I just love being looked after by a man.'

Anne, 33: 'I would like to get married but cannot even find the right man for an affair. Men want sex on the second date. After a while I run out of excuses. When I tell the truth, that I am a virgin, they drop me like a hot potato.'

Claire, 30: 'I despise myself for wanting a man so desperately when I feel I ought to be a completely independent woman – so much for intellect! Lonely women must exude some off-putting pheromone, I think.'

However, 40 per cent of women alone would only 'quite like' a man in their life.

Some see a man as a pleasant extra rather than the be-all and end-all – usually because they are quite pleased with the way of life they have created for themselves.

Gwen, 44: 'I'm slim and attractive. I like men very much indeed but I'll do without unless I can get the kind of man I want. Some women put up with awful slobs rather than be alone.'

Shona, 29: 'By choice I live alone, in my own flat, and work full-time. My job is highly demanding – the hours elastic at the end of the day, though I'm up at 6.00 every morning. As I do not have a wife to put a meal on the table for me, do the shopping, iron my clothes, my social life comes a poor second to a successful and satisfying career. A woman will put up with a man's erratic hours and unscheduled delays, but how many men will tolerate the situation in reverse?'

Judy, 31: 'It depends whether you like going out with divorced and/or damaged men. That's about all there is at my age.'

Some are shy and nervous of men – some are very sad because they feel it is now too late.

Sarah, 30: 'I have never had an emotional or sexual relationship with any man. I have never lost the shyness and awkwardness most people overcome in their teens over affairs of the heart – or body! I still shy off sexual relationships through embarrassment. My reasons: (a) not wishing to admit I have not done it before, (b) fear of getting a poor reputation, (c) fear of pregnancy or sexually transmitted infection.'

Molly: 'It is assumed that middle-aged women have some sexual experience, but in the body of a knowledgeable and, I hope, broad-minded woman of 47 I feel like a naive 16-year-old. How does a woman of my age approach a relationship for the first time? I feel less of a woman than others, and ashamed. I never tell anyone of my lack of experience, and I feel it is too late now. I have been able to fill in your questionnaire because it is anonymous, but I fear you will be laughing as you read this. I am writing it in tears.'

Ten per cent of women alone definitely don't want a man, and this was slightly more common among those who had been married.

Anita, 36: 'I've had no dates for five years, but don't feel sorry for me. I prefer a life with no hassles, no *Match of the Day* and other boring sport. I don't dream of finding a man. I dream of having an enormous windfall and living in luxury for ever. Contrary to popular opinion, men are not necessary or even conducive to happiness. I am a happy divorcee!'

Ellen, 62 and a widow: 'I think men and women are better apart, preferably on separate islands. Most men would like harems, and women can be hateful and jealous. I speak from experience. Never again! I prefer to live alone.'

Love and marriage?

Only half of those who have been married want to try it again.

Catherine, 29 and divorced: 'I tried too hard for too long to please others, often pushing my own needs into the background, and I failed. After my divorce I learned to like myself and I no longer feel guilty when I do as I wish. I have a good job, earn good money and, within reason, I please myself.'

On the other hand, 85 per cent of those who have never been married would like to be. Many of them, however, are wary.

Denise, 25: 'I have not been married but I did live with my boyfriend for six months. I decided that for the time being it is best to live separately, as I found it hard work! I felt as though I had taken on another job and had less free time to myself to do as I please. No matter what, the woman still ends up working a lot harder. I am glad I did live with him, but I've learnt a lot and I would now think a lot more seriously before marriage. It's made me more single-minded.'

Shirley, 46: 'Have you noticed how marriage-minded men are? I'd like a lover rather than a husband, someone who also likes living alone. I often like to be alone and that's difficult if you're working and living with someone.'

There are signs that women in the older age groups are more choosy than teenagers or women in their early twenties. They would rather not get married than risk it with the wrong man.

Janet, 28: 'I am strong, career-oriented and independent. Sometimes I feel I will never meet the right guy. I know what I want and will not settle for anything less, even if it means never settling down and having a family, which I must add is what I want most with the right man!'

Anna, 31: 'Because I was 27 when I had my son, many people believed it was a last-ditch attempt to get married. I did not marry his father even though he asked many times. I've had other marriage proposals before and since. But I have never met anyone who I have wanted to marry. I used to be ashamed of saying I wasn't married, because I am a mother. One day I thought: I am 31 and not a virgin. So what? I am a good mother. I have worked hard and never turned my back on anyone in trouble. What the hell am I ashamed of?'

Some, though never married, haven't let it cramp their style and are perfectly happy to remain that way.

Brenda, 49: 'I was engaged three times but I am extremely happy at being unmarried. I regret nothing about my love life, which has always been fantastic – only about four of my eighty lovers have been married. I can do without sex but enjoy it enormously. I never wanted children and adore living on my own.'

But it's more common for single women in their forties and fifties to talk wistfully of what might have been.

Audrey, 50: 'As an only child I am solely responsible for my mother. She is nearly 85, in good health and likely to go on into her middle nineties. I shall not be free to lead the life I desire until I reach retirement age. I did not take the two opportunities I had for marriage and remain single and unloved, except in the sense of family loving.

'It was the accepted norm of my generation to care for elderly parents, but I cannot see my friends' children giving up their lives as we did. Times have moved on, and a good thing too. I filled in your questionnaire but my life is reflected most by the blank sections.'

Finding the right man

More than 80 per cent of the over-25s say it's hard to meet the right kind of man.

'My husband left me two years ago. Friends ask me out with them, but I don't want their sympathy. Am I to resign myself to the scrap heap? I could make some man so happy and really love him tenderly, but where can I meet him?' Going out is difficult if you are not already half of a couple.

Jo, 29: 'I force myself to go out almost every night, but men and women are suspicious of a woman on her own. The predatory female image is too strong, even if you're there only to enjoy the music or film. There are very few places a woman can feel comfortable alone.'

Sheena, 28: 'My first ventures into the land of the divorcees were fraught. You soon find there is nowhere to go. Many clubs are just pick-up places for married men. You're too old for discos but too young for most divorcee clubs. Married friends politely enthuse about their happy marriages, discreetly warning me off their husbands.'

It's particularly difficult if you're like Elaine: 'There seemed to be nothing else in my life, only him. I had let all my friends go and built my life around him. We broke up because I smothered him.'

Women aged 26 to 40 find they are most likely to start successful new relationships through friends or at work. Work is the most likely meeting place for the over-forties, too, though meeting through friends is less common.

Helena, 28: 'Although we had worked together for two years we only got together about two months before he left the company. I wasn't aware of my attraction for him until, of all the corny situations, we had too much to drink at a Christmas lunch.'

Joy, 45: 'It started by my answering a letter he'd written to my firm. It was my job to sort out his complaint; after that first letter we felt as though something was drawing us together and kept on writing. Eventually, though this must seem odd, we fell in love. He lived in Canada at the time but he came over to England and we set up home together with my two children.'

Over-forties form the bulk of the customers for friendship and marriage agencies.

While only 1 per cent of the under-forties had started a successful relationship this way, the comparable figure for the over-forties was 13 per cent.

Sonya, 27, said, 'I would recommend this form of meeting to anyone. In all, eight people contacted me before I resigned my name – with all of whom, I think, I could have made "friends".'

But Muriel, 56, said, 'I joined an agency and met five men through it, but none that I would like a friendship with.'

The statistics are loaded against older women looking for a partner. Nevertheless, one in seven among the over-40s manages to start a successful relationship through a social club.

Tessa, 42 and divorced: 'I was introduced to my manfriend at a Divorced, Separated and Singles Club. I was very nervous to be with someone else. We met two or three times a week from then on.'

Some people seemed to be making a comfortable living trading on older women's desperation to find a man.

'Having paid £30 for six months membership I was appalled at the lack of organization. The nearest contact was 18 miles away and some they gave lived 75 miles away. The women outnumbered the men five to one. Some of the men were married and looking for a bit on the side. Only one of our group has married after meeting a man who came along to our club,' said Sylvia, 43.

Many women feel they need to be careful at social clubs. Jackie, 38: 'The club I went to was age-group thirtyish to late fifties. This type of club is OK, but there are many odd characters and you have to be careful.'

Linda, 40, met a man through her local singles club: 'He tried to turn me on by describing everything he would like to do to me while making love – only he didn't use that phrase. This was during our second meeting, and not said in a loving or caring way. I was scared I would be raped with my daughter in the next room. I have not been to the club since, in case he's there.'

Time and time again, women complained of men just looking for sex: 'They seem to think it is their right to sleep with you if you are single and unattached, especially if they have paid for the evening.'

Heather, 27: 'Several men who knew I had been living with my boyfriend before we split up started making advances when we parted – they were mostly married. They thought I was dying for sex no matter what. Some men can't accept that women can live without sex – and are always willing to provide it without giving anything of themselves. Even at dances a lot of the men stand at the bar and pounce at the last dance expecting something in return.'

Three out of four women who had lost a man through separation, divorce or widowhood found men assumed this meant that they were sexually available.

Ruth, 38: 'While I was going through my divorce I was treated like a bitch on heat. The number of married men who made advances was horrifying.'

Alice, 47: 'A week after my husband died one of his friends wanted to take me out but he had only one thing in his mind.'

Trisha, 25: 'When we finished, men, including friends, assumed I needed sex to help me over my loss. One mutual friend showed a great deal of interest in me until he'd had his one-night stand and made sure my ex knew about it. He was pleased to have upset him so much. After him, I steered clear of friends and casual one-night stands.'

Irene, 43: 'Having been twice married and now alone again, but still attractive, I receive constant sexual harassment at work

165

and from my dentist, doctor, bank manager, etc. It takes the form of innuendo, slightly blue jokes, even touching. They feel it's their role and their right! I laugh and pretend to enjoy it but I find it offensive; it is hard, without becoming masculine, to be taken seriously.'

Perhaps Irene would feel better if she said, 'I don't enjoy blue jokes,' or, 'Don't touch me like that.' Men who crowd women rely on our embarrassment and sometimes assume we enjoy it; it is important to make our true thoughts clear.

The search for satisfaction

The situation is complicated by the fact that 50 per cent of women who have lost a partner miss him sexually.

Some find that 'the less you have sex the less you want it', but to start with, at least, it is often very difficult.

Isabel, 45: 'When my husband died after twenty-three years of marriage, there was a void in my life. He was very loving and we had intercourse about five times a week. I missed it a great deal and became nervy and brittle.'

Lillian, 42: 'I was very lonely after my divorce. I longed for sex and I longed for someone to whom I mattered again.'

Establishing a new sex life is particularly difficult for those left as single parents.

Helen, 40: 'My husband walked out twelve years ago and left me with two babies. Three men asked me to give up my kids. I said no, but it's difficult. I have no privacy now they are teenagers and men seem threatened by their presence. All the men I meet seem to want sex, but they are afraid of marriage and taking on other men's children.'

Dawn, 25: 'It is difficult to meet men when you live alone with a child. My son doesn't take kindly to visitors because he has all my attention at other times and constantly seeks attention when others are here.'

Nearly three quarters of lone female parents find that their children hamper their developing new relationships.

Muriel, 56: 'My 17-year-old daughter is very critical of anyone I bring in, though she has her boyfriend in every evening. One man I might have had a chance with was very hurt by her attitude and told me so. He doesn't phone any more.'

Young women who live at home with their own parents can find them as restricting as their children.

Madelaine, 24: 'I would prefer to live away from my parents. They support me in a way, and I'm grateful, but I do not wish to be reminded of this fact for the rest of my life. I would rather be independent.

'I hardly ever go out because leaving my mother to babysit makes me feel guilty. She says she doesn't mind, but jokingly complains if I go out more than once a week. Just lately I've been lucky to go out more than once a month.'

Gossip can make you feel like a 'loose woman'. 'Neighbours' talk gave me a "reputation",' said Penny. 'And as a divorcee I found that many men felt they were guaranteed sex, often on the first date. I did not want my children harmed by this so I met men away from home, never telling friends if or whom I was dating.'

Even after divorce, some women feel the simplest solution is to continue having sex with their husbands.

Lynn, 29: 'We carried on sleeping together about once a fortnight. That was all I wanted from him. I need sex regularly and had enjoyed a very good sex life with him. I felt it was better to have sex with someone I knew. One of the hardest things for me is now doing without.'

Some rely on masturbation. Christine, 27: 'I have gone for maybe a year without sex. I don't use sex as a relief; masturbation gives me that. I would rather masturbate than have sex with a bloke for the sake of it.'

Others adopt what they often refer to as a 'more masculine' attitude to sex.

Gillian, 28: 'I divorced my husband only six months ago. I have one-night stands but I'm not interested after I have had what I want. I get enjoyment out of changing roles and picking men for sex. I don't feel I've been used but that I've used them.'

Margaret, 26: 'After an inhibiting and emotionally unsettling relationship, I wanted a fling with no strings attached, to satisfy my sexual needs. For a while all were one-night stands. I've calmed down now but still regard myself as having a man's attitude to sex. I have lost all the feelings of guilt about sex which used to cripple me. I don't think I'm missing anything by not having a permanent relationship.'

Lorna, 38: 'My husband's leaving me eight years ago had a much greater effect on me than I realized. I do not trust men and I do not allow myself to become emotionally dependent or involved. I decided to adopt a different attitude to men and treat it as my right to enjoy myself; since then I have slept with many men. It is only now that I am acknowledging the problems I've hidden from myself since my marriage break-up.'

It is clear that many unmarried women over the age of 25 have a series of sexual partners. When we asked unmarried women aged 26 to 40 whether they'd had any lovers before their current one, and if so how many, only a third replied that they had had fewer than four. (See Figure 19.) Women who have been married in the past are more likely to have had many lovers than those who have never married.

Some relish having a sequence of lovers, or having several at the same time.

Valerie, 43: 'I felt very lonely and dying for sex after my divorce. During the last year I have had relationships with more than one man at a time. I've enjoyed the situation, though there are practical, organisational problems involved! Not many women I know have had anything like my varied sex life.'

This cool, detached attitude to sexual relations often fails to bring satisfaction.

Libby, 29: 'I have had quite a few sexual encounters since we broke up but these have been under the influence of alcohol and usually for physical relief, without emotion. I feel unable to give anything more to another man. I am closing myself off.'

Barbara, 43: 'My husband was killed in an accident at work. He was only 37. We had a very good sex life, which I still miss. I have been out with men since, because when you have had a good sex life you do miss it, but what worries me is that I don't feel any emotion whatsoever when making love with another man. Afterwards I feel cheap.'

Some have sex with many men in search of affection and reassurance, and to regain self-confidence.

Lizzie's fiancé died in his twenties of cancer. 'Though I didn't really miss him sexually, I minded very much that he wasn't there to hold and kiss me. I felt empty, lost. I slept with people after a while, anyone, just one-night stands. It seemed the price I had to pay to have someone to hold and, more important, to hold me. I didn't enjoy sex with any of them, and there were a lot – I can't count how many.'

If you miss sex after losing a partner, try to decide what you want from it. If all you are seeking is a one-night stand, why feel guilty about it? (Though it is worth remembering that casual sex puts you more at risk of contracting sexually transmitted infections, and you need to be sure about contraception.)

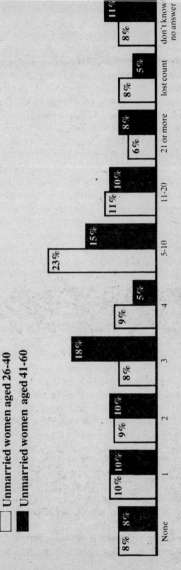

Figure 19 How many lovers had you had before your present relationship?

☐ Unmarried women aged 26-40
■ Unmarried women aged 41-60

None 8% 8%
1 10% 10%
2 9% 10%
3 8% 18%
4 9% 5%
5-10 23% 15%
11-20 11% 10%
21 or more 6% 8%
lost count 8% 5%
don't know/no answer 8% 11%

Number of previous lovers

169

However, when they are looking for love, affection, reassurance, women may find that casual sex leaves them more hurt than before.

Helen said: 'I used all the men I met for sex only. I couldn't get close to them because I thought they'd leave me like my husband did. The more lonely I became, the more I had sex. Then I realized I was the one being used and I do not sleep around now. I regret having done so. I was discreet – the family do not know – but I feel used and dirty. So now I pretend it didn't happen and hope one day to meet a man and fall in love.'

If you're having sex you don't really want, it helps to have someone to talk it through with, especially a trained counsellor. (See Help Directory.)

Jill, 28: 'Although I missed my boyfriend sexually I didn't have sex with anyone for a few months. Then I started on a series of one-night stands with men I met at parties when both of us were usually drunk. I began to despise myself for what I was doing. My self-esteem was virtually non-existent and to punish myself I slept around – it was a vicious circle.

'Luckily for me, one of the men I picked up at a party was a counsellor and once back at my flat refused to go to bed with me; instead he talked about why I was doing it. After many more sessions with him, I realized it all stemmed from the break-up of my relationship months before. Then I was able to start changing my life and I'm much more stable now.'

It's not only women who get hurt by casual sexual encounters.

Angela, 30: 'After I was separated from my husband I was very unhappy. I loved him a great deal and I was sexually very frustrated. Once something is taken away from you, you want it more and more. I masturbated frequently. Then I met a man at a party – not particularly attractive but a nice person. When it came to leaving, he started to kiss me goodbye and touch my neck. I get turned on very easily and thought that since I would not see him again – he lived three hundred miles away – I would take advantage of the situation and make love.

'He tried to put me off but in the end I persuaded him. I was purely out to use him for sex and never see him again.

'He made love to me and it was fantastic. I was extremely selfish because I just let him do all the work and I orgasmed about eight times that night.

'However, the tables were turned. The red roses started arriving. He phoned every day and asked me to marry him

170

when my divorce came through. I had only known him for two weeks! I think because I acted so strangely – I have never done this sort of thing before – he took it to mean that he meant more to me than he did.

'I have learned that some men have very deep emotions and you cannot play around with people. I shan't try that sort of "sexual fulfilment" game again.'

12 Women – and Children – Abused

Incest, rape, assault and harassment

Incest

One in ten of the unmarried women taking part in our survey had had sexual advances made to her by a member of her own family.

More than one third felt unable to describe what had happened: 'These are bad memories I do not wish to recall,' said one.

Of those who did feel able to tell us more about a quarter had experienced what appeared to be relatively innocuous incidents. Most often this was sex-play with a brother or sister while young, attributable to normal sexual exploration at that age.

Peggy: 'It was silly harmless games in bed when I was about 7 or 8. I wasn't shocked or bothered at all.'

Eve: 'My sister (a year younger) and I used to masturbate each other, always in conjunction with fantasies about relationships with girls. This happened some time between the age when I reached puberty and when my sister had her first boyfriend.'

Occasionally the brother and sister were older, but generally, as long as the sex was freely entered into, the women were not particularly troubled by it.

Kim, 23: 'My sister and I "slept together" out of curiosity when I was 16 and she was 23. It was fun! I slept with my other brother when I was 16 and he was 18 – curiosity again. It doesn't worry me.'

Again, adult incest, if indulged in voluntarily, doesn't seem to cause lasting damage. Peggy again: 'It happened about three years ago. I'm 48 and my older brother was visiting on business and staying at my flat. Friends joined us for a drink and when they left we continued to drink. Then somehow we were in bed. I felt very badly about it at the time but not for the usual reasons. One reason was that I don't like making love to older men – they give me the creeps. The second was that I am like my mother in appearance. He hated her and I felt that he was literally laying the ghost. I know she made sexual advances to him when he was in his teens. I've rationalized these ideas now and am quite happy about it and him, though I wouldn't do it again.'

One or two other women mentioned sexual approaches being made by older women in a family to boys or young men, but this was far rarer than men making approaches to girls or young women.

A few women told us of relationships with a cousin, though this is not incestuous. Cousins are free to marry.

In some cases, the advance was made by a brother-in-law. If this happens when the woman is grown up, it is not very different from any other sexual approach. She is free to respond or not. However, if the brother-in-law is considerably older and/or has been welcomed into the family and trusted as a brother, it may be traumatic for the woman.

Lindsay, 29: 'I was 18. My brother-in-law, in his mid-forties with a child the same age as me, turned up one morning and made a grab for me. I was shocked. I thought of him as a brother and had known him all my life. He left and I fell apart. The whole family soon found out and there was hell to pay. We don't see them any more.'

Roughly three-quarters of the cases of sexual advances by a member of the family were made by someone, usually older, in whom the girl or young woman should have been able to trust, and who abused his relationship with her in order to pressurize her into sexual contact she couldn't freely refuse. Some used force. In other words, this means that one in twelve unmarried women had suffered sexual abuse from a member of her family.

Jane, 27: 'I have never told anyone, but my brother raped me when he was thirteen and I was nine. I still cannot bear to be alone with him and hate him to touch me. I have felt guilty about it ever since, although I suppose I didn't know what I was doing.'

Anjana, 30: 'In Indian schools and homes there is no sex

education. At 16, I knew nothing about sex, nor that you are not supposed to have sex before marriage. My half-brother had sex with me. I behaved like a five-year-old kid.'

Fathers

The women who were most traumatized by their incestuous experiences were those who had been molested by their fathers.

Mandy, 27: 'I've never, ever told anyone before – I suppose because I feel in some way it was my fault. Even though logically, I know this isn't true, I still feel guilty. When I was 15 my mother was in hospital having a baby. My parents have always been and still are sexually active and very loving towards each other. They were quite young, having married young – my mother at 16 for the usual reason and my father 22.

'After my younger brother and sister had gone to bed, I sat up watching television. My father asked me to sit closer to him. He pulled my blouse and and undid my bra. He caressed my breasts, remarking on their firmness. I remember being totally confused and guilty, and feeling that this was inevitable and I could do nothing to stop it, that I couldn't protest and say it was wrong, because this man was my dad.

'He continued to do this all the time my mother was in hospital, although on occasion I escaped by going to bed with my sister. He even did it when my mum was out of the hospital. I was so ashamed and embarrassed. I began wearing baggy things – what my mother called my hippy clothes – to hide my body because I felt I must have provoked him somehow.'

Time and again women who were abused by their fathers blame themselves for what happened. They worry that they didn't protest more at the time, but how can a girl in this situation be expected to stand up to her own father, whom she loves, and whom she's probably encouraged to obey?

Kerry, 18: 'When I was between the ages of 6 and 10 my father started to pet me. We lay naked in the bath and in bed together. I was too frightened to refuse him. He told me it was a secret and not to tell anyone, even my mum. I didn't, until one day he arranged that I was to stay in the house all day while my mother and brother went visiting.

'At night in bed I started crying and told my mother. We left my father for a while but we are all back together now. Everything is forgotten – I think they have forgotten it, too. I daren't speak to my mother about it. I think they think it didn't really happen, it was my fault, I was making it up or something. I couldn't understand my mother being friendly with him after the horrible things he did. It doesn't affect me now except that, when my boyfriend and I make love, I feel quite indifferent to his touch.'

Even though she told her mother and it caused a rift for a while, in the end Kerry, the victim, was the one left feeling to blame and cut off from sympathy and understanding. Many girls never have the courage to tell anyone. It's too easy to convince a child that, if she tells, then it will be her fault if this leads to her father being taken away or the family breaking up.

Bridget, 29: 'My father assaulted me up until I had my first period at the age of 12, when he was 33. I then had the courage to say no. It always happened when my mother was not at home – she worked nights. Sometimes I was offered money, but I was always warned that if I told anyone the police would take him away. He stopped short of intercourse – only just.'

Some women had been molested by more than one member of the family.

Lisa, 21: 'When I was about 6 years old one of my uncles used to babysit for us. He used to encourage me to fellate him. My father found out – I don't recall how – and he banned this uncle from the house and made it very clear that he had been wrong to involve a child in such a practice.

'But when I was 12 my father came into my room and asked if I would sleep with him. It was the first time I had had the bedroom to myself; my sister had gone away. I told him I was tired and to leave me alone. The next night the same thing happened. Since then, whenever I've been upset, I get night-mares about my father. I've never been alone with him in a room since and would not trust him. My mother doesn't know.'

Sometimes, if the girl does protest, the father is violent.

Celia, 24: 'My father started molesting me at the age of 14 or 15. He started touching me more and more, "putting me to bed" and kept on coming to "talk" to me when I was revising. He didn't attempt intercourse but used to say he'd like to. I didn't tell my mother but did argue with him to stop. Then he would call me frigid, and once he hit me, causing my nose to bleed. He followed me to the bathroom and then got upset when I wanted him to go away. He dug me in the ribs sharply. My boyfriend came back after a few beers one night and dug me in the ribs when I didn't want to have sex. All my feelings of fear and being trapped came back in a split second.

'I hate my father. He is the only man I could shoot cold-bloodedly. He abused my love and trust and trapped me.'

Uncles and grandfathers

Uncles, even those with teenage daughters of their own, sometimes terrorize their nieces.

Julie, 18: 'My cousin and I are like sisters so I stay there quite often. One night about four years ago everyone went to bed except my uncle and me. When I was about to say goodnight to him he touched my breasts. As I was only 14 I didn't know what to do. I cried myself to sleep because he frightened me so much. Ever since, it has been getting worse. If I go to bed early, he will come up and get into bed with me, start touching me up and then try to have sex with me. I feel sick, dirty and cheap every time he looks at me or touches me.'

It's hard enough for young girls to cope with unwelcome sexual advances from any older man. When he is also a loved and respected relative, what is she to do?

Fiona, 25: 'I was 15 and during the school holidays went to work for my favourite uncle. After work we'd all go and swim in his pool. One day my uncle kept "grabbing" me in the pool. I didn't have the first clue how to deal with his advances so I left the pool and went indoors to change. He followed me and, without my knowledge, watched me undress.

'When I saw him watching, I tried to cover myself but he came over and started kissing and touching me. I tried to pull away in what I thought was a grown-up way. I felt it wasn't "mature" to make too much fuss! Then, thank goodness, my young cousin came home from school and my uncle rushed from the room. I never got too near him again.'

Incestuous fathers may become incestuous grandfathers. Perhaps because the ties between grandfather and granddaughter aren't as close as between father and daughter, it seems to be more likely that the girl will tell someone if her grandfather makes a sexual approach. Some mentioned that it subsequently emerged that he had molested their own mother when she was a child.

Cheryl, 18: 'I was left with my grandfather one afternoon when I was 5 and he was 50. He made several sexual advances towards me. He tried to have intercourse with me but I don't think it took place as I was very frightened and kept crying and asking him to stop.

'Although he was kind afterwards and told me not to tell

176

anyone, I told my grandmother as soon as she returned and he was forced to go to his GP and have treatment. It came out later that my grandfather had done the same to my mother when she was a child but my grandmother had never been told.'

Moira's feelings after an experience with her grandfather emphasize yet again how girls feel guilty just for being the object of sexual attraction. 'My grandfather tried to kiss and cuddle me – french kissing and not harmless cuddling. He was slightly drunk. I was only 13 and was scared to death. After I'd managed to get away from him, I felt dirty and ashamed. My upbringing had indoctrinated me with a feeling that I would somehow be disgusting if my sexuality was expressed. A child in those circumstances inevitably feels guilty merely for attracting sexual attention. That incident and the inhibitions it created – or reinforced – have marred my sex life. For years I was terrified of men and boys.'

Long-term effects of forced incest

One third of the women who said they definitely didn't want ever to get married had had a sexual advance made them by a member of their family. An incest victim was also less likely than other women to have a special boyfriend or man in her life.

Di, 18: 'My stepfather used to get me to go into his bed when my mother was at work. He told me it was OK to do it but to keep it as "our secret". I trusted him and it wasn't for quite a while that I realized that it was wrong. I then had a hard time convincing him that I did not want to do it any more. Luckily for me, I was strong-willed. Now, though, I don't trust men at all and think they are after one thing only. I do not enjoy sex as much as I should because I think subconsciously that it is wrong, although I know it isn't.'

Many women wrote about horrifying experiences with their stepfathers.

Viv, 17: 'I've never told anyone what happened to me when I was 12. Five years ago my mum married again. She got pregnant and ended up in hospital for three months. Dad was very good to me and one day I asked him about babies being born: was it very bad? Then I asked him if it was true what they said in school about getting pregnant. He said he would show me what people did to start babies. I thought he would draw me a picture or something.

'Anyway, he took me upstairs, lay me on his bed and took down my pants. Then he lay down by me and fumbled with his trousers. I was scared but didn't think he would hurt me. I could feel something warm pushing at me, then he put his finger inside me for a bit, then he tried again. He was panting a lot. Then he pushed really hard. He said he'd never had a cherry before. He pushed again and I screamed. He picked up my bottom and went really mad. I was crying and begging him to stop. He still does it when he can. I hate it.'

Michaela's stepfather wanted to have sex with her even though he had a young girlfriend. It's not true that men who sexually molest young women in their family are always frustrated. 'My mother died when I was 10. When I was 13, my father told me he was not my real father. I had already suspected that. A few days later he started hinting about sex, saying it would be perfectly all right as we were not related.

'The whole idea was revolting to me: I couldn't even understand it. His girlfriend, who more or less lived with us, was only six years my senior. I didn't make much comment, thinking that, if I ignored his hints, he would drop the subject. I was wrong.

'Over the next few weeks he went on and on about it, promising the moon and the stars if only I would go along with what he wanted. One night he got into my bed, saying we could take it easy and just get used to each other. I pushed and kicked him out of my bed. After that I wrote to an aunt and asked to go and live with her. When he found out he started threatening me if I ever told anyone of this.'

We didn't raise the subject of sexual abuse within the family in our questionnaire for wives, but many volunteered that this was spoiling their married sex lives.

Brenda, 47: 'When we are going to have intercourse, I dread it and pick a stupid row with my husband over nothing. When he is lying on top of me during intercourse, I want to scream! I just feel all this hate for him at the time. I have never fancied any other man but I wonder if it is normal for me to feel the way I do.

'When I was a child I was sexually abused by my stepfather. I never told anyone until I confided in my husband a few years ago. When my husband asks me to touch his penis I hate it, thinking of how I used to feel when my stepfather made us do it.

'We all left home and rushed into marriages because of our

unhappy childhood. One of my sisters was married and divorced after three years and has never wanted to remarry. The other sister was divorced and remarried but is still not happy.'

Andrea, 20: 'I feel very nervous and strange writing this. No one knows that my father made sexual advances towards me from 5 to 20 years old. It was worse when I was younger. I couldn't escape. Later on he used mental cruelty to make me masturbate him (e.g., "I'll be rotten to your mum"). He would touch my breasts, etc. He tried to make love to me as a child (9–14 years old) but always failed to keep an erection. He was always much happier when he had some physical contact with me. That was partly why I did it. I have never enjoyed it.

'I am crying as I write this now as it is an evil secret that I have to endure forever. My relationship with the man I live with suffers because I have to work hard at not being repulsed. He does not know about my father's feelings towards me. I wish someone could help me get over this dark depression which hits me sometimes.

'I must say my dad deeply regretted doing anything to me. He would cry afterwards. But once or twice he physically hit me if I tried to escape from his advances. What really gets me is that my mum doesn't know. She is so sweet and kind and knowing about this would destroy her.

'At 18, when I was just getting to petting with my boyfriend, my father was still pestering me. I was just a sexual plaything. I can never come to terms with the dual role I had to fulfil then. I wanted to enjoy my man's relationship but deep down couldn't.'

Talking helps

If women can manage to talk about such an experience, it helps them shed the feelings of guilt and shame and can free them to enjoy sex without being haunted by the memory.

Sadie, 21: 'When I was 15 my eldest brother came into my room. I was woken by his hand feeling my breasts and other parts. He had an erection and kept rubbing it and groaning. He asked to come into bed beside me. It made me feel quite sick. I screamed at him to get out of my room, so he told me not to tell anybody and left.

'When I had sex with my fiancé, he always wondered at how I used to shake from head to toe. I didn't want to tell him but when I did he was annoyed with my brother. When we have sex now it's great because I don't have this worry on my mind.'

However, some women do find that their partner feels they

must have been in some way to blame. Anjana: 'I told my husband after living with him for eight years. He would not believe me. He thinks I went to bed with my half-brother because I wanted to. I assured him for over a year but he wouldn't believe me. In the end we separated.'

If such an experience is haunting you and you're not sure how your partner will react, the wisest course of action is to find someone safe to confide in. Don't continue to bottle it up. There's little doubt that simply talking will help – time after time women said they felt better for expressing their views on paper. If you're unsure where to turn, see the Help Directory.

Obviously, all mothers who have daughters living at home can try to make it easier for them to talk to us openly – and the same goes for our sons, for it is not just girls who are victims of incest. Those counselling victims point out that there are many male children who are homosexually abused within families. Talking with the children is not to point a finger of accusation at our husbands. Children come into contact with many older men both inside and outside their families. Unless we ensure that it feels easy and natural for them to bring their worries to us, we have little hope of being able to protect them. 'I daren't tell my parents as they were staunch Catholics and the word sex was completely taboo in our household,' said Mary, who was being molested by her elder brother.

It is often assumed that when a man is molesting his daughter it must be because the mother is denying him sexually and that she turns a blind eye to what is happening. This is far from always true.

Alex's husband was infatuated with a girl at work at the same time as he started molesting their 14-year-old daughter. Alex managed to find out what was happening by talking to her daughter about why she seemed to hate her father being near her. In her letter to us, Alex pointed out that she had never refused her husband. It was he who had lost interest in her: 'All my daughters were innocents yet I get jealous of them, because of the way their father still puts them before me.'

Many mothers will be far more sympathetic than their scared daughters realize. Even if they are not, if the girl tells her mother it frequently seems to put an end to the abuse. However, some girls find that telling means the family is as likely to close ranks against them as around them.

Sally, 18: 'When I was 11, four years of sexual harassment

started from my father. I was in bed one night. When this hairy hand used to move up and down over my duvet, I was too scared to move or even look. My mother was always in the house. He used to come upstairs and gradually go a bit further, going under the covers, touching me, hitting me, kissing me, making me touch him. I cried and shouted but no one ever woke up to come to me. I wish now I had told someone – why didn't I?

'You think it only happens to poor deprived people but it doesn't. We are a respectable family with all the latest luxuries, a five-bedroomed house and cars. I used to cry every Friday at school because I was dreading the weekend when my father was home. If only everyone knew why I was disruptive and did so badly at school.

'He managed to get me alone in the house once and told me to stand in the middle of the room naked. I ran out of the house screaming. This experience has spoiled my whole outlook on sex and men. As soon as a man starts getting serious or tries to go too far, I chuck him, even if I like him. Will all my relationships end for the same reasons?

'Last year, during an argument with my dad, I told my mum. He was scared. He denied it, of course, and my mum doesn't believe me. I think she hates me. Their marriage has never been rosy; now she wants to leave home. I have been left alone to fight this battle. A real friend would have made all the difference. My parents seem to feel no love for me. I am being punished in a way, treated badly for something which I would have done anything to avoid.'

There are people outside the immediate family who may be in a position to spot when incest is happening – the GP, a teacher who realizes that a pupil's work has suddenly fallen off for no apparent reason, a social worker, or perhaps a relative or close friend who is not so directly involved. The professionals are beginning to acknowledge that they shy away from tackling the problem, partly because they are unsure what to do if their suspicions are confirmed. Do you try to get a culprit sent to prison, which may punish and impoverish the whole family? Is he best left within the family after a warning? There is far from general agreement about the best way to tackle incest, particularly if the molester is the father.

However, this survey confirms that if the girls could tell someone sympathetic, it made a huge difference to how the experience continued to affect them. Even though telling may

181

mean the man – usually the father – getting into trouble, they were left feeling less guilty and ashamed if they did tell.

Children and strangers

Of course, it is not only within the family that children are at risk.

Caroline, 23: 'I was only 4 years old, but it's haunted my lonely and quiet moments ever since. It's like a never-ending nightmare. I was out playing with my brother and three of his friends when a man asked us to look for his lost dog. He leg us into a back alley. He sent the boys away to look for the dog so he and I were left alone.

'I have no memory of the following hours. The next thing I do remember is being in the police station talking to a policewoman. Then I remember being examined, probably by a police doctor, around my private parts. After that it's all a blank. I tried to bring myself to ask about it. Everybody thinks I've forgotten about it but I still cry and wonder, why me?'

Gay, 20: 'I was about 10. I told my parents that this man at the cinema was rubbing his penis up and down. My dad discussed with Mum whether they should call the police or not. They asked me to repeat my story. Dad said, "If we call the police, you know you'll have to say 'penis', don't you?" I felt very ashamed; nothing was done about it.'

Marianne, 27: 'I was about 8 and walking home with four other Brownies. Suddenly a young man stepped out in front of us, unzipped his trousers and held his penis out in his hand. We were all shocked and stopped in our tracks. He said, "Who wants to suck on this?" We ran home crying. I remember standing outside my house, trying not to cry, breathing deliberately slowly, trying to compose myself. I smiled as I went indoors and never told my parents. I felt in the wrong. I thought I would be punished for this "dirty" experience.'

Parents sometimes prefer to let an offender get away than subject their child to cross-questioning and perhaps intimate examination. Some women spoke with horror of having to attend an identity parade as children, terrified that if they could not spot their attacker he would 'get' them.

Once more the stories emphasized how important it is that we don't treat sex as a taboo subject so that our children dare not mention anything that may have happened to them. They need comfort and reassurance even if we don't take any action.

182

If you are ever undecided what to do, get advice quickly. A rape crisis centre (see Help Directory) will provide assistance in an emergency and continuing advice.

Rape and assault

Sadly, many women have good reason to continue to be nervous of men.

One in ten of those taking part in our survey of unmarried women had been sexually assaulted; in a fifth of these cases they were raped.

As with the cases of incest, there was no particular reason why our survey should attract replies from women who had been subject to sexual attack. According to our figures, two women in every hundred are under threat of rape; many others may be in danger of assault or attempted rape.

There is often debate about to what extent women can be said to have brought about their own rape or assault. Hundreds of women wrote in about their experiences and their accounts made it clear that generally rape and assault are not simply questions of forced sex but are crimes of violence, involving suffering that no woman would bring on herself.

In a minority of cases of rape the attacker was a stranger.

Bernice, 19: 'I was a virgin when I was raped. I hurt and bled for several days. I had a bottle pushed inside me and was beaten up and scratched and bitten all over my body. I was forced to have oral sex. Afterwards I suffered extreme nervous tension; I had nightmares and was depressed and cried at the slightest thing. I did not know anything about sex and felt that I was dirty and had been used and that I could never tell anyone. My parents still have no idea what happened to me.'

More commonly, the rapist was known to the woman.

Jan, 23: 'When I was 15, I accepted a lift home from the village disco with a friend of the family aged about 30. He drove the Land-rover into the woods and raped me. I was frightened to tell my parents.'

Juliet, 28: 'I was raped when I was 17 and a virgin by a man of 21 I vaguely knew. He shared a flat with some friends of mine and I went there after school one night a week for a couple of hours before going on to teach dancing at the local leisure centre.

'That evening he was the only one in and we went into his bedroom to have a drink – we always sat in someone's bedroom because there wasn't a communal sitting room. After a while he began to make advances and I repulsed him. He became violent, tore my clothes and tied me to the bed. He must have been in the habit of tying people up because the ropes were close at hand under the bed.

'He was very strong and I didn't stand a chance. Anyone who thinks a girl can stop a determined man attacking her, even if she really wants to, must be crazy. It was done completely against my will. He took no precautions at all and I felt sullied and very frightened afterwards. Apart from anything else, I was worried sick I might be pregnant or have picked up VD. I had nightmares for a long time afterwards and was very difficult to get on with.

'I was sexually scarred for many years. I didn't tell my parents for about six months. I was terrified they'd go to the police, and I couldn't face going through that rigmarole of examinations, etc. I felt defiled enough as it was.'

Pregnancy can add to the horror of rape.

Linda, 37: 'I was raped by three youths at the age of 20. I washed myself and pretended it hadn't happened. After missing my next period I knew I was pregnant but delayed a further month before going to my GP – complaining of stomach ache. When he told me I was pregnant I collapsed. He was very sympathetic when I told him what had happened and arranged for me to see another doctor within twenty-four hours. The nurses at the clinic knew why I was there and their lack of understanding dejected me completely. The second doctor, though, was patient and kind. I had an abortion on the NHS and was treated with total discretion and sympathy. I told my parents because the doctor said I ought. My father was a policeman and could only ask why I hadn't gone to the police. My mother was shocked but concentrated only on my well-being. We've never discussed the rape or the abortion since.'

Even if the woman has previously had sex with her attacker, forced intercourse is still rape.

Gemma, 21: 'I was engaged at 18 to a soldier. I was on the pill and we were having quite a good sex life when he was home on leave. Once when he was on leave I was taking a break from the pill on my doctor's advice. I explained why I couldn't have sex with him and he said he understood.

'On his last evening home we went out for a meal. When we got back to his house we went upstairs to his room, where we usually sat and chatted. He had his arm around me, then he suddenly pushed me to the floor, his hand on my throat. I couldn't breathe very well and I struggled to get free, but he was six feet tall and about three stone heavier than me, so it was pretty useless. I tried to look him in the eye but he was looking straight past me, horribly inhuman.

'In the end I was so exhausted I could hardly move, and I remember thinking that I couldn't shout for help because his parents were downstairs and I couldn't bear them knowing what their son was doing, that he was such a despicable animal. Anyway, he raped me but it didn't last very long. Afterwards I felt an extreme revulsion for him. He tried to act as if nothing had happened but I broke off the engagement.

'I couldn't let anyone know what he had done, although had I been a bit braver I could have spoken out and tried to ensure he would never treat any future girlfriends like that. It's been such a relief telling someone.'

A few wives have been raped by their husbands. Marjorie, 52 and married thirty years: 'If he wants intercourse and I don't, he won't be put off. He forces his way in, even if I say it hurts, and continues to his climax. At that moment I hate him.'

Joan, 36: 'He was aggressive and insisted on sex even when I had a broken arm, caused by him pushing me and making me fall on the same day.'

Most of the women who told us about being assaulted were the victims of strangers – a fear common to many of us.

Gwyneth, 20: 'I was phoning my father from a phone box near my digs when a man came in and tried to rape me, then to kill me. I got away because he was a bit drunk, but he caught up and rugby-tackled me, scarring my leg in the process. I was screaming and crying for help but the great British public drove and walked past, ignoring me. Then a man came out of a nearby house and I ran behind him.

'The police were wonderful. My only complaint is that the men in the photography department were a little callous in saying to me, "He's probably out on bail now, not a serious offence anyway." His "not serious offence" has scarred my leg for life. I have nightmares about it almost every night, though thankfully these are getting fewer. He pleaded guilty and was jailed for nine months. With good behaviour he could be out by now, as he will have served six months. I am seeking compensation for my scar from the Criminal Injuries Board. This won't punish him, I know, but it will help me feel he's "paid" for it in some way.'

Monica, 22: 'I was sexually assaulted when fifteen or so skinheads got into my railway carriage. The guards on the train were too scared to intervene. The boys involved were charged and brought to trial but I've complained that the alarm signal was out of reach. At one point this year I got afraid to go out and I had to give up my job because of it.'

Long-term effects of rape and assault

Attacks such as these may affect a woman's attitude to sex for many years. Hilary, whose boyfriend raped her at knifepoint, said: 'Sometimes during sex I cannot feel a thing, pain or otherwise. I often freeze before sex or tense up so much I bleed. I never actually touch myself with bare fingers, except in the shower, and I wouldn't dream of actually entering myself. I had no orgasms for a long time but I do now, sometimes.'

Adriane, 33: 'My first introduction to sexual experience was a man on the train when I was 16. He fell to his knees and put his hand up my skirt. It made me feel sick and still does now. This plays on my mind every time I have sex with my husband.'

One in four of those women who said they were determined never to marry had been sexually assaulted.

Belinda, 28, was assaulted when she was 16. 'I was horrified, revolted. I had never seen an erect penis before. We had quite a fight. As a result, I became very withdrawn, I didn't trust anyone. Two years later I was admitted to a psychiatric hospital for six weeks but I couldn't tell anyone what had happened to me. I still have flashbacks which spoil sex for me.'

As we saw with incest, though nothing can lessen the horror of the ordeal, being able to talk about what happened does help lessen its emotional after-effects. Zoe, who was raped when she was 16, said, 'I am lucky it has not affected me now in my life. I was able to talk about my experience to my mother and close friends. I feel lucky I am not scarred mentally like so many others.'

Davina's father was unsympathetic. Assaulted at a bus station when she was 15, she suffered a fractured nose and bruises. She said: 'The police were very nice but my dad came and read the statement. When we got home, he hit me again and said it was my fault, that I was studying for my "hole" levels instead of my "O" levels, and that I was a cow. After that evening it was never spoken of again. Though it all happened ten years ago I cannot get over it. I am frightened of going out in the dark. I feel as though all men use me, even the ones I love. Deep down, because my dad says it was my fault, I blame myself that it happened and feel cheap if I make love with someone willingly.'

Many cases of rape and assault go unreported to the police. In fact, the more serious the offence the less likely it is the woman will tell anyone. One in eight of those raped kept it secret compared with only one in twenty of those suffering attempted rape.

Sharon, 25, was raped: 'I had a tear in the vaginal wall that required suturing. I visited a special clinic the next day because I was bleeding heavily. Probably the worst part was doctors' questions as to how I got the injury. They said they could call the police as they suspected rape. I felt that I couldn't go through with a court case and the publicity in a small town. Like most women, I felt dirty and almost guilty, as though it was my own fault. Now, five years later, I know that to protect other women I should have called the police but at the time I couldn't have stood the examination and the questioning.'

Of those who do tell someone, fewer than one in five of those raped, and a slightly higher proportion of those suffering attempted rape, told the police.

Iris, 33, was raped by three men who offered her a lift home: 'I didn't inform the police or any authority as I felt that I would have been blamed for accepting the lift in the first place.'

One place where women can be assured of a sympathetic hearing, often from women who have themselves been raped or assaulted, is from rape crisis centres. Talking to someone who understands can be a tremendous relief. They can help you decide whether to report the matter to the police, and support you through the ordeal if you do. The London Rape Crisis Centre says that women who have obtained such help have even found that – though nothing can lessen the horror of being raped – like any crisis it can be seen in retrospect as a strengthening experience. It makes them take a fresh look at the world around them and their own feelings, which can result in a new self-confidence and determination.

Defending ourselves

It is impossible to be 100 per cent safe but women can learn both how to defend themselves in case of attack, and how not to look like a victim.

Nina saved herself: 'He had me pinned to the wall and was touching me sexually. I threatened to scream, to which he replied laughing, "Do you really think anyone will listen?" I eventually got away, physically unharmed apart from a couple of bruises, though in a frightened and emotional state, by kicking him with all the strength I could muster in his testicles. He was doubled up in agony and I ran like hell.'

A fierce double-finger poke in the eyes can also be effective. However, it is advisable for women to learn self-defence in a properly run class. Women can defeat a far heavier opponent, but lashing out in panic may only enrage him and make your own situation worse.

Knowing how to defend yourself will make you look and feel more confident. Even before you go to a class, stand in front of a full-length mirror and examine the way you stand. Walk around. Do you hold your head up and look people fairly and squarely in the eye? Do you hold your back and shoulders straight so that you walk with an assured air, or do you scuff or mince along? The way we talk and move gives others messages about ourselves that may make all the difference.

However, remember this is far from complete protection. Rape stems from hatred of women and self-confidence doesn't change your sex – in fact, it's just possible it will anger some men even more.

The most important protection of all is to trust your intuition. Intuition or instinct, often belittled, is a valuable gift. We can pick up unconscious signals that we are under threat. If your instincts tell you to get out, run or scream, do it, and do it fast.

'Look at the tits on that' – sexual harassment

A milder, but often distressing, form of abuse suffered by many women is sexual harassment. Learning to handle ourselves with confidence can cut down the frequency with which it happens to us and our own irritation with it.

One in four women said they had been sexually harassed.

Of course, some women don't mind things that others object to. Trudi, 19: 'What is classed as sexual harassment? I'm an engineering apprentice working in a male environment. I'm constantly whistled at, which is a great boost to my ego. My colleagues often make rude comments about my bum – hardly surprising as I often wear tight jeans! They are very complimentary on the odd occasion I wear a skirt. I take it all with good humour. If anyone goes too far with comments (I've never been physically harassed), I jokingly warn them I'll get my diary out, and they understand.'

Some women are flattered at first but then find that they are irritated by endless innuendo and excuses to touch them.

Lesley, 21: 'Sexual harassment is the plague of the working woman. I used to see it as a compliment – someone smacking my bottom, trying to kiss me, grabbing me and making suggestive comments. It was a real ego boost, until I got tired of it. If you smile and take it in good humour, you're OK. If you smile too much, it's seen as a come-on. When this "come-on" is rebuffed, you're a "tease".

'If you react angrily to begin with, refrain from laughing and reprimand whoever is harassing you, you're miserable, you're a virgin (used in a derogatory sense) or you're "gay". Why do men feel they can treat us this way? Why do they need to comment on us? Why do they react so aggressively when we don't pretend to enjoy it?'

May, 34: 'I have a large bust and often get harassed because of this. When I was younger I hated this and was embarrassed. Now I am older I get very annoyed and show it.'

Some objected most fiercely to harassment in public places.

Frances, 17: 'I've had my bottom pinched and fondled on a number of occasions, usually during rush hour – the main offenders tend to be middle-aged businessmen. I find that this is more annoying than anything and can usually cope with it either by saying in a loud voice, "Will you kindly remove your hand from my left buttock," or by pinching the offending person's bottom. Both produce a red face and mumbled "sorry".

'What I do hate and find degrading is being shouted at in the street. Comments vary from "Hello, gorgeous" to "Look at the tits on that". This I find difficult to cope with. It serves to remind women that men own the streets. The only women safe are those accompanied by other men. It makes me so angry that men can comment upon your appearance and ridicule you.'

Women who retaliate firmly seem pleased with the effect they have. Glynis, 28: 'I've felt very satisfied by getting my true feelings across to these men – for example, screaming, "Fuck off!" at the top of my voice to a kerb crawler and seeing him feel embarrassed and drive off hurriedly instead of my scuttling away.'

Paula, 26: 'My boss tried to touch my breasts. I made it clear I wasn't interested, but when he next buzzed for me he again tried to touch me. I brought my knee up to his groin and, although I missed, he stopped his harassment. I said I wasn't interested in his games and that as managing director and as my employer I had lost my respect for him. I told him that if he ever tried it again I would have no hesitation in shouting it to all and sundry. The matter was never mentioned by either of us again. I continued working there for some time. He was just seeing how far I was prepared to go. He did not force the issue once I had made myself clear.'

Many of us find it hard to be bold. We let the harassment continue until we are so upset by it that it shows. That in itself undermines our chances of stopping it.

Get 'in touch' with your anger

Following the suggestions given below will give you more strength and confidence generally.

Have you been in situations where you felt numb at the time – but angry and upset afterwards? Have you gone along with situations, not necessarily sexual, that you didn't want to? This may not necessarily be with a stranger. It can happen with a man (or woman) you know well, your partner, your husband. Think back. What was the room like? What sounds can you hear? What were you wearing?

Breathe deeply, emptying your lungs when you breathe out. Watch your face in a mirror. Think of what he said or did, how you responded, and how it all turned out.

You will probably feel emotions rising from your stomach. If you feel tearful, let yourself cry, but keep breathing deeply. See where it leads. You may well start to feel angry. Let it go! Tell the person exactly what you think of him. He is not here to hurt or punish you. Punch a pillow, wring a towel, shout, growl, anything to help you release your feelings.

You'll be less tempted to tell yourself you feel nothing the next time you feel pressurized and it may give you the courage to act firmly. However, it's not always best to show too much anger in the middle of a situation. Feel it, know it's there, and decide how to use it.

It's best to avoid the first use of physical violence, since it may be returned with greater force. You can use your anger to fuel firm words. Especially with an excited man you don't know well, in a situation which might be physically risky, you can put your anger in your feet, and leave.

190

To use our anger effectively means controlling our body language. Angry women are often frightened – men are, after all, physically stronger – so instead of looking impressively angry, we may cringe and squeak. This casts us in the role of the victim, which can feed the other's aggression.

If you want to, say why you're angry. Be bold. Breathe, relax, face them squarely and say it. If your instincts are telling you to leave, don't hang around to make apologies or explanations. Say you're going; and go.

If you show you were angered rather than crushed, you will be treated with more respect, and respect yourself more.

Dealing with harassment ourselves, on the spot, is often the most effective approach. In theory, if we are harassed at work, we should find support through our employer (but sometimes the employer is the harasser), through the trades union (but we may have no union) or through an industrial tribunal (but how many of us want to go to an industrial tribunal, especially over harassment?). One snag is that many men, even those close to us, don't take harassment seriously.

Hazel, 27: 'A young man pulled into the kerb in a van and asked directions. I leaned forward to give the directions. Suddenly he bent over, grabbed the front of my T-shirt and pulled it down, then sped off at high speed. I was taken aback and embarrassed. I turned round and started to hurry home, hoping no one had seen anything. Then fury hit me and I turned back in an effort to see his registration number, but it was too late.

'My T-shirt was low but nothing shocking – I haven't that kind of bust. I told the girls I lived with. They were great – angry and understanding. I told my boyfriend and his dad. They said I should feel flattered!'

The same happened to Tracy, who was pestered at work by the office wolf: 'At first he made comments and lewd suggestions, but when he realized I was not responding he began grabbing at me and touching me. I informed my immediate boss, a man, who laughed and treated it like a smutty joke. He said I ought to be flattered. I became angry and went to one of the company directors. He said he would do something straight away but nothing came of it.'

Some women end up leaving their job because of harassment.

Jill, 20: 'I was harassed at work by an older man. When I reported the incidents to my superiors I was told that I was silly, that this behaviour was normal because the man was "one of the boys", and that if I pursued it any further, to the union representatives, it would cause a lot of problems. Consequently, I found an excuse to leave work and I am now on the dole.'

Sometimes official channels are more reliable than direct action. Kirsten, 19: 'A boy I knew only slightly came up behind me at work one day, grabbed me by the breasts and held on. All his mates were near and that gave them a great laugh. When I finally got rid of him I threw a bucket of water over him, which gave my mates a laugh. I was sacked.'

If the harassment is such that you can't stop it yourself and get no backing at work, you can get help rather than quit your job – see Help Directory.

13 *Unlucky?*
Sexual problems and how to solve them

The majority of couples are troubled by sexual difficulties at some point. Only two out of five couples say that they have never been.

Twenty-three per cent of wives said that they or their husband or both are suffering from sexual problems now, a further 36 per cent that they had done in the past.

The most common problem by far, affecting more than a third of those who have ever had difficulties, is the wife's lack of interest in sex (see Figure 20).

What worries you most about your sex life?

37%	Your lack of interest in sex
18%	His lack of interest in sex
8%	The quality of your lovemaking
18%	The quality of his lovemaking
19%	Your lack of orgasm
2%	His lack of orgasm
14%	His premature ejaculation
13%	His erection difficulties
18%	Problems connected with pregnancy, childbirth
12%	Problems connected with the menopause
10%	Other difficulties

Figure 20

The next most common problems, each affecting nearly one in five couples, are the wife's lack of orgasm, the man's lack of interest in sex, the quality of his lovemaking, or difficulties connected with pregnancy and childbirth.

193

We have already discussed all these subjects and considered some ways of dealing with them. Above all, we have seen that simply being willing to talk to each other about sex and our feelings helps us resolve problems. Only one in eight of those who often talk openly about sex is currently troubled by a sexual problem compared with nearly half of those who never do.

Toni, 22: 'I am very dissatisfied and unhappy about my sex life. For some months my husband has been off sex. He gives no explanation and is always very evasive. If I try to discuss it, he changes the subject. As well as his lack of interest, he suffers from premature ejaculation and I never reach orgasm.

'We used to kiss and cuddle but now I find it hard to approach him for fear of being pushed away. Does it mean he doesn't love me or has lost interest in me? I sometimes feel like a new toy – great at first, but then the newness wears off and you throw it in the back of the cupboard.

'I realize he doesn't want to discuss it because he's sensitive, but where does it leave us?'

Many wives said that their husbands were very reluctant – or refused point-blank – to seek help to overcome sexual problems. Of course, our survey was confined to women, and it could be that many men would say the same of their partners. However, marriage guidance councils, sex-therapy clinics and GPs all agree that women are usually more ready to look for help than men are.

Elaine, 28: 'My husband seems to sense when I am approaching orgasm; at this point he always climaxes and is unable to continue, leaving me very frustrated. He refuses to admit we have a problem – after all, he is "a robust, healthy serviceman and has had no complaints elsewhere" – end of quote. Marriage guidance is available and I know it is a 100 per cent confidential service, but he lives in dread of anyone finding out that we have a sexual problem.'

Some people, women as well as men, prefer to try to live with sexual problems rather than to confide them. Ma, who still suffers from lack of orgasm, first saw her GP in 1957: 'He was acutely embarrassed about my asking him anything of a sexual nature, as I was.

'In 1978 a different GP referred me to a sex therapist. She wanted me to attend weekly sessions in mid-afternoon. I was working full-time and was not going to risk embarrassment by asking for time off for such a purpose. She suggested I could attend marriage guidance, but I was not prepared to recount my sexual difficulties all over again.'

Monica is obviously bothered enough about her problem to be still seeking help after twenty years, but when it is offered she finds reasons not to accept it; she can't face exploring the details.

Of course it is not compulsory to want or try to achieve a satisfying sex life. There are some people to whom it is not important. However, we should realize that there may be a price to pay for ignoring problems, particularly if sex matters to our partner.

Lee, whose husband wouldn't admit he suffered from premature ejaculation, took a lover. 'I discovered to my surprise that, not only could I achieve orgasm regularly, but that I could do so repeatedly during one act of intercourse.'

Grace, 47: 'I have been trying to get our relationship back on a good footing. I went to the Marriage Guidance Council, who advised me to talk to him. I tried, but all he did was get depressed and resentful that I should discuss our affairs with a stranger. My doctor suggested a sex therapist, but it meant we would both have to go. My husband said, "What could they do about it? We are getting too old anyway, and I have got used to not having it."

'I told him I was not happy, but if he wouldn't discuss it or go with me, I couldn't do anything about it. I told him I wasn't going to fake orgasm for him any more and didn't want sex on these terms. I moved into the spare bedroom. Since we have stopped having sex, there is no physical contact between us, just a quick peck at bedtime. I'm seriously considering leaving him.'

Of couples with sexual problems three out of ten had sought help.

The main source of assistance for more than 40 per cent was their GP; for 13 per cent, their local marriage guidance council; for a further 13 per cent, books; 10 per cent had seen a sex therapist; and 8 per cent had received most help from their family planning clinic. Sixty per cent believed they had been at least reasonably well helped.

Alison, 28: 'Sex therapy ought to be more widely available. After five years of happy marriage but unhappy sex life, I found a sex therapist who could help me with my problem: never having an orgasm, not even through self-stimulation.'

Which source of help a couple chose didn't seem to make

much difference to the success rate – but this is probably because, once on the 'help ladder', you tend to be referred to the level and type of help you need.

The encouraging results suggest that, if you have a sexual problem, it is worth seeking advice. 'Strangers' can help – after all, many of those we have mentioned, such as marriage guidance counsellors and sex therapists, are specially trained to make it easier for us to talk about subjects we find embarrassing or upsetting.

Some wives complained that sex therapy is difficult to find and that it should be more widely advertised. Outside cities, this can be a problem, but if you persist you should succeed. If your GP seems unable to assist, ask for a referral to a sex-therapy clinic. Marriage guidance counsellors, as well as often being trained themselves to help with sexual problems, can refer you to their special sexual-dysfunction clinics. In any case, it's wisest to start with a marriage guidance counsellor if there are problems in your relationship besides the sexual one. Specialist sex therapists often find that a couple's sex life so closely reflects their whole relationship that they need help with this before they can really tackle the sexual aspects.

A large number of wives complained that their husband said that, if they weren't sexually satisfied, that was 'their problem'. In fact, most sex therapists will only treat couples – not to be awkward, but because they have found they so rarely get good results from seeing only one of a couple.

Premature ejaculation

Just how soon is 'too soon' is hard to define. To most couples who suffer from the problem, it means that the man climaxes before intercourse has lasted long enough for them to feel satisfied – perhaps even before intercourse has started.

Yvonne, 28: 'He climaxes within a minute or two of entering me and then says it's not possible to stay inside me and become aroused again.'

Andrea, 26: 'He always comes before me. Although he stimulates me I feel he's lost interest. I'd love him to do cunnilingus but he's not keen.'

Just three out of ten women – wives and unmarried women alike – say that their partner never climaxes too soon for them. However, to some extent, it's a problem if you make it a problem. Some couples manage to find ways to adapt their love making so that the fact that the man can't last very long isn't important.

Vicky, 23: 'He came in five seconds and I felt nothing but frustration and hurt. However, we are uninhibited and usually I come by manual/oral sex and then we have intercourse during which he comes.'

'Hair-trigger trouble' is more likely the less frequently a couple make love. It's twice as likely to be a problem if they have intercourse once a week compared with four or five times a week. A couple can get trapped in a vicious circle, especially if they are both expecting to gain most of their sexual satisfaction through intercourse rather than in other ways. She is unsatisfied, he feels a failure, so they tend to leave lovemaking longer, which makes it all the more likely he will suffer from premature ejaculation when they try again.

Lindy, 20, found 'His premature ejaculation has stopped since I have wanted to make love more often.'

Sexual difficulties interact – another reason why therapists usually want to see a couple together. If she has a particularly low sex drive, it is likely to make his premature ejaculation worse. Equally, a woman may be frustrated because she cannot climax during intercourse when she would like to, but who's to say whether her orgasmic response is slow or his climax too early?

Teresa, 40: 'Before I was married I slept with four other men, each of whom reached orgasm in three minutes or less. With them I rarely reached orgasm through intercourse alone. I am lucky in that my husband takes seven to ten minutes to reach orgasm without any effort at self-control, and I nearly always climax, even if I haven't been particularly aroused when we started.

'There must be a lot of women who would like to reach orgasm during intercourse, with or without additional stimulation, and who blame themselves for being difficult to arouse, when in reality they have a husband who reaches orgasm too quickly.'

One way to stop that being a problem is not to worry too much about reaching orgasm during intercourse. However, if intercourse is so short that it is emotionally unsatisfying even if you have reached orgasm another way, there are self-help ways for a man to try to slow his responses.

One simple method is for the man to reach climax once, to lessen his urgency, allow himself time to recover and then have intercourse. There is a good chance this second orgasm will take longer.

Both of you should learn to recognize his sexual responses. Try the sensate focus exercises explained on pages 201 to 203. While one or other of you stimulates the penis, he can try to spot the point of no return, beyond which climax is inevitable. When he can do this, probably after a few mistakes, stop the stimulation at the relevant moment and resume when he feels it is safe. Once he can recognize the point of no return, he should eventually be able to pause during intercourse when necessary to delay climax.

Premature ejaculation is one of the simplest sexual difficulties to resolve, but if these measures don't work for your partner, there are other techniques, which are explained in books listed in the Help Directory or can be taught by a sex therapist.

Erection difficulties

Most men experience the odd occasion when they fail to get or keep an erection. It becomes a problem if they worry about it to the extent that anxiety itself blocks their sexual responses, so making erection difficult the next time. (The cause may be medical, though this is relatively uncommon.) Of course, if the woman blames the man for his difficulty, it can make it far worse.

Dawn, 30: 'He was very much in love with his previous girlfriend and she left him for someone else. Before the end she started to reject him sexually, telling him that he wasn't doing it right any more. He now has trouble maintaining an erection and the only way he can orgasm is by manual stimulation. I think that, when he tries to enter me, he immediately worries that he's going to lose his erection, so of course he does! I've tried to make him see that it is not important and that because he was all right before he can be all right again. Also, I can orgasm without intercourse. Although I prefer intercourse I can be quite happy in a relationship without it.'

The best way to treat impotence is to take the stress off intercourse. You could agree not even to attempt intercourse for a month, meanwhile giving each other as much pleasure as possible in other ways. Again, sex therapists usually recommend sensate focus exercises as an excellent way of getting more in tune with your own and your partner's sexual responses; these exercises are also relaxing and ease anxiety about sexual performance.

However, if the impotence persists, it is important to have a medical check-up. Conditions which affect the blood flow into the penis and nerve pathways can cause impotence – or it can be a side-effect of some medical treatments. Even if your doctor says there is a medical reason, however, don't just give up. GPs don't always know about all the help that is available. Ask for a referral to a sex-therapy clinic.

However, couples who find they are going to have to live with erection difficulties can make adjustments and continue to enjoy making love.

Sylvia, 48: 'Because of an unsatisfactorily diagnosed medical condition he has always experienced difficulty in maintaining an erection. Now, when either of us does not reach a climax during intercourse, we use manual stimulation.'

Vaginismus

Another sexual problem which prevents intercourse is vaginismus, the involuntary tightening of the muscles at the mouth of the vagina. Nita, 37: 'I had such an inhibited childhood that though I married at 20, I did not manage to have sex until I was six months married. Fear was the main reason.'

Some couples enjoy a happy married life and making love without intercourse. Rene, 48: 'Believe it or not, he never makes entry. We had problems when young with vaginal spasm and premature ejaculation (and worried about contraception) and finally realized that neither of us particularly valued penetration as such. Yet we have a very good time in bed and spend a lot of time on sex.'

With the right help, however, this problem can often be solved – which may be particularly important if a couple wants to start a family.

Loren, 26: 'My husband and I first attempted to make love on our honeymoon. This attempt and many subsequent ones proved doomed to failure. I blamed myself and allowed the problem to continue. If you cannot make love, it corrodes the very roots of one's humanity and I got seriously depressed.

'After two years I saw my doctor for depression and several probing questions brought the whole matter out. She examined me and got me going with a series of dilators. This worked. Within a week I felt confident enough to suggest to my husband that we make love. We had no problems at all. We had a much better marriage and relationship as a result, and my confidence increased.'

Often, practical demonstration that it is safe and comfortable to introduce first one finger, then two, into the vagina can help women over their fears that intercourse will hurt or may be dangerous. This can be included in love-play, and is probably most effective if a couple agrees they will not try intercourse until the woman is comfortable and relaxed with two or three fingers inserted, and is lubricating freely.

Differing sex drives

This is the most common sexual difficulty and probably the trickiest to resolve.

Pauline, 31: 'My husband has no interest in me as a lover. Marriage without sex is a sham. I sleep every night in the same bed as a man who is healthy and in his prime, yet I lead the life of a nun. In fact it's even more frustrating when the person you love is lying next to you.

'I think there are three categories of people: those who are attracted to males, those who are attracted to females, and those who are not attracted to either sex. I am sad to say my husband seems to belong to the last category.'

Sheelagh, 36: 'We are poles apart in our needs. He'd be content to make love every day, whereas I'd be happy with once a month. We have had great difficulty in finding a working compromise. I'm swamped with the feeling that his appetite is insatiable. I have tried to make the effort to make love more often but because it is not really spontaneous I begin to dread it more and more.'

It may be that all you can do is accept that you have fundamentally differing sex drives, and compromise, but there are many things you can try first.

Earlier in the book we have looked at various ways to give yourselves the best chances of feeling open to sexual arousal: relaxing together, clearing any disagreements or worries out of the way, talking together openly about sex, trying to make sex as enjoyable as possible for both of you. But if your differences seem to lie too deep for you to be able to resolve them yourselves, seeing a marriage guidance counsellor or sex therapist should help. Many wives seemed to think they couldn't seek assistance for this sort of problem.

Deane, 26: 'If there isn't a specific problem, such as impotence, it is difficult to ask for help. No one can make my husband more interested in sex.'

Lily, 46: 'I wish I was not so inhibited. I don't know how to let myself make love. Being an outgoing person, I wish there was someone to talk to. Doctors and clinics are not very helpful if you yourself can't say what is wrong.'

Doctors are mainly trained to recognize physical symptoms and treat them rather than explore all the background emotions which may be strongly affecting our sex drive. Again, seeing a marriage guidance counsellor – which you can do even if you're not married, by the way – is the best course of action, and should at least identify the cause of the problem.

Sex therapists often suggest couples try the sensate focus exercises described below: as well as exploring your feelings, you explore your own and your partner's body. This stimulates the sex hormones and may also uncover new ways of making love which you hadn't thought of and which rekindle a new interest in sex and each other.

These exercises encourage a kind of constructive selfishness. You learn to tune into your own sexual responses and accept pleasure rather than worrying all the time about whether you are 'performing' well. This, of course, in a sound relationship, adds to your partner's pleasure rather than detracts from it.

Almost anyone who feels that their sex life isn't as satisfying as it might be, for whatever basic reason, will be helped by trying these exercises. In fact, even people who reckon they have a pretty good sex life often find that doing sensate focus exercises helps their loving become more sensitive, tender and deeply satisfying.

Sensate focus

If you are going to help someone else give you pleasure, you need first to discover for yourself what gives you pleasure. Don't think you know it all. Many men and women are quite surprised to find how sexy it feels to have certain parts of their body caressed which they have never thought of as remotely erotic. You and your partner should do this exercise separately.

It is pleasant to do it in a warm bath or bed, having made sure that you will not be disturbed, even by your partner. Stroke yourself all over. Experiment with soft stroking or firmer massage. It is important that you do not chafe your skin, so use soap – in the bath – or cream or body lotion.

Perhaps after a week or so, with your partner choose a time when you won't be interrupted. Start early enough so that you both have some energy. Get the room warm. Have a drink or put on some background music – whatever helps you to relax. Leave the light on so that you can see each other. Choose which one of you is to start – you take it in turns. Using a little cream or oil, massage and stroke one another all over. Don't be afraid to show your pleasure at what feels good. Say whether light stroking or firm massage feels good where. Keep your thoughts on how your body feels. Don't worry about looking funny, or whether your partner is getting tired – his turn will come.

The first time you do this sensate focus exercise, do not touch one another's sexual areas. This should wait until you are both comfortable doing the exercise. The important thing is not to hurry the stages. Don't give up, thinking: this isn't going to improve our sex life. Eventually you will begin to see – or rather, feel – the benefits. In the meantime, the massage will be deeply pleasurable if you concentrate on what is happening now or the good feelings now, rather than wondering where it will lead in the future. The exercises are about focusing your mind, your attention, on what your body is feeling rather than on the possible outcome.

When you both feel ready – and you must be honest; there must be no pressure to agree before one of you is ready or the exercises will fail – then you can move on to touch the more sexually sensitive parts of one another's bodies. Begin showing one another how to give the most pleasure by stroking and massaging the penis, the breasts, round the anus (if you enjoy that), the clitoris and vagina. Lick one another all over, if that feels good. Experiment with kissing and licking one another's sexual parts. Remember, the only rule is that you should both enjoy it.

Again, talk. Tell one another what feels good. Being able to communicate about sex is an important part of this therapy. Use the words that come most naturally to you. Don't feel you must use the 'proper' names. Try to concentrate on the positive – not 'That doesn't do anything for me' but 'Do more of that wonderful thing you were doing before.'

If one of you becomes very eager to climax before the other is ready for intercourse, that person can help by caressing the

202

other in the right way. If you're not sure, ask. Feel free to show one another what feels good, what works for you. It is important that neither of you feels pressured into intercourse before you really want it. In fact, it is usually thought to be crucial to the success of these exercises that you agree beforehand that you won't have intercourse for a fortnight, or whatever length of time seems reasonable.

That is something to remember for the future, too. Even if these exercises do stimulate your appetite for intercourse, don't feel that from then on sex must always mean intercourse, that intercourse must always be the goal. Many couples with differing sex drives work out a happy compromise: while there are times when one is longing for sex and the other doesn't feel like it, the less eager partner may be willing to join in some massage like this, and so bring their partner to climax.

Medical problems and/or the treatment for them can lie behind a seriously declining sex drive, however, and until these are, if possible, cleared up you probably won't recover your interest in sex. It's always sensible to have a medical check if you have lost interest in sex for no apparent reason, and also to query with your doctor whether any drugs he may prescribe are likely to affect you sexually. Sometimes it is unavoidable – if the drug is needed to make you well – but sometimes there may be an alternative.

Hayley, 31: 'When our business was going through a bad patch and we were desperately short of money, I suffered a bout of severe depression as a result. I went off sex completely, although I still needed the cuddles.

'My husband didn't react in the same way, but was very sympathetic and understanding. I was treated by my doctor for my depression and our sex life gradually re-established itself. My mother helped, too, by letting me talk it out, but my husband was the greatest help.'

Physical disability

The commonest physical disability affecting sex we were told of is back trouble.

Stephanie, 27: 'Because of my husband's back problem we cannot have full intercourse. We do make love once a fortnight – manually! After my husband had had his back problem for nearly a year I felt very unhappy because of his lack of interest in me and my feelings. I fell for a young man at work – a real infatuation. After a month I told my husband I was going to leave him. We talked it out and I realized I could not love and enjoy living with anyone as much as I did him. Our marriage has been stronger and happier since then.'

Muriel, 55: 'My husband is very kind and considerate; he prefers sex in the missionary position and so do I – but this causes problems with my weak back which has given pain for many years. Can you come up with a solution to this problem? When the osteopath asks, "How did you do this?" I cannot tell him what caused the trouble!'

In fact, Muriel's best solution by far would be to tell her osteopath just what is the problem. He knows her back, its particular weakness, and it won't be news to him that people with back pain can have trouble making love.

He may not have raised the subject himself because it has been realized that some people with back pain who haven't enjoyed their sex life are rather glad of the excuse. If you tell him that your only problem is your back, he will advise you how to minimize discomfort.

It may be, however, that you have to accept that you either make love in the missionary position with pain or in a different position without it. Standard advice given to back-pain sufferers is that the one with the bad back should take the top position. However, a firm bed, a board under the mattress and a pillow in the small of the back can help. Some people take a painkiller half an hour in advance. Starting lovemaking with some relaxing massage can help prevent muscle spasm, too. (I've suggested a source of further guidance in the Help Directory.)

The more severely disabled often have to cope with a double handicap. Not only do they have to overcome their own physical problems but the prejudice of many able-bodied people who find the idea of the disabled having a sex life unsettling.

Irene, 30: 'My husband is paraplegic following an accident eleven years ago. There is very little help available regarding sexual fulfilment. It is still considered not quite nice for an able-bodied person to marry a disabled partner.'

Obviously each disabled person needs specialized advice and aids to help them overcome their particular problem. These days there are many aids available, and I have suggested a source of expert advice in the Help Directory.

The idea that only the physically attractive and complete

should enjoy sex also affects women who suffer from disfiguring operations such as mastectomy.

Gale, 36: 'I had a mastectomy operation three years ago. Before, I had a 39-inch bust; it was my best asset. Now I have nothing. When I get down beneath the sheets I feel ugly, freaky. My husband loves me as I am very much, but I can't seem to accept the situation at all. I have always felt insecure and I'm still muddled up.'

It's very common for women to suffer from depression after mastectomy and hysterectomy. Self-confidence and self-esteem may be low, particularly since so much stress is generally laid on women's appearance and bodies. They have suffered a loss and often don't get enough chance to talk through their feelings. Hospital staff may see the operation as essential for life and health and simply believe that that overrides other concerns – without realizing that the feelings have to be worked through.

Reassurance from your partner that he still loves and desires you obviously makes a tremendous difference but often the best source of understanding is others who have experienced the same operation – contact addresses in the Help Directory.

Sexually transmitted diseases and infections

There is widespread alarm at the increase in sexually transmitted diseases, particularly among the young. One in eight of the unmarried women taking part in our survey had suffered from an STD or infection.

In a quarter of cases, however, this was thrush (yeast infection). This is rarely sexually transmitted. It certainly causes discomfort during intercourse but it often plagues those who are faithful to one partner and even those who don't have intercourse at all. The same is true of cystitis.

10%	Genital warts
25%	Thrush
17%	Gonorrhoea
14%	Urinary infection/NSU
5%	Trichomoniasis
8%	Herpes
12%	Pubic lice
2%	Cystitis

Figure 21

As Jill pointed out, 'Anybody who sleeps around must stand a higher chance of getting sexually transmitted diseases.' However, it doesn't follow at all that, if you catch a sexually transmitted disease, it means you are promiscuous.

Sharon, 21: 'My husband had a one-night stand and I only found out because I caught gonorrhoea. I forgave him but I'll never forget the humiliation of going to the clinic and so on. I would leave him if it happened again and he knows it!'

Gabrielle, 20: 'I caught herpes after sleeping with my boyfriend – it was my first time – last May. The doctor at first diagnosed it as honeymoon cystitis but it turned out to be herpes. We are mystified as to how I caught it because my boyfriend doesn't suffer. Since the second attack it has not come back, so I rarely think about it now. At first it made me feel dirty and cheap because it is usually connected with people who sleep around and I don't.'

If you develop any unusual symptoms, you shouldn't agonize about them or be embarrassed, but hurry to get treatment. Joanna said of her doctor and special clinic she was referred to, 'I must stress how kind and understanding everyone was.' STDs are unpleasant but you are very unlikely to suffer any permanent ill-effects as long as you get treatment quickly.

One very dangerous problem with gonorrhoea is that it is symptomless in 50 per cent of women. You may not know you have it but it can be causing serious damage.

Karen, 23: 'I contracted gonorrhoea because my boyfriend of eighteen months made love to another woman. I forgave him and the thought of VD never crossed my mind. I had no symptoms for six months. I'm not easily embarrassed and would have no qualms about seeking medical advice about unusual discharges or similar problems.

'When I eventually noticed some vague stomach pains I saw my GP, who thought I was having ovulating pains and recommended a painkiller.

'It was only when I collapsed at work that I was taken into hospital and found to have gonorrhoea. At that stage it had caused severe salpingitis – so severe that I had to have an immediate hysterectomy, including removal of both ovaries and fallopian tubes. My boyfriend left me because he couldn't cope with his guilt and I lost my job because I was too ill to work.'

Karen's case was particularly severe but if left untreated gonorrhoea can cause blockage of the fallopian tubes and infertility. Is there any way to guard against this risk?

Fidelity on the part of you and your partner is one way, obviously. But if you or your partner has a one-night stand, or if you change partners and there is any chance your new partner may be carrying an STD, it's worth having a check-up even if you have no symptoms. If you do often have sex with different partners, then it's wise to have a check at least every three months.

There is a lot of fear of herpes, too, which has attracted a great deal of attention in the press because it is said to be 'incurable'.

Josie, 24: 'I suffer from recurrent herpes, getting an attack about once a month. The actual physical discomfort is minimal. The only horror of it is the terrible fear you have of passing the infection on to someone else and the longing to discuss it with a fellow sufferer. No one will admit to the disease because it is so dreaded and blown out of proportion by the media. I have to sit through endless dinner-party jokes about herpes and laugh glibly, hear people talking about it as if it is something only the worst sort of promiscuous slags get. Before I began my affair with the man who passed it on to me, I had not had sex for nine months and would not consider myself at all promiscuous.

'One boyfriend of mine constantly joked about herpes. When I gently pointed out that you could only get it from someone if you had sex at the time of an attack he replied, "Well, if I found out someone had herpes I wouldn't touch them with a barge pole, even if they hadn't had an attack for years."

'I have slept with three men since and have never passed it on. There is no need to, so long as you make sure not to have sex during an attack.'

There is hope for herpes sufferers. A new treatment, acyclovir, lessens the severity of the first attack and can prevent or lessen the severity of recurrent attacks, though its use is not fully evaluated as yet. Herpes has also been found to be stress-related. The more you worry about it and its effects, the more likely you are to have recurrent and more severe attacks. The reverse is also true.

Caroline, 21: 'I was very inexperienced when I got herpes. He was only the second man I'd been with. I used to find that I'd get so worked up agonizing over whether or not to have sex with a boyfriend, and whether or not to tell him, that I'd bring an attack on. I would finish with him rather than explain. Over the three years I've had herpes I've learned not to let myself become stressed, and as a result have not had an attack for more than a year, despite potentially stressful events like university finals. I still find it extremely difficult to talk about, though.'

See the Help Directory for more information about herpes and how to contact fellow sufferers.

Only 30 per cent of unmarried women generally said that VD scare stories have any effect on them. It doesn't make most of them think twice before having sex.

Of those who had suffered from some sort of sexual infection 42 per cent said that worry over STDs had changed their sex lives.

Overwhelmingly, these changes consisted of being more cautious about one-night stands, making sure they got to know their partner better before having sex, and being generally more wary.

Debbie, 19: 'After having warts six months ago I now think I have VD all the time, which I haven't. The thought is always in my mind. I'm worried I will catch something. I never sleep around. I have got to like someone a great deal before I sleep with them.'

Thrush

Though not strictly a sexually transmitted disease, many women find that thrush causes a great deal of suffering. It helps to avoid wearing tights, which encourages the 'greenhouse' atmosphere the yeast infection thrives in. Cool and dry is the motto for thrush sufferers – so warm baths or preferably showers are better than long soaks in a steaming tub.

Even so, many find that the pill or a course of antibiotics brings on an attack. Lucy, 27: 'The first time we slept together was long overdue. I was on the pill and when we tried intercourse it was so dry it was impossible. The first time we managed it we had to stop quite soon because I was so sore. Afterwards I discovered I had thrush, for which I had almost continuous treatment for a year to no avail – until I came off the pill and it cleared up. When I got a cap it was a revelation to discover that it wasn't normal to feel very sore after intercourse!'

New and more effective treatments for thrush have been developed, and Sara thought it worth braving the special clinic: 'I suffered from thrush for the first six months of our relationship – we are getting married soon. These attacks put a great strain on a relationship. Because the thrush is brought on by intercourse, you become more and more uptight about making love, which results in a vicious chain of making love, getting thrush, not making love for a couple of weeks, making love, getting thrush.

'My GP offered various creams, which had no real effect. The family planning clinic told me about a special clinic – formerly the VD clinic – at the hospital. They did an internal examination and a smear test and could make a definite diagnosis within ten minutes. The clinic was far better than my GP, as they deal solely with sexual problems.'

A lot of the stigma that used to attach to 'VD clinics' has now been removed. These days the clinics treat the whole range of genito-urinary problems and some sexual difficulties – though if it's continuing sex therapy which would best help you they will refer you. There's no need to fear that doctors and nurses will have a disapproving attitude. You can go along even if you have no symptoms and it's reassurance you need, and these clinics have the great benefit, as far as some people are concerned, that you can just turn up there without a doctor's referral.

The most important message about sexual problems is that help is available as long as you have the courage to seek it. It may take persistence; the first person you ask may not know the answers, but if you keep trying you will find someone who understands.

Help Directory

When writing to any of the organizations listed, please remember to enclose a stamped addressed envelope. Many, particularly those which are charitably funded, are often short of funds as well as of helpers. Some organizations and practitioners have to charge for their help, so always check about fees before making any appointments or arrangements.

Great Britain

I am sorry that, because of lack of space, I have rarely been able to give contact addresses for Scotland, Wales, Northern Ireland and Eire. Usually, however, the head office given here will be able to refer you where necessary.

Books mentioned on pages 230 to 232 can be ordered from good bookshops if not in stock. If it is hard for you to reach a bookshop you could phone your nearest and see if they will supply you by mail order. The Family Planning Association and National Marriage Guidance Council both supply advice books by mail order.

Sex and relationships

Your GP can refer you for specialist help for relationship and sexual problems to a psychotherapist, or clinic for psycho-sexual problems.

Family Planning Information Service. A very comprehensive source of further information and advice, not only about family planning but also about sexual and women's health problems. They can often refer you to your nearest source of specialized help – well women centres, PMT and menopause clinics, for example. You can write or phone, and at the same address the Family Planning Association Book Centre runs a mail order service supplying a wide range of guidance books. They will send you their booklist but will also supply other books on request. Family Planning Association, 27/35 Mortimer Street, London WIN 7JR (01-636 7866).

National Marriage Guidance Council can give you details of your nearest MGC if you want counselling for any relationship problem. Some MGCs provide specialist sex therapy. They help people of all ages, single as well as couples – and couples don't have to be married. Some councils ask you to make a donation towards the cost but this is never more than you can afford. You may have to wait a few weeks for an appointment but don't let this put you off. Most couples have lived with their problems for years before seeking help and can manage to last another few weeks, and once your appointment is made at least you know you have taken a positive step towards improvement. The NMGC bookshop will supply books on relationships and sexuality on their mail order list and supply special requests in this field. National Marriage Guidance Council, Little Church Street, Rugby CV21 3AP (0788 73241).

Scottish Marriage Guidance Council, 58 Palmerston Place, Edinburgh EH12 5AZ (031-255 5006).

Northern Ireland Marriage Guidance Council, 76 Dublin Road, Belfast BT2 7HP (Belfast 223454).

Catholic Marriage Advisory Council, 15 Lansdowne Road, London W11 3AJ (01-727 0141). Counselling, education for relationships and natural family planning advice.

Jewish Marriage Council, 4a Somerset Road, London NW4 4EL (01-203 6311).

British Association for Counselling, 37A Sheep Street, Rugby CV21 3BX (0788 78328), can put you in touch with a counsellor near you if you feel strongly that a MGC counsellor would not be suitable.

Brook Advisory Centres for Young People, 153A East Street, London SE17 2SD (01-708 1234), specialize in helping the under-25s in confidence on all problems connected with sex and relationships, including contraception and pregnancy. Head office will put you in touch with your nearest branch.

National Association of Young People's Counselling and Advisory Services, 17-23 Albion Street, Leicester LE1 6GD (0533 554775), also specialize in helping the under-25s by acting as a referral service. They will find you help to work through any relationship problems, including those with your parents. If there is no young people's centre near you – and there are far from enough – they may be able to suggest an alternative source of help.

Samaritans, 17 Uxbridge Road, Slough SL1 1SN (0753 32713). Local numbers are listed in the directory and the operator will put you through if you don't know the number. No matter what your worry, the Samaritans will always provide a sympathetic listener and are particularly helpful in an emergency.

Association of Sexual and Marital Therapists, PO Box 62, Sheffield S10 3TS, can put you in touch with your nearest practitioner.

Skills with People, 13 Liberia Road, London N5 1JP (01-359 2370), organize workshops and courses for those who want to develop more confidence in relationships.

Redwood, 83 Fordwych Road, London NW2 3TL (01-452 9261), can put you in touch with women's sexuality and assertiveness groups.

Women's Therapy Centre, 6 Manor Gardens, London N7 6LA. Offers workshops for women in London.

Sexual and Personal Relationships of the Disabled (SPOD), 286 Camden Road, London N7 OBJ (01-607 8851).

Albany Trust, (01-730 5871), helps with psycho-sexual problems in all relationships, especially those of sexual minorities or those worried about their sexual orientation.

Identity, Beauchamp Lodge, 2 Warwick Crescent, London W2 6NE (01-289 6175). For those worried about their sexual orientation.

Friend, 274 Upper Street, Islington, London N1 2UA (01-359 7371), provides counselling and contact for lesbians.

Lesbian Line, BM Box 1514, London WCIN 3XX (01-251 6911). Mon & Fri, 2.00 to 10.00 p.m.; Tues, Wed, Thurs, 7.00 to 10.00 p.m. For advice and information, and they can refer you to local lesbian lines.

Glasgow Lesbian Line, GLL, PO Box 57, Glasgow (041-248 4596). Mon, 7.00 to 10.00 p.m.

Parents Inquiry, 16 Honley Road, Catford, London SE6 2H2. Counselling and support for the families of gay people.

Sigma, BM, Sigma, London WCIV 6XX, is for the 'straight' partners of homosexual men and women.

Gemma, BM Box 5700, London WCIN 3XX. For disabled lesbians.

Gay Christian Movement, BM6914, London WCIV 3XX (01-283 5165).

Women of the Beaumont Society, BM/WQBS, London, WCIN 3XX, for the partners and families of transvestites.

Against your will . . .

National Council for Civil Liberties, 21 Tabard Street, London SE1 4LA (01-403 3888), can advise on cases of harassment.

London Women's Aid, 52-54 Featherstone Street, London EC1 (01-251 6537) and *National Women's Aid*, same address but 01- 251 6429, provide advice and refuge for women suffering from violence.

Rape Crisis Centres, PO Box 69, London WCIN 9NJ (01-837 1600), and c/o The Peace Centre, 18 Moor Street, Birmingham 4 (021-233 2122/2655), give support and sympathy to those who have suffered assault and harassment as well as rape.

Incest Survivors Campaign, c/o A Woman's Place, Hungerford House, Victoria Embankment, London WC2. For female victims of incest.

Incest Crisis Line, (01-890 4732 and 01-422 5100) for anyone who has suffered as a result of incest, either recently or in the past.

Health and fertility

Women's Health Concern, Ground Floor Flat, 17 Earls Terrace, W8 6LP (01-602 6669), provides information on PMT, the menopause and gynaecological problems.

Well Woman Centre, Marie Stopes House, 108 Whitfield Street, London W1P 6BE (01-388 0662/2585), provides advice and treatment on a wide range of women's health and family planning problems.

British Pregnancy and Advisory Service, Austy Manor, Wootton Wawen, Solihull, West Midlands B95 6BX (05642 3225). For problems connected with pregnancy, including counselling for abortion, sterilization, artificial insemination.

Life, 7 The Parade, Leamington Spa, Warwickshire CV32 4DG (0926 21587). For problem pregnancy when abortion is not an option you would consider.

Sexually transmitted diseases and infections: Phone your local hospital and ask for the nearest special clinic or clinic for genito-urinary infections. Treatment is confidential; it doesn't even go on your medical record. They are experts at treating infections such as thrush and cystitis.

National Association for Pre-Menstrual Syndrome, 23 Upper Park Road, Kingston Upon Thames, Surrey KT2 5LB.

Depressives Anonymous, 36 Chestnut Avenue, Beverley, N. Humberside HU17 9QU, organize friendly local groups which meet weekly and publish a quarterly newsletter.

Tranx, 17 Peel Road, Wealdstone, Harrow, Middlesex HA3 7QX (01-427 2065). For women worried about dependence on tranquillizers and wanting to taper off their use.

Foresight, The Old Vicarage, Church Lane, Witley, Godalming, Surrey GU8 5PN (042879 4500). For the promotion of pre-conceptual care.

National Childbirth Trust, 9 Queensborough Terrace, London W2 3TB (01-221 3833). For problems connected with pregnancy, childbirth, post-natal depression, etc.

Association for Post-Natal Illness, 7 Gowan Avenue, London SW6, and c/o Institute of Obstetrics and Gynaecology, Queen Charlotte's Hospital, Goldhawk Road, London W6 (01-741 5019).

National Association for the Childless, 318 Summer Lane, Birmingham B19 3RL (021-359 4887). For those with fertility problems.

Miscarriage Association, Dolphin Cottage, 4 Ashfield Terrace, Thorpe, Wakefield WF3 3DD (0532 828946).

Stillbirth and Neonatal Death Society (SANDS), Argyle House, 29-31 Euston Road, London NW3 ILA (01-833 2851).

Mastectomy Association, 26 Harrison Street, King's Cross, London WCIH 8JG (01-837 0908).

Hysterectomy Support Group, Rivendell, Warren Way, Lower Heswall, Wirral, Merseyside L60 9TU (051-342 3167).

Women's National Cancer Control Campaign, 1 South Audley

Street, London WIY 5DQ (01-499 7532). For free information about breast examination, smear tests and local screening clinics.

Cancer Link, 46A Pentonville Road, London N1 9HF (01-833 2451).

Association for New Approaches to Cancer, 28 Blythe Road, London W14 OHA (01-603 7751).

Royal Association for Disability and Rehabilitation, 25 Mortimer Street, London WIN 8AB (01-637 5400).

Back Pain Association, 31–33 Park Road, Teddington, Middlesex TW11 OAB (01-977 5474).

Endometriosis Society, 65 Holmdene Avenue, Herne Hill, London SE24.

Pelvic Inflammatory Disease Support Group, 61 Jenner Road, London N16.

Herpes Association, c/o Spare Rib, 27 Clerkenwell Close, London EC2.

Making friends, finding understanding

National Association of Youth Clubs, PO Box 1, Blackburn House, Bond Gate, Nuneaton, Warwickshire.

National Federation of 18-Plus Groups, Nicholson House, Old Court Road, Newent, Gloucestershire GL18 IAG (0531 821210) for 18-to-30-year-olds.

PHAB (clubs for physically handicapped and able-bodied young people), 42 Devonshire Street, London WIN 1LN.

Outsiders Club, PO Box 4ZB, London W1A 4ZB (01-741 3332). For those who feel that some physical or social handicap makes it difficult for them to make friends and find someone to love.

National Association of Women's Clubs, 5 Vernon Rise, King's Cross Road, London WCIX 9EP (01-837 1434).

Women's Information and Referral Service (WIRES), PO Box 162, Sheffield 1 1UD (0742 755290), can supply details of women's consciousness-raising and mental-health groups.

Spare Rib, 27 Clerkenwell Close, London ECIR OAT. The 'notice-board' of the women's movement.

A Woman's Place, Hungerford House, Victoria Embankment, London WC2 (01-836 6081). Meeting-place for women; provides information on women's groups, activities and services, and can refer women for counselling.

Black Women's Centre, 41A Stockwell Green, London SW9 (01-274 9220).

Meet-a-Mum Association (MAMA), Mrs Sylvia Ashton, 2 Railway Terrace, Pontrilaf, Hereford HR2 OBH. For mothers at home with young children.

National Housewives Register, 245 Warwick Road, Solihull, West Midlands B91 7AH, runs local groups providing an interest out of the home.

National Federation of Women's Institutes, 39 Eccleston Street, London SW1W 9NT (01-730 7212).

National Union of Townswomen's Guilds, Chamber of Commerce House, 75 Harborne Road, Edgbaston, Birmingham B15 3DA (021-455 6868).

Pre-school Playgroups Association, Alford House, Aveline Street, London SE11 5DH (01-582 8871). For friendly contact for you as well as your pre-schooler.

Gingerbread, 35 Wellington Street, London WC2E 7BN (01-240 0953), run local groups as well as provide advice for lone parents.

National Federation of Solo Clubs, Room 8, Ruskin Chambers, 191 Corporation Street, Birmingham B4 6RY (021-236 2879) for singles over 25 – separated, widowed and divorced.

National Council for the Divorced and Separated, 13 High Street, Little Shelford, Cambridge CB2 5ES.

Scottish, Single, Widowed, Divorced and Separated Clubs, 103 McCulloch Street, Glasgow G41 (041-429 0894).

Cruse, 126 Sheen Road, Richmond, Surrey TW9 IUR (01-940 4818/9047) for the widowed.

National Federation of Old Age Pension Associations (Pensioners' Voice), 91 Preston New Road, Blackburn, Lancs BB2 6BD (0254 52606). For the retired.

National Council for Carers and their Elderly Dependants, 29 Chilworth Mews, London W2 3RG (01-262 1451/2). For those looking after elderly relatives.

National Association of Carers, c/o Medway Homes, Balfour Road, Rochester, Kent ME4 6QU (0634 813981). For all those caring for a disabled or infirm spouse, child or other relative.

Australia

If there isn't a specific organization listed for your problem, don't despair. There wasn't room to list them all. The following should be able to help you themselves or refer you to someone who can.

Health problems

Talk to your GP. Contact the major women's hospitals in your state. Many of these have women's health centres, PMT clinics, menopause clinics, sex therapy/counselling, information.

Family planning clinics (see list for central addresses) can help everyone, irrespective of age, with contraception, pregnancy counselling, abortion advice and sex therapy.

Maternity sections of large public hospitals can help with pregnancy counselling, single parents, ante-natal classes, post-natal problems including feeding problems, and depression.

Speak to the sister at the local infant welfare centre – if she can't help, she should be able to refer you to someone who can.

Contact your municipal council for details of community health centres, women's health centres and the like in your area.

Others

Look in your local paper for details of support groups (e.g., for single parents), courses for self-awareness, assertiveness, personal growth, etc. (Courses are often advertised in major daily newspapers too.)

Contact CAB, TAFEs for details of courses.

Contact local municipal council for details of Youth Refuges, Youth Counselling, Women's Refuges, and emergency accommodation.

Women's Liberation Switchboard in each state is one of the best sources of information. They offer advice, support and referrals on all women's matters, including health, sex, relationships, incest, harassment. Can also refer to feminist doctors, lawyers, dentists, psychologists, and will have details of women's groups.

Victoria

Marriage Guidance Council of Victoria, 46 Princess Street, Kew (861 8512/5354/5974).

Family Planning Association of Victoria, 270 Church Street, Richmond (428 1414, 429 1177/1868). Contraception, pregnancy counselling, abortion advice. Also sex education for the intellectually handicapped.

Family Planning Association of Victoria Action Centre, 35 Elizabeth Street, Melbourne (61 3445) – adolescent counselling and referral centre.

Catholic Family Planning Centre, 20 Brunswick Street, Fitzroy (419 6355).

VD Clinic, 364 Little Lonsdale Street, Melbourne (602 4900).

Gay Line Telephone Advisory Service, 126 Franklin Street, Melbourne (329 5555).

Women's Liberation Switchboard and Lesbian Line, 295 Victoria Street, West Melbourne (329 8515).

Rape Crisis Centre, Queen Victoria Medical Centre, 172 Lonsdale Street, Melbourne (665 5111).

WIRE (Women's Information and Referral Exchange), Flinders Lane, Melbourne (63 6841). State-funded. Advice and referrals on all women's matters.

Women's Health Resource Collective, 199 Sydney Road, Brunswick (380 9974). Women's health information centre.

The Cairnmillar Institute, 993 Burke Road, Camberwell (82 1361). Courses in personal growth, self-awareness, women's assertiveness.

Birthright (Victoria), 238 Flinders Street, Melbourne (63 2364). Supports single parents.

Parents Without Partners, 220 Canterbury Road, Canterbury (836 3211).

Council for the Single Mother and her Child, 246 Collins Street, Melbourne (63 7225).

Catholic Family Welfare Bureau, 491 Nicholson Street, Carlton (347 6066).

South Australia

Marriage Guidance Council of South Australia, 55 Hutt Street, Adelaide (233 4566).

Family Planning Association, 17 Phillips Street, Kensington (31 5177).

Family Life Movement of Australia, 252 Kensington Road, Leabrook (31 9486).

COPE (Centre of Personal Encounter), 114 Hutt Street, Adelaide (223 3433). Courses in all areas of human relationships.

VD Clinic, 275 North Terrace, Adelaide (218 3557).

Gay Counselling Service Association, and *Gayline,* Kilkenny (268 5577).

Rape Crisis Centre: 268 8888; Northern Districts: 250 8874

Women's Information Switchboard, 122 Kintore Avenue, Adelaide (223 1244). State-funded. Advice and referrals on all women's matters.

Women's Liberation Movement, and *Women's Community Health Centre,* 6 Mary Street, Hindmarsh (46 6521).

Women's Community Health Centre, 2 King William Road, North Adelaide (267 5366).

Childbirth Education Association, 11 Wingfield Street, Clovelly Park (276 9810).

Birthright, 88 Currie Street, Adelaide (212 6241). Supports single parents.

Parents Without Partners, 17 Currie Street, Adelaide (51 6660).

Catholic Family Welfare Bureau, 33 Wakefield Street, Adelaide (223 6313).

New South Wales

Marriage Guidance Council of New South Wales, 226 Liverpool Road, Enfield (745 4411).

Family Planning Association of New South Wales, 161 Broadway, Sydney (211 0244).

Catholic Family Planning Service, Rigney House, Marist Road, Parramatta (630 7404).

Family Life Movement, 41 The Boulevard, Lewisham (560 3377). Counselling, sex education.

Youthline, 153 George Street, Parramatta (633 3666); 210 Pitt Street, Sydney (264 1177).

Gay Counselling Service, 51 Holt Street, Surrey Hills (211 1177).

Lesbian Line, 3rd Floor, 323 Darling Street, Balmain (818 5630).

VD Clinic, 93 Macquarie Street, Sydney. Female: 217 5993. Male: 217 5990

Rape Crisis Centre (24 hours): 819 6565.

Darling Street Women's Health Centre, and *Abortion Access and Advice*, 323 Darling Street, Balmain (818 2994).

Women's Health and Resources Foundation, 112 West Botany, Arncliffe (59 4251).

Women's Liberation House, 62 Regent Street, Sydney (699 5281).

Women's Medical Centre, 10 Martin Place, Sydney (231 2366).

Leichardt Women's Community Health Centre, 164 Flood Street, Leichardt (560 3011).

Liverpool's Women's Community Health Centre, 273 George Street, Liverpool (601 3555).

Childbirth Education Association of Australia (NSW) Ltd, 38A Allenby Park Road, Allambie Heights (29 1328).

Birthright, 121 Pitt Street, Sydney (232 6455). Supports single parents.

Parents Without Partners, 316 Pitt Street, Sydney (267 5177).

Queensland

Marriage Guidance Council, 159 St Paul's Terrace, Brisbane (221 2005).

Family Planning Association of Queensland, 239 Brunswick Street, Fortitude Valley (52 5151/2).

Family Life Movement, 120 Rode Road, Wavell Heights (266 6933). Counselling, sex education.

VD Clinics, 484 Adelaide Street, Brisbane. Male: 224 5634. Female: 229 8264

Youth Care and Counselling, 4 Tully Street, Keperra (355 4073).

Homosexual Information and Advice Service, 379 George Street, Brisbane (221 9373).

Rape Crisis Centre, 54 Browning Street, West End (44 4008). Also Women's House Shelta.

Women's Liberation, 65 Stanley Street, South Brisbane (391 2556).

Childbirth Education Association, 861 Gympie Road, Chermside (359 9724).

Birthright, 174 Queen Street, Brisbane (229 4186). Supports single parents.

Parents Without Partners, 19 Clarence Street, South Brisbane (44 8567).

Catholic Family Welfare Bureau, Morgan Street, Fortitude Valley (52 8585).

Australian Capital Territory

Marriage Counselling Service Inc Canberra, 115 London Cct, City (48 0530, 47 0603).

Family Planning Association ACT Inc, Childers Street, City (47 3077).

Catholic Family Planning, Canberra Avenue, Manuka (95 2484).

Youth Advice Line, 2 Mort Street, Braddon (49 7668).

Rape Crisis Centre: 47 8071.

Women's Information Service, Women's Liberation, Abortion Counselling Service: all at 3 Lobelia Street, O'Connor (47 8070).

Childbirth Education Association: 82 3614.

Birthright (ACT), Griffin Centre, City (47 4282). Support for single parents.

Parents Without Partners (ACT) Inc, 72 Antill Street, Dickson (48 6333).

Northern Territory

Citizens Advice Bureau, 247 Trower Road, Casuarina, Darwin (27 2511).

Family Planning Association of NT Inc, PO Box 3158, 42 Stuart Highway, Darwin (81 5335).

VD Information Service, Peel Street, Darwin (81 5460).

Rape Crisis Centre, 42 McLachlan Street, Darwin (81 4454).

Childbirth Education Association, 78 Nightcliff Road, Nightcliff (85 1497).

Parents Without Partners (NT) Inc, 6 Beatrice Street, Darwin (81 8503).

Western Australia

Marriage Guidance Council of Western Australia, 27 Victoria Square, Perth (325 6644).

Family Planning Association of WA Inc, 104 Colin Street, West Perth (321 2701).

Youthline Samaritan, 60 Bagot Road, Subiaco (381 2500).

Homosexual Counselling and Information Service, 329 Pier Street, East Perth (328 9044).

Centacare (Catholic), 25 Victoria Square, Perth (325 6644).

VD Clinic, 69 Moore Street, Perth (325 6466).

Rape: Sexual Assault Referral Centres: 380 1122.

Women's Liberation and Lesbian Line, 323 Pier Street, East Perth (328 5717).

Childbirth and Parenthood Association, 1186 Hay Street, West Perth (321 4821).

Birthright, 504 Hay Street, Perth (325 7343). Support for single parents.

Parents Without Partners (WA) Inc, 504 Hay Street, Perth (325 4575).

Tasmania

Marriage Guidance Council, 192 Charles Street, Launceston (31 9157); 22 Main Road, Penguin (37 2334).

Family Planning Association of Tasmania Inc, 73 Federal Street, North Hobart (34 7200).

Lifeline (North West) Counselling: Burnie 31 1330. If outside local area, ring 008 00 1188 (charged at local-call rate).

Youthline: 31 4477.

Centacare (Catholic Family Welfare), 19 Canning Street, Launceston (31 6811); 44 Sandy Bay Road, Hobart (23 2428;.

Parents Without Partners: Burnie 31 6303.

Canada

For a list of counselling services, sex therapy and advice on family planning and pregnancy, clinics, organizations and self-help groups useful to women in your province, write to the Women's Programme, Secretary of State, Ottawa, Ontario KIA OM5 (819 994 3190). This will give you very detailed information. The addresses listed here give an indication of the range of help available, though you may need to consult your Women's Programme list or local telephone directory or operator for a local contact.

Planned Parenthood Federation of Canada, 151 Slater Street, Suite 2000, Ottawa, Ontario K1P 5H3, will give details of local branches offering advice on family planning, pregnancy alternatives and sexuality counselling.

Canadian Guidance and Counselling Association, c/o University of Ottawa Faculty of Education, 651 Cumberland Street, Suite 212, Ottawa, Ontario K1N 6N5 (613 234-2572).

Canadian Association of Marriage and Family Life, 271 Russell Hill Road, Toronto, Ontario M4V 2T5 (416 968-7779).

Marriage Encounter, 129 Hannaford Street, Toronto, Ontario M4E 3G9 (416 694-8700) for marriage guidance and counselling.

Sex Information and Education Council of Canada, 423 Castlefield Avenue, Toronto, Ontario M4N 1L4 (416 691-3499).

Planned Parenthood of Toronto, 58 Shaftsbury Avenue, Toronto, Ontario M4T 1A3 (414 961-8290), operate a phone-in for teenagers with sexuality problems.

Youth Counselling Services. For details of what's available in your area, contact the Women's Programme, Ottawa, or ask at your Provincial Department of Health and Welfare.

223

Distress Centres perform the same functions as the Samaritans in helping the suicidal and depressed: their actual name may alter from province to province, but the telephone operator will put you through.

Canadian Mental Health Association, National Office, 2160 Yonge Street, Toronto M4S 2Z3 (416 484-7750).

Montreal Gay Women, CP 128, Succ. G, Montreal, Quebec.

Lesbian Organization of Toronto (LOOT), PO Box 70, Station F, Toronto, Ontario M4X 2L4 (416 960-3249), operates a help-line.

Lesbian Society, c/o Gay Community Centre, Box 1662 Saskatoon, Saskatchewan S7K 3R9 (306 652-0972).

Lesbian Info Line, 1501 West Broadway, Vancouver, BC, V5Y 1P8 (604 734-1016).

Rape Crisis Centres and Transition Houses. Women's Programme, Ottawa, will send on request a list of help available in your area, or consult your telephone book or operator.

Committee Against Rape and Sexual Assault (CARSA), 5017 Victoria Avenue, Niagara Falls, Ontario L21 409.

Canadian Association of Sexual Assault Centres, c/o 4-45 Kingsway, Vancouver, BC V5T 3H7 (604 872-8212).

Women's Health Education Network (WHEN), PO Box 1276, Truro, Nova Scotia B2N 5C2 (902 895-2140).

Women Healthsharing, PO Box 230, Station 'M', Toronto, Ontario M6S 4T3 (416 968-1363). Publishes quarterly national magazine on women's health care.

Childbirth Education Association, 33 Prince Street, Toronto, Ontario M4W 1Z2 (416 924-1628).

Canadian Mothercraft Society, 32 Heath Street West, Toronto, Ontario M4W 1T3 (416 920-3515). Promotes child care and health education, pre-natal classes.

Parents Experiencing Perinatal Death Association, c/o Gael Gilbert, 47 Alberta Avenue, Toronto, Ontario M6H 247.

Queens Birth Control, VD and Abortion Information and Referral Service, 51 Queens Crescent, Kingston, Ontario K7L 3N6 (613 547-2806).

Canadian Abortion Rights Action League, PO Box 6282, Depot C, Victoria, BC V8P 5KS (604 474-1482/382-6001) and Box 935, Station 'Q', Toronto, Ontario, M4T 2P1 (416 961-1507) run an education programme and give counselling on contraception, sexuality and fertility.

ADDICS (Alcohol and Drug Dependency Information and Counselling Services), No 209, 818 Portage Avenue, Winnipeg, Manitoba R3G ON4 (204 775-1233).

Canadian Cancer Society, 130 Bloor Street W, No 1001, Toronto, Ontario M5S 2V7 (416 961-7223) and 1118 St Catherine Street W, No 700, Montreal H3B 1H5 (514 866-1112).

Canadian Rehabilitation Council for the Disabled, Suite 2110, 1 Yonge Street, Toronto, Ontario M5E 1E5.

Women's groups. Women's Programme, Ottawa, publish up-to- date lists of all national and regional women's groups and women's centres available on request.

Black Women's Sisterhood Organization, 1918 Davenport Road, Toronto M6N 1B7 (416 656-3465).

Immigrant Women's Centre, 348 College Street, Toronto, Ontario M5T 1S4 (416 924-7161). Free, confidential own-language medical help and counselling on all topics.

Anduhyaun House, 106 Spadina Road, Toronto, Ontario M5R 2T8 (416 920-1492). Canadian Indian women's residence offering counselling and 'life skills' training.

One Parent Families Association, 218 Kent Street, Charlottetown, Prince Edward Island (902 894-3050).

Carrefour des Associations de familles monoparentales du Quebec, 890 rue Dorchester est, Suite 2320, Montreal, Quebec H2L 2L4 (514 288-5224/5225).

Housewives Register, Karen Panfili, 75 Hollyberry Trail, Willowdale, Ontario M2H 2N9, and Mrs Elizabeth Dalgleigh, 399 Sunset Drive, Oakville, Ontario L6L 3N3 (416 827-6196). For 'lively-minded women'.

Housewives Association, 220 Parkridge Place SE, Calgary, Alberta T2J 5B7 (403 278-1878).

MAMMA (Modern Activities for Mother's Mental Awareness), PO Box 308, Station 'A', Willowdale, Ontario M2W 5S9 (416 977-1408).

Women Alone, 136 Avenue F, South Saskatoon, Saskatchewan S7M 1S8 (306 244-7702).

Women Helping Women, PO Box 121, Station 'B', Sudbury, Ontario P3E 4N5.

Widows Outreach Network (WON), 179 Queen Street, Kingston, Ontario K7K 5Y2 (613 542-4497).

Community Contacts for the Widowed, 1643 Yonge Street, Toronto, Ontario M4T 2A1 (416 486-9945).

Widows Information Centre, 421-620 View Street, Victoria, BC, V8W 1J6.

Canadian Pensioners Concerned Women's Committee, Tower 1, Suite 200, 7001 Mumford Road, Halifax, Nova Scotia B3L 2M9.

New Zealand

Mental Health Foundation of New Zealand, The secretary, PO Box 37-438 Parnell, Auckland 1, NZ. Information on nearest Parents Centre/Parentline/Marriage Guidance/Citizens Advice/Family Planning/Lifeline/Women's Health Centre, and will help set up discussion groups, self-help support groups, etc.

National Marriage Guidance Council of New Zealand, Box 2728, Wellington, NZ; Box 8781, Auckland; Box 640, Hamilton; Box 10-234, Wellington; Box 2428, Christchurch; 226a High Street, Dunedin.

New Zealand Family Planning Association Inc., 218 Karangahape Road, Auckland 1, or write to Box 68-200, Newton, Auckland 1.

Samaritans, 9 Herbert Street, Greymouth, South Island, and PO Box 448 (6611); 69 Woburn Road, Lower Hutt and PO Box 27294 (644 591/664 252); YMCA Premises, Church Street, North Masterton (81259); 15 Amesbury Street, North Palmerston and PO Box 1963 (74400); Hakiaha Street, North Taumaranui (6664); PO Box Brooklyn 6309, North Tauranga (81001); 120 Guyton Street and PO Box 4116 Mid-Av. PO North Wanganui (55090); Cathedral Building, Molesworth Street and PO Box 12041, North Wellington (49600).

Lifeline, Nat. Sec., Box 5104, Auckland.

Lifelink, c/o Social Service Centre, Rotorua.

New Zealand Homosexual Law Reform Society Inc, Box 9458, Courtenay Place, Wellington.

New Zealand Council for Civil Liberties Inc, Secretary, Box 357, Wellington.

Women's Refuge Inc, Box 8044, Dunedin.

National Council for Women of New Zealand Inc, Mrs M. Salas, Box 12-117, Wellington.

New Zealand Women's Health Network, Secretary Sarah Calvert, Gondollin, R.D.4 Newstead, Hamilton.

Pregnancy Help Inc, General Secretary, Box 13-012 Johnsonville, Wellington. Fourteen branches across New Zealand. For those needing emotional/practical help in pregnancy now or in the past.

Abortion Law Reform Association of New Zealand Inc (ALRANZ), Box 10-351, Wellington, and Box 13-129, Christchurch.

Birthright, PO Box 347, Wellington. Supports one-parent families.

Federation of New Zealand Parents Centres, Secretary, Box 11-310, Wellington. Thirty-three centres across New Zealand. Information centres: help with all aspects of pregnancy and child care.

Council for the Single Mother and her Child, Secretary, Box 437-090, Auckland.

Cruse, for the widowed: Mrs M. Wallace, 8 White Street, Taradale, H. Bay; Mrs R. E. Flannery, 18 Menin Road, Onekawa, Napier; Mrs M. Drown, 303 Sylvan Road, Hastings.

New Zealand Widows' and Widowers' Association Inc, Mrs Valerie Austin, PO Box 12-160, Wellington. Help and advice – branches throughout New Zealand.

60's-up Movment, PO Box 3143, Auckland.

Disabled Citizens Society Inc, Box 5062, Auckland 1.

Cancer Society of New Zealand Inc, Secretary, Box 10-340, Wellington.

Mastectomy Association Inc, Secretary, c/o Auckland Division of Cancer Society, Box 1724, Auckland.

National Society on Alcohol and Drug Dependence NZ, Secretary, Box 1642, Wellington.

South Africa

National Council for Marriage and Family Life, 114 MBA Building, 413 Hatfield Street, Pretoria.

Famsa – Pietermaritzburg Society for Marriage and Family Life, 14 Leathern Street, Box 928, and at Health Welfare Office, 248 Church Street, Pietermaritzburg.

Family and Marriage Society, Suite 525, Fifth floor, 320 West Street, Durban (031 68991), will also advise young people on contraception, pregnancy and abortion and give general counselling.

Family Planning Association of South Africa, 412 York House, 46 Kerk Street, Johannesburg 2001: *of Natal Region*, 705 Commercial City, Commercial Road, Durban (031 322588).

Family Planning Clinic, 43 Werdmuller Centre, Main Road, Claremont (64 4330).

Institute for Child and Adult Guidance, Rand Afrikaans University, PO Box 524, Johannesburg 2000.

Indian Youth Advisory Centre, 263 Road 240, Chatsworth (031 431425).

Durban Indian Child and Family Welfare Society, Pioneer Buildings, Berea Road, Durban (031 314265).

Durban African Child and Family Welfare Society, Old Fort Road, Durban (031 325506).

South African National Council for Mental Health, PO Box 2587, Johannesburg 2000.

South African Psychological Association, PO Box 4292, Johannesburg 2000.

Samaritans, PO Box 2201, Bloemfontein, Orange Free State (83000), and 305 Old Mutal Building, Oxford Street, E.L. 5201 (27559).

Lifeline, Head Office, 56 Roelandts Street, Cape Town (46 1111), and 38 Adrian Road, Stamford Hill, Durban (031 333-333), can also put you in touch with local Rape Crisis Centres, and offer counselling and referral for sexual minorities and the disabled.

Selby Lodge, c/o The Rectory, Main Road, Kalk Bay 7975. Shelter for girls and women needing temporary assistance.

Allison Homes, Queen Mary Place, 488 Burger Street, Pietermaritzburg. Homes for women.

The Women's Hospice for Battered Wives, Stamford Hill Road, Durban.

ARAG. Abortion Reform, Assertiveness, Pregnancy and Counselling, c/o June Cope, PO Himeville (03392 32).

Women's Health Centre, 43 Werdmuller Centre, Main Road, Claremont (64 4330).

GASA (Gay Association of South Africa), Box 3330, Johannesburg 2000.

LILACS, PO Box 93, Salt River, South Africa. Organization for lesbians.

Rape Crisis Centre, PO Box 11496, Vlaeberg, Cape Town 8018 (21 5400), and c/o POWA, PO Box 93416, Yeoville, Johannesburg 2158 (783 5027). Numbers of local centres can be obtained from your nearest branch of Lifeline.

United Women's Organization, 3 Hare Street, Mowbray 7700 (69 1055). For details of assertiveness and sexuality groups. (Rape Crisis Centres can also give details of these.)

Women's Bureau of South Africa, PO Box 705, Pretoria 0001 (47 6176), and at Mutual Building, Darling Street, Cape Town (45 8911), will give details of all women's groups, women's health centres and family planning clinics.

The Woman's Group, c/o Ingrid Shevlin, Durban (031 215645).

The Cape Town Feminists, PO Box 11486, Vlaeberg 8018, hold consciousness-raising meetings.

Women in Action, 63 Vause Road, Durban 4001.

Women's Movement of UCT, c/o 2 Possen Road, Newlands 7700. To spread consciousness of women's liberation.

Feminist Action Group, 302 Margate Court, c/o Banket and Kapteijn Street, Hillbrow, Johannesburg 2001.

Clubs for single women: Robert E. Lee Entertainment, Durban (031 211351), and The Warehouse, Durban (031 377271).

Pathways Institute of Thanatology, c/o Jenny Kender, PO Box 391037, Bramley, Johannesburg 2018. For information on problems related to dying, death and bereavement, widow-to-widow basis.

Widows Information Service (Weduwees-Inligtingsdieds), Mrs Hilda Powell, 501/503 CTC Building, Plein Street, Cape Town 8001.

Independent Living Centre, 1st Floor, Happiness House, corner of Loveday and Wolmarans Street, Braamfontein, Johannesburg, and PO Box 7289, Johannesburg 2000. Help for the disabled. Lifeline also have information to help the disabled.

National Cancer Association of South Africa, 11th floor, 1107 Shepstone House, Shepstone Arcade, Box 2186, Pietermaritzburg.

National Housewives Register, c/o Ann Moroney, 48 Ninth Street, Linden 2195, Johannesburg.

Black Housewives League, 1288 Mofolo N., PO Kwa Xuma, 1868.

Union of Jewish Women of South Africa, French Bank Building, 4 Church Square, Cape Town 8001. 60 branches across South Africa.

Further Reading

Sex and relationships

Make It Happy: What sex is all about by Jane Cousins (Penguin). A frank and reassuring guide for teenagers.

Love and Sexuality, ed. Romie Goodchild (Octopus). Answers young adults' questions openly and straightforwardly.

So You Think You're Attracted To The Same Sex? by John Hart (Penguin). For those worried about their sexual orientation.

Parents and Teenagers. A helpful guide for parents by the Open University, Health Education Council and Scottish Health Education Group with a readable, practical approach (Harper and Row).

Help, I've Got a Teenager by Jean and Robert Bayard (Exley). A light-hearted but very reassuring guide for parents.

A Woman In Your Own Right: Assertiveness and You, by Anne Dickson (Quartet). A practical self-help course.

Fat is a Feminist Issue by Susie Orbach (Hamlyn). Shows how our weight and body image reflect our feelings about our relationships and ourselves – for all of us on the dieting see-saw.

Meeting People is Fun: How to overcome shyness by Dr Phyllis M. Shaw (Sheldon Press).

Making Marriage Work by Dr Paul Hauck (Sheldon Press).

The Massage Book by George Downing (Penguin). A clear, step-by-step explanation.

The Art of Sensual Massage by Gordon Inkeles and Murray Todris (Allen and Unwin) is more lavishly presented.

In Our Own Hands by Sheila Ernst and Lucy Goodison (Women's Press). A book of self-help therapy for women.

Treat Yourself to Sex by Paul Brown and Carolyn Faulder (Penguin). A self-help guide to treating common sexual problems.

Lesbian/Woman by Del Martin and Phyllis Lyon (Bantam).

Better Lives for Disabled Women by Jo Campling (Virago). Discusses the social, sexual and psychological problems.

Enjoy Sex in the Middle Years by Dr Christine Sandford (Martin Dunitz). For couples in mid-life.

Divorce and Separation: A guide to a new life by Angela Willans (Sheldon Press).

One-Parent Families by Diana Davenport (Sheldon Press). A practical guide to coping.

Against our will

Stand Your Ground by Kaleghl Quinn (Orbis). On how not to be a victim.

Self-Defence by James Shortt (Sidgwick and Jackson). A practical handbook.

Incest: Fact and Myth by Sarah Nelson (Stramullion). On a new approach to helping incest victims.

Sexual Violence: The reality for women, from the London Rape Crisis Centre (Women's Press).

Health and fertility

Choices in Contraception by Zandria Pauncefort (Pan), Guidance on all traditional and new methods of contraception, plus how to minimize their effects on your relationship.

The Pill by John Guillebaud (Oxford Paperbacks). Contains detailed information, especially useful for those with particular health worries.

Natural Birth Control by Katia and Jonathan Drake (Thorsons). A detailed guide to up-to-date methods.

Lifting The Curse: How to relieve painful periods, by Beryl Kingston (Sheldon Press).

Understanding Pre-menstrual Tension by Dr Michael Brush (Pan).

Women and Depression by Deidre Sanders (Sheldon Press). A practical guide to beating depression and relieving anxiety, when possible without drugs.

Your Body, Your Baby, Your Life by Angela Phillips with Nicky Lean and Barbara Jacobs (Pandora Press).

Sex During Pregnancy and After Childbirth by Sylvia Close (Thorsons).

Depression After Childbirth by Katharina Dalton (Oxford University Press).

Why Us? by Dr Andrew Stanway (Thorsons). An excellent guide for the childless.

Miscarriage by Ann Oakley, Dr Ann McPherson and Helen Roberts (Fontana).

When Pregnancy Fails: Coping with miscarriage, stillbirth and infant death by Susan Borg and Judith Lasker (Routledge and Kegan Paul).

The Menopause: Coping with the change by Dr Jean Coope (Martin Dunitz).

Prime Time by Helen Franks (Pan). A positively cheering look at mid-life for women.

Hysterectomy: How to deal with the physical and emotional aspects by Lorraine Dennerstein, Carl Wood and Graham Burrows (Oxford University Press).

Breast Cancer by Dr Michael Baum (Oxford University Press).

Mastectomy: A patient's guide to coping with breast surgery by Nancy Robinson and Ian Swash (Thorsons).

Thrush: How it's caused and what to do about it by Caroline Clayton (Sheldon Press).

Cystitis: A complete self-help guide by Angela Kilmartin (Hamlyn).

Herpes: What to do when you have it by Dr Oscar Gillespie (Sheldon Press).

Avoiding Back Trouble (Consumers' Association).

The Love Life of the British Wife

Circle the number next to your answer. Remember, this is anonymous

Setting the scene

1 How long have you been married?

Less than 5 years	1
6–10 years	2
11–20 years	3
21–30 years	4
More than 30 years	5

2a How often do you and your husband usually make love?

Less often than once a month	1
About once a month	2
About once a fortnight	3
About once a week	4
2–3 times a week	5
4–5 times a week	6
Every day	7
More than once a day	8
We never make love now	9

2b Would you and do you think your husband would like to make love:

	You	Husband
More often	1	1
Less often	2	2
Happy as you are	3	3

2c If you wish you made love more often what gets in the way? RING ALL THAT APPLY

Lack of privacy from parents, others	1
Lack of opportunity because of the children	2
You are often too tired	3
Your husband is often too tired	4
You don't feel like it that often	5
Your husband doesn't feel like it that often or doesn't seem to	6
You find it hard to be responsive	7
Your life is too busy, you haven't time	8
Your husband's life is too busy, he hasn't time	9
Your husband is often away	0
Other, please write in	V

....

2d If you wish you made love *less often* what forces you?

Your husband wants to more often than you do	1
You feel that you ought to have an active sex life	2
You are trying to get pregnant	3
Other, please write in	4

....

3a What is the longest time you have gone without making love (excluding times when you were apart for some reason).

1–3 days	1
4–7 days	2
8–13 days	3
2 weeks–month	4
More than a month, write how long	5

....

3b Why was this?

Menstruation	1
Pregnancy	2
After childbirth	3
Sexual relationship problem	4
We are/were both happy not to	5
Other, write in	6

....

4 How do you rate your husband as a lover?

Excellent	5
Good	4
Average	3
Passable	2
Poor	1

5 How do you rate yourself and how do you think your husband rates *you* as a lover?

	You	Husband
Excellent	5	5
Good	4	4
Average	3	3
Passable	2	2
Poor	1	1

6 I love you. How often do you tell him or does he tell you?

	You	Husband
Every day	5	5
Once a week	4	4
About once a month	3	3
About once or twice a year	2	2
Never/can't remember the last time	1	1

7 Do you and your husband often kiss and cuddle apart from before having sex?

Very often	4
Fairly often	3
Not very often	2
Not at all	1

8 Is this often enough for you and your husband?

	You	Husband
Yes	1	1
No	2	2

9 Is kissing and cuddling as important to you both as sexual intercourse?

	You	Husband
More important	3	3
Equally important	2	2
Not as important	1	1

10 Do you have difficulty becoming sexually aroused?

Always	5
Often	4
About half the time	3
Occasionally	2
Never	1

11 Do you and your husband go to bed at the same time as each other at night?

Always	5
Usually	4

Occasionally	3
Almost never	2
Never	1

12 Do you have:

Double beds	1
Twin beds	2
Separate bedrooms	3

13 Do you ever make love anywhere else besides the bedroom?

No	1
In the living room	2
In the kitchen	3
In the bathroom	4
In the garden	5
In the car	6
Other, please write in	7

....

14 When do you usually make love?

Last thing in the evening	1
During the evening	2
During the day	3
Early in the morning	4
During the night	5
It varies often	6

15 Who makes the first move towards making love?

It's always him	5
Usually him	4
It's about 50/50	3
Usually me	2
Always me	1

In the mood?

16a Do you ever refuse to make love?

Never	1
Occasionally	2
Often	3
Always	4

16b If you do, how do you refuse?

Very directly (I don't feel like making love now)	1
Indirectly (I'm too tired now/I've got a headache)	2
Other, please write in	3

....

16c If you do refuse, what's usually the reason?

You don't want sex as often as your husband	1
To get back at him	2
His approach puts you off	3
You're not in the mood	4
Other, please write in	5

....

17 Do you ever make love wishing you weren't?

Always	4
Often	3
Occasionally	2
Never	1

18 Do you ever make the first move when your husband is not interested?

Always	4
Often	3
Occasionally	2
Never	1

19a Does your husband ever turn you down?

Always	4
Often	3
Occasionally	2
Never	1

19b If so, how does he refuse?

Very directly	1
Indirectly	2
Other, please write in	3

19c If so, what do you think is usually the reason?

He doesn't want sex as often as you	1
To get back at you	2
Your approach puts him off	3
He's not in the mood	4
Other, please write in	5

....

20 Do you ever do any of the following to help you or your husband to get in the mood for love? RING ALL THAT APPLY

Put on perfume	1
Put on make-up	2
Wear pretty nighties	3
Wear certain clothes	4
Cook favourite/special meals	5
Drink more than usual	6
Put on music	7
Other, please write in	8

....

None of these	9

21 How do you and your husband usually initiate sex?

	You	Husband
Direct request – I want to make love	1	1
Start cuddling, kissing, touching	2	2
Indirect request (I'm going to bed now)	3	3
Wake up your partner	4	4
Other, please write in	5	5

....

Never initiate sex	6	6

22 Do you like and do you think your husband likes your taking the lead sexually?

	You like to lead	Husband likes you to lead
Always	4	4
Often	3	3
Occasionally	2	2
Never	1	1

23 In what kind of light do you like to make love?

Darkness	1
Low lights	2
Bright light	3
Don't care	4

24a Do you use a method of family planning?

Always	4
Usually	3
Occasionally	2
Never, I don't bother with that	1
Never, I'm trying to get pregnant	V
Never, my periods have ceased	X
Never, it's against my religious beliefs	0
Other, please write in	9

....

24b If you do, which method(s) do you use? RING ALL THAT APPLY

Pill	1
IUD (coil)	2
Cap or diaphragm	3
Sheath	4
Female sterilisation	5
Vasectomy	6
Safe period (rhythm)	7
Spermicides	8
Other, please write in	9

....

24c If you use family planning, does your method interfere with your enjoyment of your love life?

Yes, considerably	3
A little occasionally	2
Never	1

25a Do you fantasise while making love (such as imagine yourself in an exotic situation or with another man)?

Always	5
Often	4
About half the time	3
Occasionally	2
Never	1

25b If you do fantasise please write your favourite fantasy on a separate sheet of paper and attach to questionnaire.

26 Do you find that your mind wanders on to other things when making love (e.g. day-to-day worries, the children etc).

Always	4
Often	3
Occasionally	2
Never	1

27a Do you use any of the following to increase your sexual pleasure?

Vibrator	1
Other sex aids	2
Reading/seeing erotic material	3
Specialist underwear	4
Other, please write in	5

....

27b Does your husband know about this?

Yes	1
No	2

27c And does/would he mind?

Yes, a lot	1
Yes, a little	2
No, he accepts it	3
No, he encourages it	4

28a Do you or your husband masturbate?

	You	Husband
Often	3	3
Occasionally	2	2
Never	1	1
Don't know	–	0

28b If you do, does your husband know?

Yes	1
No	2
Not sure	3

29 Does masturbating make you feel guilty?

Always	3
Occasionally	2
Never	1

How important is orgasm?

30 Is it important to you or your husband whether or not you usually reach orgasm when you make love?

	You	Husband
Very important	4	4
Fairly important	3	3
Not very important	2	2
Not at all important	1	1

31 Do you reach orgasm when you make love:

Always	5
Usually	4

About half the time	3
Occasionally	2
Never	1

32 Are you, and do you think your husband is happy with the frequency with which you reach orgasm?

	You	Husband
Yes	1	1
No	2	2

33 Do you have difficulty reaching orgasm when you want to?

Always	5
Usually	4
About half the time	3
Occasionally	2
Never	1

34 Do you ever fake orgasm?

Always	5
Usually	4
About half the time	3
Occasionally	2
Never	1

35 Is it important to you and your husband whether he usually reaches climax when you make love?

	You	Husband
Very important	4	4
Fairly important	3	3
Not very important	2	2
Not at all important	1	1

36 Does he climax when you make love?

Always	5
Usually	4
About half the time	3
Occasionally	2
Never	1

37 Are you, and do you think your husband is happy with the frequency with which he reaches climax?

	You	Husband
Yes	1	1
No	2	2

38 Does he have difficulty reaching climax when he wants to?

Always	5
Usually	4
About half the time	3
Occasionally	2
Never	1

39 If you and your husband reach orgasm, what usually causes it?

	You	Husband
Intercourse	1	1
Manual stimulation	2	2
Vibrator	3	3
Oral sex	4	4
It varies	5	5
Other, please write in	6	6

....

40 How often does your husband climax before you would really like him to?

Never	4
Occasionally	3
Often	2
Always	1

41 How often does your husband have difficulty keeping an erection?

Always	4
Often	3
Occasionally	2
Never	1

42a Do you ever do anything during love-making that your husband likes but makes you feel uneasy?

Always	4
Often	3
Occasionally	2
Never	1

42b If so, what is it usually? Please write in

....

43 Do you ever refuse your husband's requests to try a new position or technique?

Yes	1
No	2

44a Do you think your husband ever does anything during love-making to please you which makes him feel uneasy?

Always	4
Often	3
Occasionally	2
Never	1

44b If so, what is it usually?

Please write in ....
....

45 Do you ever make requests your husband refuses?

Yes	1
No	2

46 Have you ever held back from making a request for something particular during love making?

Yes	1
No	2

• If you can tell us more about anything mentioned in this section, please write on a separate sheet.

47 How happy is your marriage generally?

Very happy	4
Reasonably happy	3
Not very happy	2
Not at all happy	1

48 How satisfied are you with your sexual relationship?

Completely satisfied	4
Reasonably satisfied	3
Not very satisfied	2
Not at all satisfied	1

49 If you could change the way you and your husband make love would you want to/want him to:

	You	Husband
Be a more tender lover	1	1
Be a more forceful lover	2	2
Take more time in the beginning	3	3
Be a more passionate lover	4	4
Be a more skilful lover	5	5
Be a more spontaneous lover	6	6
Be more experimental	7	7
Be more relaxed during love-making	8	8
Find you/him more attractive	9	9

Be keener to make love more often	0	0
I wouldn't want to change/change him	V	V
No idea	X	X

50 How often do you and your husband openly talk about sex or your sexual feelings?

Often	3
Occasionally	2
When we have a problem	1
Never	0

51 Have you ever been troubled by sexual difficulties?

Yes, we are now	1
Yes, in the past	2
No	3

52 If YES, was or is this difficulty:

Your lack of interest in sex	1
His lack of interest in sex	2
The quality of your love-making	3
The quality of his love-making	4
Your lack of orgasm	5
His lack of orgasm	6
His premature ejaculation	7
His impotence (loss of erection)	8
Connected with pregnancy, childbirth	9
Connected with menopause	0
Other, please write in	V

....

53 If YES, did you or your husband seek help or advice for this problem?

Yes	1
No	2

54 If YES, from whom. RING ALL THAT APPLY (a). And of those, which one source gave most help (b)

	(a) All sources	(b) One main source
GP, doctor	1	1
Family planning clinics	2	2
Marriage Guidance	3	3
Sex therapist	4	4
Books	5	5
Magazine or newspaper problem page	6	6
Family	7	7
Friends	8	8

55 How well did this one main source help with solving the problem?

Very well, solved the problem	4
Reasonably well	3
Not very well	2
Not at all well	1

56 If you went to a sex therapist, how did you find him or her?

Referred by your GP	1
Referred by Family Planning Clinic	2
Referred by Marriage Guidance	3
Referred by problem page	4
Family or friend	5
Other, please write in	6

....

Other lovers?

57 Did you make love with your husband before you were married?

Yes	1
No	2

58 Did you or your husband have any lovers before you met?

	You	Husband
No	1	1
Yes, write in how many	—	—
Don't know	—	X

59 Do you or your husband wish you had had more sexual experience with other lovers?

	You	Husband
Yes, lots more	3	3
Yes, some more	2	2
No	1	1
Don't know	–	X

60 Do you or your husband wish he had had more sexual experience with other lovers?

	You	Husband
Yes, lots more	3	3
Yes, some more	2	2
No	1	1
Don't know	–	X

61 Have you or your husband (as far as you know) had any other sexual relationships since marriage?

	You	Husband
No	1	1
Yes, please write in how many	—	—
Don't know	–	X

62 What is the longest time such a relationship has continued?

	Your affair	Husband's affair
A day/night	1	1
A few days	2	2
A few weeks	3	3
A few months	4	4
More than six months	5	5
Write in how long	—	—
Don't know	–	X

63 Did the affair(s) have an effect on your marriage?

	Your affair	Husband's affair
No	1	1
Improved the sexual relationship	2	2
Worsened the sexual relationship	3	3
Improved the emotional relationship	4	4
Worsened the emotional relationship	5	5
Other, please write in	6	6

....

64 How did this sexual experience of yours compare with your marriage? RING ALL THAT APPLY

More satisfying	1
Less satisfying	2
More exciting	3
Less exciting	4
More emotionally rewarding	5
Less emotionally rewarding	6
Same as marriage	7
Just a change	8
Don't know	–
Other – please write in	0

....

65 Are you or your husband (as far as you know) having an affair now?

	You	Husband
No	1	1
Yes	2	2
I'm suspicious	–	3

● **If you can tell us more about anything mentioned in this section, please write on a separate sheet.**

And finally . . .

66 How important do you and your husband think sex is in your marriage?

	You	Husband
Very important	5	5
Important	4	4
Reasonably important	3	3
Not very important	2	2
Not at all important	1	1

67 Has your sex life with your husband changed over the years?

No, it's always been good	1
No, it's always been average	2
No, it's always been poor	3
Yes, it's had its ups and downs	4
Yes, it's steadily improved	5
Yes, it's steadily worsened	6

68 Think about this list of events. For each of them say whether your sex life was better or worse than average at these times:

	Better	Average	Worse	Doesn't apply
Early days together	3	2	1	X
Being engaged	3	2	1	X
First being married	3	2	1	X
Pregnancy	3	2	1	X
Having babies	3	2	1	X
Children growing up	3	2	1	X
Children leaving home	3	2	1	X
Your job demanding	3	2	1	X
Husband's job demanding	3	2	1	X
Other, please write in	3	2	1	X

....

69 Which of the following statements do you think are true? RING THOSE YOU THINK ARE TRUE.

You can have a happy marriage without an active sex life	1
Sex is more important to men than women	2
It's time that women's sexual needs were better understood	3
Press and TV coverage of sex makes people feel inadequate	4
Understanding each other's sexual needs is important in marriage	5
Greater openness about sexual matters saves people suffering problems in secret	6
Sexual fulfilment is as important to women as men	7
It's difficult to get expert help if you have a sexual problem	8
Sex isn't something women discuss with their friends	9
It's quality not quantity that counts in sex	0
Women are more inhibited than men	X

242

How old are you?

Under 18	1
18–24	2
25–34	3
35–44	4
45–54	5
55–64	6
65+	7

Do you have children under 16 living with you? RING ALL THAT APPLY

Child/children under 3	V
Child/children 3–5	X
Child/children 6–11	0
Child/children 12–16	1
No children at home	2
We have no children	3

Which region?

North of England	1
Midlands and Wales	2
South of England	3
Scotland	4
Other, please write in:	

....

Love and the Unmarried Woman

Setting the scene

1 How old are you?

Under 16 years	0
16–18 years	1
19–21 years	2
22–25 years	3
26–30 years	4
31–40 years	5
41–50 years	6
51–60 years	7
over 60 years	8

2 How easy do you think it is these days to meet the right kind of boys/men?

Very easy	4
Fairly easy	3
Not very easy	2
Not at all easy	1

3 Which would you say are the most likely ways of meeting them?

At discos/dances	1
Through friends	2

At work	3
At school/college	4
Through hobbies/interests	5
Through social clubs	6
Through friendship/marriage agencies	7
Other _____	8

4 Where did your most successful relationship start?

At a disco/dance	1
Through friends	2
At work	3
At school/college	4
Through hobbies/interests	5
Through a social club	6
Through a friendship/marriage agency	7
Other _____	8

5 Please tell us, on a separate sheet, more about your first meeting and the start of your relationship.

Marriage

6 How do you feel about marriage?

Hope to marry one day	1
Have definite plans to marry within 2 years	2
I am living with my man with a view to marriage	3
I am living with my man but not bothered about marriage	4
Not bothered about living with a man or marriage	5
Determined not to get married	6
Other _____	

7 Have you been married before?

| Yes | 1 |
| No . . . **Go to Question 10** . . . | 2 |

8 If YES, have you been married:

Once	1
Twice	2
More than twice	3

9 How did your previous marriage(s) end? CIRCLE ALL THAT APPLY:

I was widowed once	1
I was widowed more than once	2
I was divorced once	3
I was divorced more than once	4
I am separated from husband	5

Your parents' view of sex

10 Are you living at home with your parents now?

| Yes | 1 |
| No | 2 |

11 Can you talk openly about sex with your mother and father?

	Mother	Father
Very openly	4	4
Fairly openly	3	3
Not very	2	2
Not at all	1	1
Not applicable	X	X

12 Would your parents allow/have allowed you to sleep with your boyfriend in their house?

Yes	1
Only if engaged	2
Only if a regular boyfriend	3
No	4
Don't know	5

13 Have/did your parents discuss(ed) contraception with you?

Yes, fully	1
A little	2
Not at all	3

14a Has any member of your family ever made sexual advances towards you?

Yes	1
No	2

14b If YES, and you feel able, please write on a separate sheet saying which relation it was, their age and what happened.

15a Have you ever been sexually assaulted or harassed?

Yes, assaulted	1
Yes, harassed	2
No	3

15b Did you tell anyone about your experience?

No	1
Yes	2

Who did you tell? Please write in

_____

15c If YES, and you feel able, please write on a separate sheet of paper saying what happened to you.

Sexual experience

16 Have you ever had sexual intercourse?

Yes . . . Go to Question 18 . . .	1
No	2

17 If NO, is this because:

You feel you're too young	1
You've not had a boyfriend yet	2
You haven't met the right man	3
You don't feel ready yet	4
You want to be married first	5
You want to but are scared	6
Your relationship is not close enough	7

Just don't want to	8
Other _____	

Now go to Question 33

18 If YES, when was the last time you had sex?

Within the last week	1
Within the last month	2
Within the last year	3
More than a year ago –	4
please write in how many years ago	

19 Do your parents know you have had sex with your boy/man-friend(s)?

Yes, they're happy about it	1
Yes, they're unhappy about it	2
No	3
Not applicable/left home	4

The first time

20 How old were you the first time you had sexual intercourse?

Under 16	0
16–18	1
19–21	2
22–25	3
26–30	4
31–40	5
Over 40	6

21 What mainly made you decide to have sex on that occasion? CIRCLE ONE ONLY:

We were deeply in love	1
He talked me into it	2
He threatened me with violence	3
I'd been drinking	4
All my friends had had sex	5
I wanted to see what sex was like	6
I wanted to with that boy/man	7
Other _____	8

22 Did you enjoy the first time?

A great deal	4
Reasonably well	3
Not very much	2
Not at all	1

23 Was it better or worse than you expected?

Much better	4
A little better	3
A little worse	2
Much worse	1

24 Did either of you use contraception then?

Yes	1
No	2

25 Please write and tell us about this first time on a separate sheet of paper.

26 Have you ever regretted having sex?

Yes	1
No. . . Go to Question 28 . . .	2

27 Why did you regret it?

I gave in too easily	1
I'd had too much to drink	2
I felt used	3
It proved to be a one-night stand	4
I was being unfaithful	5
It was a disaster sexually	6
Other _____	

Contraception

28 Have you ever had sexual intercourse without either of you using a method of contraception?

Yes	1
No	2

29 If YES, how did it happen?

I was carried away	1
We decided to risk it	2
I decided to risk it	3
I thought it was the safe time of the month	4
I wanted to get pregnant	5
My boyfriend said it would be OK	6
Other (please write in) _____	7

30 Who feels most responsible about using contraceptives?

I feel more responsible	1
He feels more responsible	2
We both feel equally responsible	3

31 Do you (or your partner) use any method of contraception?

Yes, always	1
Yes, sometimes	2
No, I don't bother with it	3
No, I don't need it	4
No, I'm trying to get pregnant	5
Other _____	6

32 If YES, which method?

Pill	1
IUD (Coil)	2
Cap or diaphragm	3
Female sterilisation	4
Spermicides only	5
Vasectomy	6
Sheath	7
The safe period/rhythm method	8
Withdrawal	9

33 Do you feel you know enough about contraception?

Yes	1
No	2

34 Where have you got most of your information from?

The doctor	1
Parents	2

Older brothers/sisters/friends   3
Family planning clinic   4
Lessons at school   5
Books/magazines   6
Other _____ 7

35 Would you be frightened of going to your doctor about contraception if you thought he might tell your parents?

Yes   1
No   2
Not applicable – left home   3
Other _____ 4

36 Do you ever masturbate?

Yes   1
No . . . Go to Question 38a . . .   2

37 Do you feel guilty about masturbating?

Yes, very guilty   3
A little   2
No   1

A special man in your life

38a Do you currently have one special boy/manfriend in your life?
Yes   1
No   2

38b If NO, would you like one?

Yes – very much   1
Quite like one   2
No *Now go to Question 43   3

39 If YES, how long have you been together?

Less than a month   1
One to three months   2
Three months to a year   3
More than a year –   4
write in how long _____

40 How often do you usually meet?

We live together   1
Several times a week   2
Once or twice a week   3
Less than once a week   4
Less than once a month   5

41 Do you think you are both in love?

	You with him	He with you
Yes	1	1
No	2	2

42 How old is he?

Under 16	0
16–18	1
19–21	2
22–25	3
26–30	4
31–40	5
41–50	6
51–60	7
Over 60	8

43 Are you going out with more than one boy/manfriend?

Yes   1
No, just one boy/man   2
Not going out with men at all
   . . . Go to Question 77 . . .   3

44 If YES, how many?

Two   2
Three   3
More than three   4

Making love

● Answer the next questions about your relationship with the most important boy/manfriend in your life:

45 How far has your lovemaking with your boy/manfriend developed? CIRCLE ONE ONLY:

We don't get close at all	1
We kiss	2
We kiss and cuddle	3
We kiss and caress over our clothe	4
We kiss and caress under our clothes	5
We do everything but have intercourse	6
We have intercourse	7

46 Do you feel your lovemaking has gone:

Too far too soon?	3
Just far enough?	2
Not far enough?	1

47 Do you enjoy lovemaking with your boy/manfriend? CIRCLE YOU COLUMN
And do you think your boy/manfriend enjoys it? RING HIM COLUMN

	You	Him
A great deal	4	4
Reasonably well	3	3
Not very much	2	2
Not at all	1	1

48 'I love you'. How often do you tell him or he tell you?

	You	Him
Very often	4	4
Fairly often	3	3
Not very often	2	2
Never	1	1

49 If you could change things about you and your boy/manfriends' lovemaking would you want to/want him to:

	You To	Him To
Kiss and cuddle more?	1	1
Be less inhibited?	2	2
Be more skilful?	3	3
Be more gentle?	4	4
Be more enthusiastic?	5	5
Be less demanding?	6	6
Go further than we do now?	7	7
Other _____		
I wouldn't want to change/change him	0	0

50 Do you and your boy/manfriend think it is important that you are faithful?

	You think	He thinks
Yes	1	1
No	2	2
Don't know	0	3

51 Do you and your boy/manfriend think it is important that he is faithful?

	You think	He thinks
Yes	1	1
No	2	2
Don't know	0	3

52 Is there only one man in your life you have intercourse with?

Yes, only one	1
There are two	2
There are more than two	3
I'm not having sex with anyone at the moment	4

● Please answer the next questions if you are having sex with the most important boy/manfriend in your life. OTHERS GO TO QUESTION 77.

53 How often do you and your boy/manfriend have intercourse?

Less than once a month	1
Less than once a week	2
About once a week	3
2 to 3 times a week	4
4 to 5 times a week	5
Every day	6
Never make love these days	7

54 Would you, do you think your boy/manfriend would like to make love:

	You	Him
More often	1	1
Less often	2	2
Happy as you are	3	3

55 If you wish you could make love more often what stops you?

Lack of opportunity – have nowhere to go	1
Lack of privacy from parents/others in family	2
Lack of opportunity because of children	3
You are often too tired	4
He's often too tired	5
You don't feel like it that often	6
He doesn't feel like it that often	7
You find it hard to be responsive	8
Your life is too busy	9
His life is too busy	10
He is married	11
He is often away	12
You are often away	13
Other _____	

56 How do you rate your boy/manfriend as a lover?

Excellent	5
Good	4
Average	3
Passable	2
Poor	1

57 How do you rate yourself? And how do you think your boy/manfriend rates you as a lover?

	You	Him
Excellent	5	5
Good	4	4
Average	3	3
Passable	2	2
Poor	1	1

58 Do you and your boy/manfriend often kiss and cuddle apart from before intercourse?

Very often	4
Fairly often	3
Not very often	2
Not at all	1

59 Is this often enough for you and your boy/manfriend

	You	Him
Yes	1	1
No	2	2

60 Is kissing and cuddling as important to you as sexual intercourse?

More important	3
Equally important	2
Not as important	1

61 Where have you and your boy/manfriend made love?

In bed	1
In the living room	2
Elsewhere in the house	3
In the garden	4
In the car	5
In the street	6
In the countryside	7
Other (please write in) _____	

62 How often do you and your boy/manfriend spend the night together?

We live together 1
Very often 2
Whenever we have sex 3
Occasionally 4
Never 5

63 Who makes the first move towards making love?

It is always/usually him 3
About 50/50 2
Always/usually me 1

64 Do you ever make love wishing you weren't?

Always 4
Often 3
Occasionally 2
Never 1

65 Do you ever worry that you don't enjoy sex enough?

Often 3
Occasionally 2
Never 1

66 Is it important to you or your boy/manfriend whether or not you usually reach orgasm when you make love?

	You	Him
Important	3	3
Not very important	2	2
Not at all important	1	1

67 Do you reach orgasm when you make love?

Always/usually 4
About half the time 3
Occasionally 2
Never 1

68 Do you have difficulty reaching orgasm when you want to?

Always/usually 4
About half the time 3
Occasionally 2
Never 1

69 Do you ever fake orgasm?

Always/usually 4
About half the time 3
Occasionally 2
Never 1

70 Does he climax when you make love?

Always/usually 4
About half the time 3
Occasionally 2
Never 1

71 If you and your boy/manfriend reach orgasm what usually causes it?

	You	Him
Intercourse	1	1
Manual stimulation	2	2
Vibrator	3	3
Oral sex	4	4
It varies	5	5
Other, please write in _____		

72 How often does your boy/manfriend climax before you would really like him to?

Never 3
Occasionally 2
Always/often 1

73 How often does your boy/manfriend have difficulty keeping an erection?

Always/often 3
Occasionally 2
Never 1

74 Can you tell your boy/manfriend exactly what you do and don't enjoy during lovemaking, and discuss difficulties?

Can't tell him 1
Find it very difficult 2
Sometimes can tell him 3
No problems 4

75 Did you or your boy/manfriend have sex with other people before you met?

	You	Him
No	0	0
Yes, write in how many	—	—
Don't know		X

76a How important is sex to you, and how important is it to your boy/manfriend?

	You	Him
Very important	4	4
Fairly important	3	3
Not very important	2	2
Not at all important	1	1

76b What is the longest time you have gone without having sex?

Please write in _____

77a Do you think that for a woman to have had sex before marriage is:

A good thing	1
A bad thing	2
Makes no difference	3

77b Do you think that for men to have had sex before marriage is:

A good thing	1
A bad thing	2
Makes no difference	3

78 From what age do you think it is all right for men and women to have sex? Write in –

Men ____
Women ____

79 When do you think it is generally acceptable for women and men to start having sex?

	Woman	Man
On the first date	1	1
Once they've got to know each other	2	2
When they think they're in love	3	3
When they plan to marry	4	4
When married	5	5

Losing your man

80 Have you ever lost an important man in your life?

Yes	1
No . . . Go to Question 86 . . .	2

81 What happened?

He died	1
He left me	2
I left him	3
We decided to finish	4
Other	5

82 Did you miss him *sexually*?

Yes, a great deal	4
Yes, quite a lot	3
Not very much	2
Not at all	1
Not applicable – no sexual relationship	X

83 Did other men assume you were sexually available?

Often	3
Sometimes	2
Never	1

84 If you can, please tell us more about your experiences after losing your man on a separate sheet of paper.

85 If you have had children living with you, have they hampered your developing new relationships?

A great deal	1
Sometimes	2
Never	3
Not applicable – no children	4

86 Have you ever had a sexually transmitted disease or infection?

Yes	1
No . . . Go to Question 90 . . .	2

87 If YES, what did you have?

Write in _____

88 Has worry over sexually transmitted diseases changed your sex life?

Yes	1
No	2

89 If YES, in what way? Please write

_____
_____
_____

90 Have you ever made love with another woman (including kissing and caressing)?

Yes	1
No	2

91a Are you having such a relationship now?

Yes	1
No	2

91b If NO, how old were you when you had the last such relationship?

Please write in _____

92 And finally here are some things people have said. Please ring all those you agree with

Girls who have sex with several boys are admired	1
Girls who have sex with several boys get a bad reputation	2
Boys who have sex with several girls are admired	3
Boys who have sex with several girls get a bad reputation	4
Easily available contraception encourages early sex	5
If contraception is hard to obtain it leads to more pregnancies not less sex	6
VD scare stories make you think twice before having sex	7
Fear of VD doesn't stop you having sex, it just makes you worry more	8
The boys have all the fun and girls all the worry	9
Boys take their fair share of responsibility sexually	10
Sex is best when you're young	11
Sex gets better as you get older	12
Sex isn't as important to women as it is to men	13
Women's sexual needs are not well enough understood	14
Sex is more exciting if you have many different partners	15
Sex is best with one man you love	16

About you

93 Have you ever had a child(ren)?

Yes	1
No	2

94 Were you married at the time?

Yes	1
No	2

252

95 Do(es) your child(ren) live with you now?

Yes   1
No   2

96 Where do you live?

North of England   1
Midlands, Wales   2

South of England   3
Scotland   4
Northern Ireland   5

Note on Methodology and Sample

We did not lightly make our decisions on which research methodology to employ for this study. Our objective was to obtain reliable and honest data about the sexual activity and experiences of women and their feelings and opinions about them. We knew from our own research experience, and believed it to be generally understood, that people overclaim their levels of sexual activity and satisfaction in the same way as they underclaim the number of cigarettes they smoke and pints of beer they consume.

We considered several options.

1. *Face-to-face interviews with a representative sample of women.* We decided against this method because previous surveys on similar subjects carried out in this way had, we understood, proved to be rather unsatisfactory. We also knew from our own previous experience that, faced with an interviewer, people do not always feel able to answer honestly questions about very sensitive, perhaps painful, areas of their lives.

When, for example, we (Deidre Sanders and Anne Rigg) once conducted a survey through interviews of a representative sample on the problems of working women, which included questions as to whether and how often working mothers left children alone at home, we were faced with almost 100 per cent denial that interviewees ever did so – even though this is known to be a significant problem in many areas, and despite the fact that the intention of the survey was not to blame but to highlight the need for help. A bound-in self-completion questionnaire on the same subject carried out earlier had revealed that significant numbers of mothers were leaving young children unattended at home for some time after school.

In the case of a survey on sex, we felt that using interviewees would have made the findings extremely liable to bias, resulting from the interviewers' own feelings and anxieties about different areas of sexual experience and how comfortable they felt in

254

asking questions about this very private side of our lives. It would have also biased the results towards those interviewees who were most readily able to discuss sex.

2. *Random-sample self-completion questionnaire by post.* We decided against this method because it would have presented enormous problems in ensuring that respondents took the survey seriously and that we received an adequate response. There is no doubt, either, that some people would have found it extremely offensive to have an unsolicited questionnaire about their sex lives dropping through their letterbox. You do, after all, exercise choice in buying a magazine and bringing it into your home which would not have applied if we had mailed out the questionnaire to a random sample.

3. *A questionnaire bound in* Woman *magazine and subsequently sampled in proportion with the population statistics for age and region.* We chose this method because we were sure we could present the study honestly and without bias. As explained in the introduction, we were careful to encourage responses from those who were content as well as the disillusioned, from different age groups, from those who thought sex important and those who thought there had been a great deal of fuss about very little. We could monitor the response thoroughly ourselves, and a consideration of the statistics of the readership profile of *Woman* led us to conclude that there is no reason to believe that the readers of *Woman* are biased in any way that might affect our results, given that we sampled from the response.

Out of a total of 15,604 completed questionnaires, we randomly selected for more detailed analysis 2,000 questionnaires from wives in proportion to national statistics for ages of married women and regions, and 2,000 of the completed questionnaires returned by unmarried women to reflect the age and regional characteristics of the UK population of unmarried women in the correct proportions for those aged 16 to 60 years old.

We undertook a number of precautions to ensure that all the questionnaires included in the computer analysis were honest and genuine replies:

1. The questionnaires were screened on receipt for the obvious 'jokers' – the type who say they're under 18 and married for more than thirty years, have sex every day and are keen on gang-bangs. There were, in fact, very few of these.

2. Each questionnaire was then individually coded by a psychologist who read all the accompanying material (many women enclosed letters with their questionnaires) and who could ensure that the questionnaires were consistent records. Any whose stories could not be reconciled with their answers were dropped from the analysis.

3. We conducted a 10 per cent quality-control check of the coding.

4. Before computer analysis the questionnaires were edit-checked by the computer for simple inconsistencies missed in coding. All queried questionnaires were checked again.

Of the unmarried women, 46 per cent were living with their parents. This included 85 per cent of the 16-to-18-year-olds and a decreasing proportion of the older age groups. Ninety-two per cent of those who replied had had intercourse.

Eighty-one per cent had a 'special boy/manfriend'. Of these, 25 per cent were living with him.

Seventy-nine per cent had never been married. Of those who had, 66 per cent were divorced, 30 per cent were separated, and 7 per cent were widowed.

Index

Abortions: help to prevent need for 102; number of performed on married women 104

Abuse of women and children 172ff.

Affairs: benefits from having an a. 132ff.; effect on marriage 135–7; percentage of wives having an a. 15; reactions from having an a. 139–40; reason for women having an a. 127ff.

Anal sex: enjoyment of couples of 80–81; participation in by women to please partner 81

Baby(ies), views expressed sex life affected by having b.117

Birth control: methods of 104; need for more education regarding 41; no perfect method invented 106; sheath as unsatisfactory method 104; withdrawal as unsatisfactory method 104

Body: exploring through touch 74–5; realisation of fertility 107

Brain, as most important organ of sexual pleasure 83

Broodiness, waves of experienced by many women 117

Change, desire for sexual change 62–4

Childbirth 119; inability to reach orgasm during intercourse 121; proportion of wives aver sexual difficulties connected with 119

Children: as restricting factor in frequency of lovemaking 124–6; difficulties in lovemaking when children at home 125; hindering lone parents to develop new relationships 166; sexual approaches by strangers to 182–3

Climaxing, premature, by husband 78

Clitoris: function of 70; sensitivity of 46, 72; stimulation of 46, 71–2

Clothes, wearing of attractive as stimulus for sexual lovemaking 54

Conception 116; as aid to reviving ailing relationship 116; close link with sexuality for many women 116–17

Contraception: arguable responsibility for 100–102; indulging in intercourse without using contraceptives 99; methods of 98; percentage of unmarried women ignorant about 103–4; taking risk when having intercourse 99–100

Cystitis, contracting 205, 206

Divorce, after, women resorting to continuing sex with husbands 167

Drink, as aid to lovemaking 53

Episiotomy, effects of 119–20

Erection, inability to achieve through anxiety 47, 198–9

Experimenting with new positions and techniques 81–2

Family planning, disagreement over method of 101

Family Planning Association, seeking help from 37
Fantasizing 83ff.; erotic f. and pornography 95–7; extreme and impossible fantasies 93–4; fantasies about rape 94–5; fantasies about another man known to wife 84–6; lovemaking on desert islands 87–8; lovemaking with film or rock stars and sportsmen 89–90; swapping partners 91–3; wives affected by worries about family affairs while lovemaking 88–9; wives not communicating with husbands about sex, indulging in 86–7; women's most common fantasies 84
Fathers, difficulty in dealing with daughter's emerging sexuality 19
Fertile periods, determining 107–8
Fidelity 127; belief in by young women 28–9
Friendship and marriage agencies, over 40s as large percentage of clients 164–5

Girls: age of first intercourse 1; enjoyment of sex 1; orgasm reached or faked 1; promiscuity of 1
Gonorrhoea, contracting 206

Herpes, contracting 206, 207; treatment for 207
Hormone-replacement therapy (HRT), as assistance during menopause 113–14
Husband, jealousy of baby by 123
Hysterectomy, undergoing 115

Impotence, treating 198–9
Incest 172ff.; abuse by fathers 174–6; advances made by uncles and grandfathers 176–7; approaches made by older women in family 173; detecting i. 181; longterm effects of forced i. 177–9; recounting experiences of i. 179ff.
Infertility problems 108–9
Intercourse: advice if pressured into 38; effect of age in enjoyment of first-time i. 33–5; factors affecting first-time enjoyment 34; importance of being aroused and relaxed before 46–7; initial experience of 31; percentage enjoying 31; percentage enjoying through curiosity 35–6; reasons given for having i. first time and enjoying 33–4; when unprepared 31–2

Kissing and cuddling: as first move by large proportion of women 59–60; asking for more before intercourse 61–2; enjoyment of when not ready for intercourse 122; lack of as objection by wives to sex in middle of night 51; more appreciated by wives and unmarried women 11–12; more welcomed by married women 56ff.

Lesbians(ism): 5,144ff.; 'coming out' 155–7; dilemma of l. with children 153–4; effect of on wives 146; enjoyment of sex with men and women by 152ff.; experimenting in 147; reason for l. enjoyment 157–9; self-analysis of l. 149–50; social disapproval as drawback 150
Lovemaking: discussion with partner during 79–81; dissatisfaction at being woken in middle of night for 50–1; frequency of 12–14; results of survey into 5–6; secret 25; time of 50–1; variations in places to participate in 25, 52–3; variations in time to indulge in 50–51; venues for secret 25

Lovers: desire by women for l. to be more skilful and experiment 73–4; definition of good 7

Marriage, unhappy, as cause of wives having affairs 130
Massage, an excellent way to relax before lovemaking 56
Mastectomy, undergoing 205
Masturbation 21, 75; by unmarried women 21–2; by women during periods 109–10; joint 76–7; resorting to after losing partner 167
Men: meeting 'right type of' 43–4; supposedly 'better' at sex 9
Menopause 111ff.; experience of m. by men 114; fears m. indicates loss of sexual enjoyment 111; many women finding m.vulnerable time 114; no indication m. cause of disruption of sexual lives 112; problems caused by 112; symptoms of 112–13
Mistress(es): happier if not full-time 143; role of 140–3; unhappiness with role of 141

Nice girls, and sex 17

Oral sex 12; shyness in indulging in 12; uneasiness by men about 80
Orgasm: by women reached after intercourse 9; causes of 68ff.; exercises to assist o. during intercourse 78; faking 10, 47, 65–6; feeling 72; importance of 72–3; lack of 194–5; overcoming worry about reaching during intercourse 197–8; problems with 73; reason for faking by women 65–6; urination during 70
Over-25s: large percentage unable to find right man 163ff.;

percentage of married desiring second try 162–3; percentages wanting or 'quite liking' man friend 160–1; small percentage not wanting men 161–2; unattached, pleasures and problems of 160ff.
Ovulation: body changes after 107; body changes before 107; checking temperature o. taking place 108

Parents: and attitude to contraception 23; discussing sex with p. by unmarried women 18ff.; double standards of 23; fear of promiscuity 28–9; need to love daughters to ensure happy love life 29; refusal by p. to discuss sex openly 20; reticence in communicating with children 28–9; worried by responsibility by being p. 123; worry about risk of pregnancy of daughters 23
Pelvis, exercises for unlocking 75–6, 78
Penis, size of: as factor in women's enjoyment 79; not vitally important to women 79
Perfume, as stimulus for lovemaking 54
Petting 44, 45; importance of 46; power of 46–8; value of 46–7
Physical disability: back trouble as commonest affecting sex 203–5; recommended assistance during intercourse 204
Pill: as method of contraception 98–9; beneficial effects of 103–4; constituents of 103
Post childbirth 121–2: improved or worsening sex life after 121; tiredness preventing lovemaking 122
Post-natal depression 124
Pregnancy 118; good for sex 118; sexual problems during p. 118

Premature ejaculation 194, 195, 196–8
Premenstrual tension 110–11; if troublesome 111
Promiscuity 15, 23; fear of by parents 28–9; periods of by women 42–3
Puberty, emergence of sexuality at 18

Quarrel, making up after as aid for sex 61–2

Self-pleasure 76
Sensate focus exercises 47–8, 76–8, 198, 201–3
Sex: before marriage 34; dissatisfaction with s. by wives 17; factors assisting towards good s. 34–5; frequency of 53ff.; secret 25–6
Sex drives, differing 200–201
Sex therapy(ists): exercise used to break down initial shyness 27; use of 195–6
Sexual arousal, building up to peak 78–9
Sexual excitement, creation of 47
Sexual experience: desire for more by wives 128; self-confidence lessened by lack of 128
Sexual harassment and assault 15–16, 188–90; aids to strength and confidence in s.h. situations 190–2
Sexual problems: lack of interest by wife as most serious problem 193; seeking help to overcome 195–6; solving 193ff.
Sexual relationship: improvement in 49; percentage stating worsening in 49–50
Sexually transmitted diseases and infections 205ff.
Sexy cycles 109–10; most desire felt around ovulation 109, 117
Sterilization, female, a very safe operation 104, 106

Teenagers: drink as reason for first-time intercourse 37–40; intercourse by 31; percentage rejecting contraception 40–41; percentage urged into intercourse 37–8
Thrush: contracting 205; treatment for 106, 208–9
Touch, learning through 44ff.

Unmarried women: belief sex important with one lover 10; curiosity as reason for intercourse 35–7; desire to become less inhibited in lovemaking 12; discussing sex with mothers 18; having intercourse with near-strangers 35; importance of sex to 4–5; large percentage who masturbate 21–2; less inhibition regarded as main change 59ff.; more frequency of lovemaking with sexual partners than wives 14; more sexual satisfaction than among wives 5; most likely ways of meeting 'right man' 43–4; percentage enjoying lovemaking great deal with special man-friend 5; proportion making love with another woman 5; proportion regretting sex 41–3; reservations expressed regarding the pill 103–4; worry at not enjoying sex sufficiently 9; would appreciate more kissing and cuddling from lovers 11–12

Vagina: lubrication for during menopause 113; structure of 70–71
Vaginismus, problem of 199–200
Vasectomy, as safe operation 104, 106
VD clinics, assistance from 209

Verbal communication, to assist
  shyness 27–8
Vibrator, use of 76, 95

Wives: affairs conducted through
  being sexually dissatisfied with
  husband 129; contrary feelings
  towards intercourse 39; desire
  for more frequency of sex 53ff.;
  effect of affair to improve
  sexual and emotional
  relationship with husband
  135–6; effect on when discovery
  made husband having affair
  138; finding affair more sexually
  satisfying 134; forties as peak
  age to have affairs 130;
  importance of sex emphasised
  by 3; improvement or
  worsening in sex life after
  childbirth 121–2; lack of desire
  in making love 7; lack of
  discussion of sex or feelings with
  husbands 79–81; main benefit
  providing a 'change' 134; many
  w. dissatisfied sexually 49–50;
  many dissatisfied with any birth
  control methods 106–7; more
  sexual experience desired by
  128ff.; number finding affair
  more emotionally rewarding
  than marriage 133; objection to
  intercourse 39; percentage
  dissatisfied with lovemaking 6;
  percentage fantasizing when
  making love 83ff.; percentage
  making first move sexually 12;
  percentage obtaining orgasm
  67, 68; question of sexual
  satisfaction among 6;
  questionnaires directed at, huge

response and results 2–4; raping
  by husband 185; reason for not
  protesting regarding husband's
  mistress 142; religious
  upbringing blamed for sexual
  difficulties 26–7; reticent w.
  more likely to have affair 131–2;
  risk taken when rating husband
  as poor lover 129; sexual
  difficulties through lack of
  communication with husbands
  17–18; sexual dissatisfaction of
  12; tiredness of husband as
  deterrent to sex 54–5; views of
  husband's affairs 137–9
Woman magazine, surveys
  conducted by 1ff.
Women: adoption of 'more
  masculine' attitude after losing
  partner 167–8; appreciative of
  their men 7; defence against
  rape 187–8; desire for partners
  to be more skilful and
  experienced lovers 73–4; desire
  to be more adventurous and
  suggest more variety in
  lovemaking 61; hurt of casual
  sex 168, 170; importance
  attached by men to w. reaching
  orgasm 9; long-term effects of
  rape and assault on 186–7; loss
  of partner a great blow sexually
  166; many cases of rape and
  assault on not reported to police
  187; need felt to be assertive 38;
  problems voiced regarding
  lovemaking 7; promiscuity by
  42–3; rape and assault on 183ff.;
  self-criticism by 2; sexual
  assaults on 15–16; underrating
  as lovers 7–8

A selection of bestsellers from SPHERE

FICTION

MONIMBO	Arnaud de Borchgrave and Robert Moss	£2.25 ☐
KING OF DIAMONDS	Carolyn Terry	£2.50 ☐
SPRING AT THE WINGED HORSE	Ted Willis	£1.95 ☐
TRINITY'S CHILD	William Prochnau	£2.50 ☐
THE SINISTER TWILIGHT	J. S. Forrester	£1.95 ☐

FILM & TV TIE-INS

SPROCKETT'S CHRISTMAS TALE	Louise Gikow	£1.75 ☐
THE DOOZER DISASTER	Michaela Muntean	£1.75 ☐
THE DUNE STORYBOOK	Joan D. Vinge	£2.50 ☐
ONCE UPON A TIME IN AMERICA	Lee Hays	£1.75 ☐
WEMBLEY FRAGGLE GETS THE STORY	Deborah Perlberg	£1.50 ☐

NON-FICTION

PRINCESS GRACE	Steven Englund	£2.50 ☐
BARRY FANTONI'S CHINESE HOROSCOPES		£1.95 ☐
THE COMPLETE HANDBOOK OF PREGNANCY	Wendy Rose-Neil	£5.95 ☐
WHO'S REALLY WHO	Compton Miller	£2.95 ☐
THE STOP SMOKING DIET	Jane Ogle	£1.50 ☐

All Sphere books are available at your local bookshop or newsagent, or can be ordered direct from the publisher. Just tick the titles you want and fill in the form below.

Name _____

Address _____

_____

Write to Sphere Books, Cash Sales Department, P.O. Box 11, Falmouth, Cornwall TR10 9EN

Please enclose a cheque or postal order to the value of the cover price plus:

UK: 55p for the first book, 22p for the second book and 14p for each additional book ordered to a maximum charge of £1.75.

OVERSEAS: £1.00 for the first book plus 25p per copy for each additional book.

BFPO & EIRE: 55p for the first book, 22p for the second book plus 14p per copy for the next 7 books, thereafter 8p per book.

Sphere Books reserve the right to show new retail prices on covers which may differ from those previously advertised in the text or elsewhere, and to increase postal rates in accordance with the PO.